full circle

Full Circle is the remarkable and moving story of three generations of Edie Wright's family. In the early 1900s, at the age of four, Alfred Brown was taken from his mother in northern Queensland and placed in Mapoon Mission. Eventually, as a young married man employed by the mission he was sent to the far north-west Kimberley. Following the death of his wife, Ina, Alf showed resourcefulness and steely determination in keeping his family together despite great difficulties and unsympathetic government policies.

Laurelle, Edie Wright's mother, and her brothers and sisters grew up on Kunmunya Mission and aboard the mission lugger her father skippered, travelling between the islands and isolated communities of the north-west coast.

After raising a large family of her own, and now a grandmother, Laurelle begins to retrace and reclaim her family's connection with the remote Kimberley coastal area and to re-establish family ties with her Cape York people.

Through its captivating description of life for an Aboriginal family in twentieth century Australia, *Full Circle* emerges as a book of hope that, despite decades of government policy and action which worked to assimilate, fragment and disperse indigenous families, the circle of kinship, land and culture need not be broken.

*Edie Wright (left) and her mother
Laurelle D'Antoine, 2001.*
(Courtesy Geoff Wright.)

Edie Wright was born in Broome and educated at Derby Junior High School and Saint Brigid's, Lesmurdie. She completed a Diploma of Education and a Bachelor of Education and is currently Principal at Wangkatjungka Remote Community School. She is married and has three sons.

Full Circle is her first book, and was inspired by listening to the rich stories of her parents and grandparents.

full circle

*From mission to community
a family story*

EDIE WRIGHT

FREMANTLE ARTS CENTRE PRESS

First published 2001 by
FREMANTLE ARTS CENTRE PRESS
25 Quarry Street, Fremantle
(PO Box 158, North Fremantle 6159)
Western Australia.
www.facp.iinet.net.au

Copyright © Edith Wright, 2001.

This book is copyright. Apart from any fair dealing for the purpose of
private study, research, criticism or review, as permitted under the
Copyright Act, no part may be reproduced by any process without written
permission. Enquiries should be made to the publisher.

Consulting Editor Wendy Jenkins.
Production Coordinator Cate Sutherland.
Cover Designer Marion Duke.

Typeset by Fremantle Arts Centre Press
and printed by Lamb Print, Perth.

National Library of Australia
Cataloguing-in-publication data

Wright, Edie, 1954– .
    Full circle: from mission to community: a family story.

    ISBN 1 86368 329 1.

    1. D'Antoine, Laurelle. 2. D'Antoine family. 3. Queensland —
    Genealogy. 4. Western Australia — Genealogy. I Title.

929.20994

The State of Western Australia has made an investment in this project
through ArtsWA in association with the Lotteries Commission.

Publication of this title was assisted by the Commonwealth Government
through the Australia Council, its arts funding and advisory body.

To the memory of
my brothers,
Gregory and Dickie,
maternal grandparents,
Alfred and Ina Brown,
and paternal grandparents,
Amy (Goodji) and
Richard (Ginger) D'Antoine.

Contents

Preface		9
1	Mapoon Mission Station	15
2	The Move to the West	34
3	Kunmunya	43
4	Life on the Mission	64
5	The Loss of Our Mother	91
6	Raising Sisters and a Brother	97
7	Last years at Kunmunya	118
8	The War Years	136
9	The Byford Home	156
10	Back to the Kimberley	172
11	Broome	187
12	Return to Derby	206
13	The Death of Gregory	235
14	Work and Recuperation	240
15	Times of Change	260
16	Dickie's Death	273
17	Some Big Moves	276
18	Grandad Passes On	286
19	Djarworrada	290
20	Going the Full Circle	306
Bibliography		316

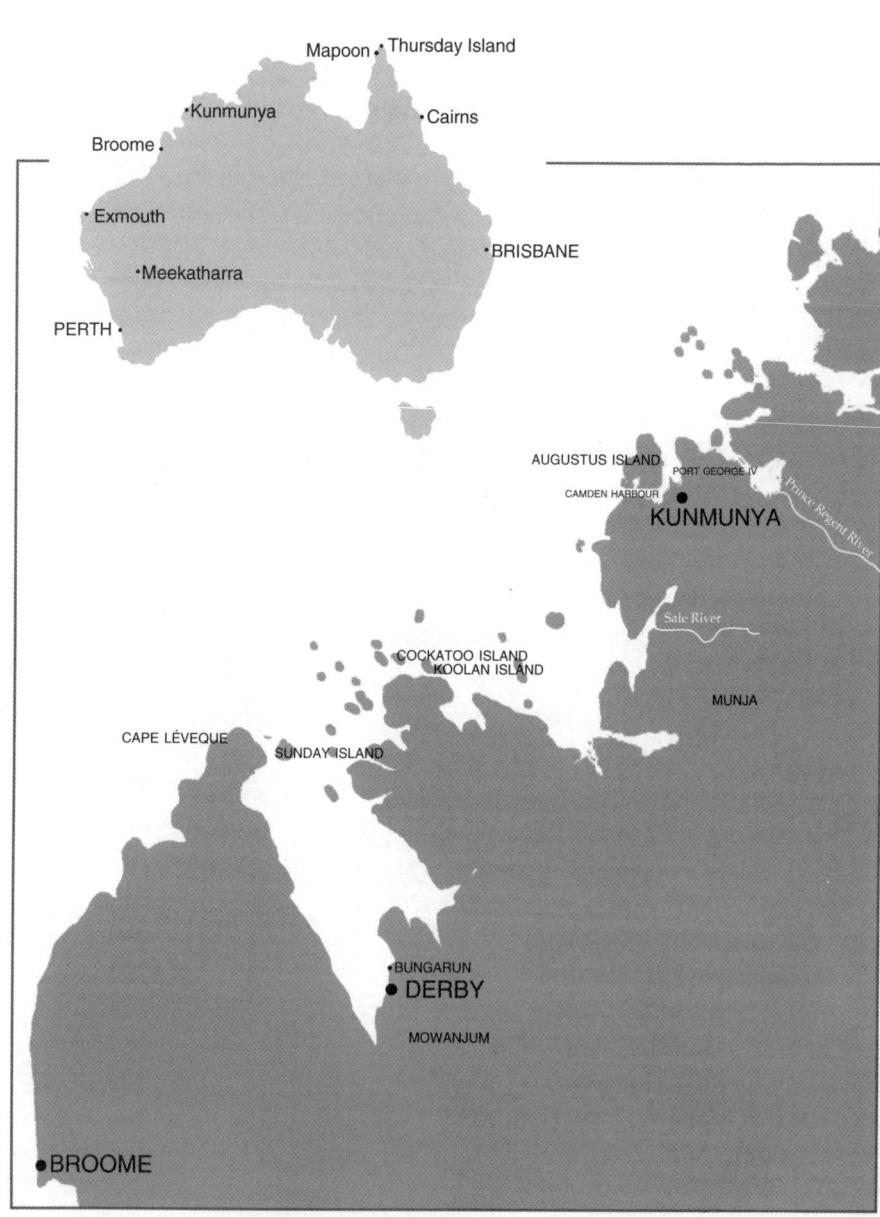

(Based on maps provided by Joel D'Antoine.)

Preface

As a child growing up I often heard Mum and Grandad recount their life at Kunmunya Mission to visitors who listened with fascination, commenting on what a good book their stories would make. The mission was established by the Presbyterian Church, initially at Port George IV, before moving to a more suitable location at Kunmunya. Mum and Grandad discussed life on the mission and sailing on the *Watt Leggatt* (the mission lugger) before the Second World War air attack on Broome led them on the droving trail to Meekatharra. They talked about their acceptance by the Aboriginal people, the Worrorra. Grandad was promised work at Byford orphanage, run by the church and situated in the foothills south of Perth, so their travels continued. In 1947 Mum and Grandad returned to the Kimberley. Occasionally Grandad opened up and talked about Mapoon Mission in Queensland but this was on rare occasions. He did not speak freely about his childhood and family and we found his early life mysterious. At the time I did not fully understand or appreciate the value of soaking up the stories he did tell.

It was not until after Grandad died in September 1986 that I realised the wealth of family history lost with his passing. He had had such an interesting life overcoming hardships and soldiering on, completely dedicating himself to his children and their families. Yet future generations might never know the elements and experiences that made his life unique.

I decided I would write Mum's story and make every effort to capture the full flavour of her life. I was determined her grandchildren would have something to cherish and pass on to future generations. But when I started the writing process I realised I could not do justice to Mum's biography without including Grandad's story.

Full Circle reflects the complete circular movement of Mum's family starting at Mapoon Mission on the west side of Cape York peninsula in Queensland at the turn of the century. Links with the Queensland family were severed when my grandparents moved to Kunmunya in 1926 and Mum grew up knowing very little about her parents' families. Her mother died when she was eight years old and Grandad seemed to shut out that part of his life.

Shortly after Grandad's death, an advertisement appeared in the *West Australian*. This led to a reunion between Mum and her cousin Waiu Uiduldam and other family members in Cairns in July 2000. The following March a huge reunion of the Brown family took place in Cairns where over three hundred people attended.

Shortly after our first visit to Cairns the Taepadhighi and Thanikwithi people of Cape York acknowledged Mum as a traditional elder. These were the Aboriginal people my grandparents came from, of which Mum was a descendant too. In traditional Aboriginal culture this is a highly honourable role, the culmination of preparation and rituals throughout life. Mum's circumstances had prevented her from singing the songs, listening to the stories and dancing the corroborees, so her acceptance as a traditional elder was exceptional. The Taepadhighi and Thanikwithi people chose to bestow this honour on Mum as the daughter of Alfred and Ina Brown, and for her this is a very moving gesture.

In mid 1995 I started taping sessions with Mum, and at the same time I decided to tape Dad's story. In the event that something happened to him I would always have the tapes to write from at a later date. The whole process was very much trial and error. The experience was new to me and I struggled with intuition, common sense and what little understanding I had of oral history techniques.

I started to exhaust all possible avenues that I thought might provide useful information. At the time I had no idea of the richness of a search that became Australia wide. Strangely enough, my earliest find was probably my most valued. It was a transcript I located in the J S Battye Library of West Australian History of an oral interview done with Grandad in 1981. It was a cooperative project between the Library Board of Western Australia and Broken Hill Proprietary Limited. After reading the transcript I realised I had made the right decision to include Grandad's story.

I was able to get Mum and Grandad's Native Welfare files from Perth. I had been advised to counsel Mum before she read them as they are extremely damaging. Mentally preparing what I would say to her, I sat her down and tried to explain the paternalistic attitudes and behaviour of government departments and churches at the time. Believe me, I felt pretty hopeless trying to explain the oppression her family had experienced, knowing she has lived through over forty different state and federal Acts and amendments that are a legacy of the way Aboriginal people were treated.

Mum's comments about the files were:

> *I got the shock of my life; I didn't know these files existed. I was disgusted and angry. I wondered who gave people permission to write these things about us. I thought, what right do they have to keep information like this on us? What sort of people write these things? If we hadn't got our files how would I know they were writing these things about us? You see, we lived on the mission and it wasn't the government who clothed and fed us. It was the mission. I couldn't understand why Dad had to write to the Native Protector every time he wanted to take money out of his bank account. I thought a Protector was there to protect us but all he did was watch every move we made. I didn't know they were keeping tabs on us, it was like being on parole. I thought Dad's file was rather a cruel file. There was only negative things in there about him.*

We gathered church records and birth and marriage registers kept by the church in Sydney. The Presbyterian Church was very supportive, allowing us access to letters, diaries and other useful correspondence. We managed to locate families of the missionaries who were at Kunmunya. They helpfully sent us copies of their parents' diaries and photos of Kunmunya. Looking over them helped stimulate Mum's memory and corroborate her stories along with the research I had done.

I found many anomalies and discrepancies with places, dates and events. My grandparents' birth certificates and government records in Brisbane were very important to me but even before I started looking for them I had a gut feeling I would not find them.

Recording statistics of this nature about Aboriginal people was not a legal requirement until after 1967 and was virtually non-existent for those born at the turn of the century.

A lot of people knew I was writing Mum's story and commented on its importance as Aboriginal history. The audience had grown to include a wider public and I knew it would be challenging and daunting to meet the more general interests of Aboriginal history, bearing in mind the primary reason for writing the book.

The judgements voiced throughout the book are based on my opinion and are not meant to be offensive. In order to write about the characters I had to try to place myself in their position and gauge their feelings and reactions when confronted with different situations.

In most Aboriginal culture it is forbidden to mention names of the deceased. I would like to thank the Aboriginal people who allowed me to use their parents and grandparents' names and photographs, especially the Mowanjum people.

While writing *Full Circle* I have been warmly supported by my husband Geoff. He encouraged me to continue when I felt down and out and always told me to keep focused on the big picture and the importance of my work as family history. I would also like to thank my family, friends and colleagues. They have assisted me in many ways from editing and constructively commenting on my early work, to participating in interviews, supplying photos and valuable information, doing preliminary sketches and maps, photocopying, showing me how to use a computer and driving me around Perth in search of further information.

I would like to sincerely acknowledge our Queensland family, from whom we have been separated for far too long. They warmly welcomed us into their family, home and hearts. There was no animosity, friction or negative judgements, just absolute gratitude in meeting all of us. I would like to thank Aunty Waiu Uiduldam and all members of the family for the utmost respect and welcome they gave Mum as the daughter of Ina and Alfred Brown.

Edith Wright
Gudumul
July 2001

1

Mapoon Mission Station

This story begins in the late nineteenth century in north Queensland at Mapoon Mission. Mapoon is on the west side of Cape York in the north of Queensland. It was a place of great importance to my grandfather, Alfred Brown, who was taken there as a very young child. As he grew from a boy to a young man his character was shaped and moulded through the Christian teachings and his experiences there.

The Mapoon story starts towards the turn of the century when interaction between the colonisers and Aboriginal people started to change. The state government sought to stop the abuse of Aboriginal people in the pearling and bêche-de-mer industry. Mistreatment was particularly prevalent along the west coast of Cape York where recruiters were keen to replace workers lost after the collapse of Papua New Guinean labour in 1885. The Queensland government felt that a number of missions strung out along the west coast would address the problem and ease the growing tension between the two races.

In 1891 two missionaries, Reverend James Ward and Reverend Nicholas Hey, set their sights on the west coast of Cape York. They were from a mission society called the Moravians and travelled with John Douglas, a government official, to select a suitable site for a mission. They settled on the Batavia River (now called the Wenlock on government maps), opposite Cullen River, more for its defence position than its quality of soil, abundance of water or aesthetic appeal.

As the missionaries set about starting the mission the Aboriginal people hid in the bush. Watching curiously they witnessed the missionaries stamp their hallmark on the area, erecting buildings, speaking a foreign language, and wearing clothes. They smelt and looked noticeably different, and they brought unusual foods and practised Christian rituals that were totally alien. The Aboriginal people observed carefully and with suspicion, wondering whether the visitors would deal them the same fate as their forefathers. Oral history has it that early cattlemen Lachlan Kennedy and Frank Jardine treated resistance by the indigenous people violently.

> Jerry Hudson (an elder from Mapoon): *Jardine and Kennedy came through Batavia River. Jardine wanted to put his station fifty miles up — you can see the stone walls he made for his footpath. They were killing people all the way up. At Dingle Dingle Creek they killed most of the tribe ... only fifty left out of three hundred ... but the Aboriginal people were fighting people ... they were fighting with spears.*

Thus, when the missionaries arrived, the Aboriginal people kept their distance, poised ready to flee should relations turn sour and their lives become threatened.

Mapoon Mission Station was started in 1891. Government assistance provided temporary rations of food, clothing, blankets and five hundred pounds for building materials. A few years later Weipa Mission was established to the south on the Embley River and Aurukun Mission further south on the Archer River. By 1914 the string of missions along the west coast was complete when Mornington Island was established. All four missions were initiated by the Moravian and Presbyterian churches.

Mapoon Mission, c. 1919.
(Courtesy Oxley State Library of Queensland, 58438.)

The response to mission life by Aboriginal people was not always in keeping with church expectations. Although many of the inmates gave the appearance of conforming to Christian principles, at the same time they continued to practice their cultural ceremonies. The missionaries found this very frustrating. They expected complete severance from the traditional lifestyle which they saw as conflicting strongly with Christian values. They disliked Aboriginal mortuary ceremonies, dances, initiations, child rearing practices and marriage rituals, and described them as wild and vulgar with streaks of satanism. Being a hunting and gathering people, Aborigines found it difficult to embrace the philosophy of farming and agriculture and were branded lazy and useless. Many fled the mission realising the two cultures had nothing in common and took to the bush, surviving on the dwindling remnants of bush tucker. They became marginalised in their own country.

Initially established to make contact with the traditional people of the area, in 1901 Mapoon became an Industrial School to cater for Aboriginal children forcefully removed from their parents. The 1897 *Aboriginals Protection and Prevention of the Sale of Opium Act*, together with the Industrial and Reformatory Schools legislation, legalised the Queensland Government's removal practices. By the turn of the century the Queensland Government was well seasoned at taking children without parental consent, especially light-skinned children of part Aboriginal descent. It was thought they could learn more quickly and blend into mainstream society more readily. Being light-skinned they would go unnoticed. Restrictive laws suffocated their ability to maintain links with their traditional culture and forced them to sever ties with their Aboriginality. Policies and practice demanded they comply with complete assimilation and pass on to the next generation the values, attitudes and aspirations of the non-Aboriginal society rapidly colonising Queensland. The cycle would repeat and the process would eventually breed out Aboriginal culture.

> Mrs Jean Jimmy (an elder from Mapoon): *The mission was a tribal grouping. Before the mission ... there were many tribes, but the missionaries took us into the dormitory at the age of three years old and there we had to learn to speak like our mission ladies. We were not allowed to talk lingo (our language), because we might learn our legends and things like that you see. That's where they cut it out. But my mother taught me some of our culture when we grew too old for the school.) She knew all the history of the different tribes.*

An extremely large number of Aboriginal children were removed and institutionalised at Mapoon and other missions throughout the state. Alfred Brown was one of these children.

According to Reverend Hey, the superintendent at Mapoon, by 1906 there were between four hundred and five hundred Aboriginal people in touch with the mission, of which two hundred were permanent residents. The government gave the mission some financial assistance and a supply of blankets for the year and although it didn't meet the cost of caring for the inmates it was better than nothing. Those capable of earning their own way did so, leaving the government benefits for the children, the sick and the aged. The health of the Aboriginal people at the time was threatened by epidemics of influenza, whooping cough and venereal and other diseases. Unsavoury sea traders visited the mission in hope of finding cheap labour. The missionaries lived in fear of these visits; the traders were often carriers of a range of diseases that had lasting, if not fatal, effects on the health of indigenous people.

In return for food and accommodation the adults worked around the mission. They were trained in basic skills with the intention of preparing them for employment; the women for domestic duties and the men for labouring positions in the pastoral or fishing industries. They were taught limited skills that prepared them for a subservient role in mainstream society. Women and girls learnt to sew, do lacework, crochet and perform domestic duties such as keeping house, cooking and cleaning. The men learnt station trades, horticulture and marine skills. Cattle were bred and sold each year to generate finance to plough back into the mission. Harvesting bêche-de-mer and sandalwood were other means of obtaining income, along with the sale of lacework and crocheting.

> Jerry Hudson: *Here is the best hunting ground from Cloncurry to the tip of Cape York — I've travelled all over. Here is swamp and sea. Cattle started on these missions here at Mapoon. I can remember the time when Dad came down with the bullocks from a station. That was when Rev. Hey was here. When he left Mapoon he said to the Mapoon people: 'Well, here's your cattle' — and from there Dad took it on and kept it going until he was called to Aurukun. Hey brought the cattle with his own money. In those days the government had very little money for this part of the country, so he had to pay for this out of his own pocket.*

With the growing presence of children a school was built. In 1906 the average attendance at the school was eighty-one students, with the female enrolment well exceeding the male. The government made an annual contribution of a hundred pounds towards the teacher's salary. The school was well run and the children were taught English, the three Rs and religious instruction. There was no recognition of their cultural needs and schooling went only as far as year three. It was thought Aboriginal children did not have the intelligence to cope with schooling beyond this level. The school boasted separate boys' and girls' bands, with the latter comprising nine brass instruments. There were two small rooms where the children changed from work to school clothes before entering the classroom. This ritual took place twice a day and each day started and concluded with prayers and hymns. The mission clothed, fed and accommodated the children in separate dormitories for boys and girls. In return the children worked around the mission, helping in the kitchen or in the vegetable garden, or tending to the domestic animals. The doors of the dormitory were connected by wire to the mission house, so that the matron could close or open them from the verandah, the better to control the movement of boarders and others after dark.

Situated in the centre of the mission were the residences for the missionaries. The simple houses were close to the beach and coconut trees grew to the water's edge, creating a tropical appearance against the raw reality of mission life. As well as the school and the church there was a hospital, a boat shed and workshop. Most of the buildings were constructed on piles with space underneath for use as storage or extra living area. Beyond the church was a village of small dwellings built by the Aboriginal people from local timber, tin and other materials they could find. The shacks were badly ventilated, quite primitive and shabby in appearance.

There was an outstation attached to the mission. It was about four miles inland and was established as an agricultural venture for young married Aboriginal couples raised on the mission. It perpetuated a false air of independence while functioning to assimilate young couples into the expectations associated with a non-Aboriginal lifestyle. Assistance was given to build a house and in return the land had to be worked, to provide vegetables, coconuts and other produce that could be sold locally. This cottage-type industry generated a meagre income for the couples. The outstation was supervised by an Aboriginal person living on site and Reverend Hey visited twice a week to monitor progress. The families were expected to work hard and develop aspirations in keeping with the church and government policies of complete assimilation.

When Alfred Brown married he did not go to live in the outstation. His destiny was different: he was sent to a remote mission in the far north-west of Western Australia.

In addition to limited financial assistance from the Queensland Government, the Presbyterian Church did its best to contribute resources and aid. Boxes of clothes and medicine appeared courtesy of generous parishioners. But although various missionaries over the years did the best they could to manage Mapoon successfully, government reports indicate life there was not as comfortable as the Presbyterian Church would have us believe. Annual reports written by government officials visiting Mapoon raised concerns on the conditions for inmates. The dormitories were not cleaned regularly and appeared dirty and untidy. The eating area was far from hygienic and did not comply with health regulations: cooking utensils were found left unwashed for several days with food scraps stuck to the bottom of the pots. The old people in the village slept on dirty blankets on the ground and there was a growing population of neglected mangy dogs wandering around. Arrangements for meals for the old people were very hit and miss, as were medical attention and general care for the aged.

Yet in spite of these reports Mapoon was a good place to grow up in compared with conditions for Aboriginal people elsewhere in the state.

At the turn of the century in Queensland Aborigines were exploited and used as a cheap source of labour for sea traders and pastoralists. The supply of convict labour to the developing colonies had ceased and settlers to the area found working in the tropics almost impossible. Employers looked to the growing number of dispossessed Aboriginal families to satisfy their need for labour. They paid for indigenous labour in alcohol and opium; Aboriginal people did not receive any form of wages. Aboriginal women and children were regularly used as servants by the settlers. Their services included physical labour and extended to sexual favours. Many children became addicted to alcohol or opium and the young girls and women were forced to pursue a life of prostitution. Venereal disease became endemic among Aboriginal people, who in nearly all cases were denied access to medical attention. The spread of venereal disease, and other diseases like dysentery, influenza and typhoid, only increased the possibility of extinction of indigenous people. In 1897, the *Aboriginal Protection Act* was introduced in Queensland. Despite its name, this did not stop the exploitation and abuse of indigenous people and was generally counterproductive as the Act was wrought with anomalies, misinterpretations and discrepancies.

ALFRED'S EARLY YEARS

He never talked much about his young childhood days. I think it hurt him to talk too much about it. All this time I thought Dad was born at Thursday Island, but he wasn't. He told me, one time when I came back from Exmouth in early 1980, for a holiday, that he was born on a station.

Laurelle D'Antoine (Alfred and Ina's daughter)

Alfred Brown was born at McDonnell Telegraph Station at Cape York in the north of Queensland. His father was a white man and his mother was an Aboriginal woman from the Taepadhighi tribe.

McDonnell Station was one of six telegraph repeater stations which ran through the middle of Cape York. Built from 1886 to 1887 and situated a hundred to a hundred and twenty kilometres apart — starting with Musgrave in the south, then Coen, Mein, Moreton, McDonnell and Peterson in the north — they served as depots and barracks for line repair crews as well as post and telegraph offices. They also provided protection for the occupants against hostile encounters with local Aborigines.

McDonnell Station was used by the Queensland government as a depot for blankets, rations and medical supplies for Aboriginal people living in the area. Traditional food was becoming increasingly scarce and the people were forced to rely on government rations to supplement their meagre diet.

Registrations of births of indigenous children were rarely kept and there is no documentation of Alfred's birth. He was told that he was born on 10 April 1900. His father was probably a worker at the telegraph station. Isolation allowed relations between non-Aboriginal men and Aboriginal women to develop. Such relationships occurred frequently on remote settlements free from external social pressures and expectations. In many instances non-Aboriginal men loved and cared for their Aboriginal wives and families as best they could in the circumstances of the day.

Alfred grew up learning his mother's language and hearing very little English. He lived at McDonnell Station for his first year or two with his mother and possibly other siblings; he had two sisters, Kitty and Jane Brown, who were also removed to Mapoon at a very early age.

When he was around four years of age, Alfred was removed from his mother by the police and taken to Thursday Island, the main administrative centre for the area. He was presented to the Court of Petty Sessions facing committal by the bench to an institution for Aboriginal children for an initial period of seven years. In Queensland this was the usual process for the removal of Aboriginal children from their families.

While Alfred was at Thursday Island he was cared for by a young Aboriginal woman called Jessica. As an old man he retained a clear memory of her kindness and of how she tried to satisfy his simple plea for a drink of water. He couldn't speak English and kept asking for ipi (water). Not understanding, she gave him food. Each time he was handed the wrong thing his frustration increased until he began to cry. Jessica gathered him in her arms and walked around and around trying to soothe him until in sheer desperation she handed him a pannikin of water. To her surprise he snatched it out of her hands and gulped it down before he'd had time to steady his grip. She watched as the water dribbled down his cheeks, then gathered him in her arms again and cried for both of them.

Alfred later became Jessica's brother-in-law when he married her sister Ina.

Within twelve months of his removal, Alfred was sent from Thursday to Mapoon Mission Station. At the time of his arrival one of the original founders, Reverend Hey, was the superintendent. The previous superintendent, Reverend Ward, had died but his widow remained at the mission as a schoolteacher.

It was common practice at Mapoon for Aboriginal people to be given the names of visitors and mission staff. A prominent member of the Society of Friends in England, who visited Mapoon Mission was called Alfred Brown.

Alfred's sister Kitty lived in the girls' dormitory.

Waiu Uiduldam (Kitty Brown's daughter): *Mum was taken to Mapoon as a very young girl. She was a dormitory girl. They had to do many jobs at the mission. She told me they made their own butter. She had to put milk in a bottle and shake it and the next morning take the cream and make butter from it. They got fresh honey from a sugar bag* [wild bees nest]. *She told us Uncle Alfred was always climbing up the coconut trees at Mapoon to cut down the coconuts for the mission. Around 1920 Mum married a Badu man at Mapoon then moved to Badu Island.*

Shortly after Alfred arrived at Mapoon he was adopted by a young Aboriginal couple, Lucy and Willy Hudson. Willy was a well-known identity, a stockman, who worked hard and believed in the work of the mission. The Hudsons lived in the village in a makeshift house made from sheet iron and whatever local timber Willy had been able to lay his hands on. Soon Lucy and Willy were the only parents Alfred knew — he grew up with their children and never saw his mother again. He was not told the reason for his committal to Mapoon but accepted the circumstances in which he found himself as normal. He was surrounded by children in the same situation. His early childhood, like that of the other children of Mapoon, revolved around school and church, performing menial tasks, and going fishing and hunting when the opportunity arose.

Alfred enjoyed school and respected his teachers, Mrs Hey and Mrs Ward. A story he was fond of telling was concerned with school. He went off to school one day feeling pretty happy with himself. It was test day and he was confident he would go up a level. Going up a level was something to feel proud of and meant the work would be challenging. Mrs Ward signalled the start of the school day with the ringing of the school bell and he entered a small room that led onto the main classroom. He quickly changed from his work to his school clothes, neatly hanging them on a peg. As he walked into the class he took in the musty smell of the room. It was distracting, but not as pungent as the mildewy odour that blanketed the class during the humid wet season. The room was badly lit, crowded and sparsely furnished with rickety wooden chairs and desks that had seen better days. Alfred took his place at his desk and when testing time arrived he sat up straight and folded his arms in front of him, knowing it would draw the attention of Mrs Ward. Sure enough Mrs Ward tested him first in the usual drill and rote method and then said, 'You've done well again Alf. Right! Up a level.' Her comment immediately drew a spontaneous smile to his face. He knew his results would win the envy of his mates and more importantly he looked forward to the challenge of the next level. With her air of confidence and superiority she wandered around the room randomly testing students and occasionally whacking the knuckles of an unfortunate child with a wooden rule for not reciting the correct answer. She stopped at the desk of a student who Alfred knew had problems with spelling. When Mrs Ward started on spelling Alfred waited with bated breath for the now familiar sound of wood on flesh and bone, but it didn't happen. He heard Mrs Ward's high pitched voice as she said, 'Say after me U P [spells], up.' The student looked nervously at her and innocently replied, 'No! I pee down.' Instantly a veil of silence hung over the class as the children tried to keep a straight face and not to wet themselves with laughter.

 At the age of fifteen Alfred left school with a strong grounding in literacy. He remained interested in reading and learning all his life.

His first job was on Thursday Island where he worked as a houseboy at the Federal Hotel. Aboriginal people were employed on pearling luggers and in the bêche-de-mer industry, earning thirty shillings per month under the government award. After two years Alfred returned to the mission and worked on the mission lugger, the *J G Ward*. This was the beginning of a lifelong career in sailing. The lugger sailed up and down the west coast of Cape York doing the mail and store run. The church had two other missions, Aurukun and Weipa and the lugger was the lifeline between the three missions and Thursday Island. Alfred acquired a comprehensive understanding of the coast and became an experienced deckhand, studying and learning about the tide, sea, stars and coastal navigation.

The education provided for Alfred benefited him as he had a working life that spanned nearly sixty years.

It is uncertain at what point Alfred and his future wife, Ina Shadforth, became interested in one another but they would have known each other from early childhood. They attended school and church together, and participated in the communal ceremonies and activities of the mission.

> Laurelle D'Antoine: *Mum must have gone to the mission as a baby because they said Nanna arrived there with a very fair baby in her arms.*
>
> *Rose Andrewina Shadforth was known as Ina to family and friends. She was born on 26 December 1900 in Normanton, Queensland. Like Alfred there is no record of her birth. She was told this information along with the ethnicity of her father, who was a German named Shadforth. Her mother was an Aboriginal woman from the area, named Georgina Lee. Ina arrived at the mission with her mother, brother and sister, Harry and Jessica. After her*

arrival at Mapoon Georgina married Jimmy Jimmy and had several children to him. Gilbert and Rachel Jimmy were their children.

Jimmy Jimmy was from the Thanakwithi tribe in Cape York. He adopted Ina when she was a small child having married her mother. This had cultural implications as Ina was accepted into the Thanakwithi tribe and is still recognised by the Thanakwithi people. She was in the unusual circumstance of having cultural links to two Aboriginal groups, through her mother's people and through Jimmy Jimmy.

Very little is known of Ina as she died when her children were young and Alfred found it distressing to talk of her.

As a young girl Ina lived in the dormitory at Mapoon with the other girls, possibly until she married. She went to school for three hours in the morning and two in the afternoon. On Wednesday and Saturday the girls learnt to sew, housekeep and garden while the boys did carpentry, agriculture and dairy work. The school was strictly run. Writing letters was encouraged and the children were expected to write to the missionaries when they went on holidays to the city.

Ina's first job was helping with the teaching of the younger children. She received

Ina Shadforth (right) and Mabel Butta, Mapoon, c. 1926.

no formal training and acquired her skills under the guidance of Miss Giles, who had taken over as teacher. It was common for the dormitory girls to work in the school and Ina worked with a good friend called Mabel Butta.

After Alfred returned to the mission to work on the lugger their relationship became serious and on the 26 March 1926 Alfred and Ina were married at Mapoon by the Reverend J R B Love. They were a well matched couple, handsome, intelligent and hard working. It is highly likely it was a double wedding, as the Reverend Love married a couple by the name of Angus and Doris on the same day. Willy Hudson and Margaret Love witnessed the marriage and the mission celebrated the occasion.

Ina was ready to marry Alfred. She had watched her older brother and sister marry. Harry was happily married to Mackie and Jessica married a local chap named Charger. She remembered blushing through the ceremony as the girls jokingly teased each other about who would be next. She had made a good choice. Alfred already had a reputation as being kind, thoughtful and hard working.

REVEREND J R B LOVE

Reverend Love was one of the straightest gentlemen I have come across. As the old saying goes, as straight as a gun barrel.

Alfred Brown

In 1922 Reverend James Robert Beattie Love arrived at Mapoon Mission Station. He replaced Reverend Hey, who by now had clocked up twenty-eight years of service.

Reverend Love made an enormous impact on Alfred and Ina's life. He guided and supported them first as a young married couple, then as young parents. He shared with them his understanding of people and relationships, finance, the law, religion and much more. It was a relationship based on mutual trust and respect at a time when Aboriginal people were usually treated as servants, without civil rights. Reverend Love was their mentor, friend and confidant.

Rev J R B Love, Kunmunya, c. 1939.
(Photograph H R Balfour, courtesy Uniting Church of Australia.)

Reverend Love was born in 1889, in Killeter, Ireland, the fifth of eleven children. He was five months old when his family migrated to Australia and settled in Strathalbyn, South Australia, where his father, Reverend George Love, was the Presbyterian minister. At an early age he was interacting with Aboriginal people, making friends with them and developing an understanding and acceptance of their culture. He became a teacher and taught for several years before the church asked him to do an assessment on the status and condition of indigenous people in the interior. He snapped up the invitation, seeing it as an opportunity to learn more about a race of people he was becoming attached to. Covering the interior and taking in Darwin to the north, Victoria River to the west and Charleville to the east, he travelled by horse and train. Full of enthusiasm, he meticulously documented flora and fauna and studiously observed the welfare of the Aboriginal people for the full twelve months of his journey. His attention to detail resulted in a comprehensive report for the church.

In 1914, after completing the assessment for the church, he was sent to Port George IV, a Presbyterian mission in the far north of Western Australia. His task was to supervise the mission while the superintendent, who had worked tirelessly under extremely harsh conditions, went on an overdue holiday. This was Love's first contact with the traditional owners, the Worrorra people. He displayed his acceptance and respect for these people by eventually documenting their language and culture through a book titled *Stone age Bushmen of Today*.

Port George IV was established in 1911 on the remote north-west coast of Western Australia. The church wanted to work with the Aboriginal people in Western Australia and operate a mission along the same lines as Mapoon in north Queensland. Christian principles were to underpin efforts to introduce Aboriginal people to a culture encroaching on their land. The only communication link between the mission and the closest town, Broome, was by sea. An old lugger, the *J G Ward* that had come from Mapoon, was used to collect freight and mail from Broome.

Numerous problems had begun to manifest when Love arrived at Port George IV. The soil was not as fertile as anticipated and the mission was unable to produce adequate crops and vegetables. The previously reliable supply of fresh water was drying up and becoming brackish. Unsavoury beachcombers were enticing Aboriginal people aboard their luggers and using them as slaves. It was necessary to a find a better location if the church wanted to continue its work with the Aboriginal people. Love and two elders, Wondoonmoi and Indamoi, set out in search of a more suitable position. After spending days exploring the area they settled on a place inland from the coast called Kunmunya. The new location for the mission was in the heart of Worrorra country whose people were the traditional owners and custodians of the land.

In 1915 Love reluctantly left Port George IV before the arduous task of moving to Kunmunya started. He took with him a very good understanding of the Worrorra people and a bonding that drew him back twelve years later.

After leaving Port George IV he joined the Light Horse Regiment and served in Palestine. He was later discharged as a result of chest and hand wounds received in battle. For his services he was highly decorated, receiving the Military Cross and Distinguished Conduct Medal. He became ordained as a Presbyterian minister in Adelaide, then in 1922 took up the superintendent's position at Mapoon Mission. He married Margaret Holinger, a schoolteacher at Mapoon, in 1923. Their first child, Bobby, was born on Thursday Island in 1925.

2

The Move to the West

There was continuous contact between the missions, and Reverend Love maintained a keen interest in the operations of Kunmunya. He was very concerned when it began to experience financial problems. Overheads and expenses to run Kunmunya — a property in excess of fifty thousand acres — were draining the church budget. The sheer enormity of operating a remote settlement hundreds of kilometres from the closest town was starting to tax the physical and emotional well-being of the staff. The situation at Kunmunya was looking very grim and its future was in jeopardy.

Reverend Love longed to return to the mission and the Worrorra people he first met over a decade before. The conviction that Kunmunya needed a strong leader got the better of him and he decided to return. Knowing he would need hard working, skilled people like Alfred and Ina to turn the mission into a viable church venture, he sent them ahead with plans to join them after he and his family had taken a well-earned rest.

Leaving Mapoon was an emotional occasion. Willy put his arm around Alfred's shoulder and said, 'Best you go with Reverend Love and make a new life for you and Ina. This place is not doing too good. There is still a lot of hookworm and sickness with whooping cough and influenza. Best you go and try your luck. Make a fresh start for yourselves.' Willy and Lucy Hudson were the only parents Alfred knew and the tears started to form as they farewelled each other.

Reverend and Mrs Love accompanied Alfred and Ina to Thursday Island. From there, on 12 June 1926, Alfred and Ina set sail for Kunmunya on the *Marella*. The Loves remained on Thursday Island for a holiday.

Alfred enjoyed the journey, but it was draining on Ina. They had been at sea for a short time and Alfred leant his lean brown body, seasoned from years of sailing, against the salt-stained rails of the *Marella*, a sturdy vessel owned and operated by the Presbyterian Church. He couldn't help thinking of the scrawny thin Chinese chap who consistently badgered Ina to buy his pathetic trinkets. It was his rude manner that annoyed Alfred. The man rudely shoved a number of items in Ina's face, not taking no for an answer. Alfred could see his wife becoming increasingly agitated with the

Ina and Alfred Brown aboard the Marella, *June 1926.*
(Courtesy John Love.)

obnoxious behaviour of the hawker and felt like putting him in his place. It had taken him a while to coax Ina out of the cabin onto the deck for some fresh air and now this hawker was intruding on their privacy. He managed to control his anger and rationality ruled as he reported the incident to the captain.

Usually Ina was more than capable of taking care of herself but her physical condition was not the best. She was pregnant with their first child and had spent most of the journey below in the cabin suffering from morning sickness and irregular bouts of vomiting, dizziness and hot and cold flushes, all of which had resulted in weight loss.

Alfred reached into his back pocket for his tin of tobacco. As he started to roll his cigarette he let his thoughts wander back to their departure from Mapoon. Leaving the mission was distressing for both of them. Ina took it hard. Leaving her mother had been very difficult. Alfred had to gently put an end to the emotional farewell, slowly guiding her towards the dinghy waiting to ferry them to the mission lugger lying in deep water ready to take them to Thursday Island. Ina's mother knew her daughter was pregnant and felt helpless knowing she wouldn't be by her side when the baby arrived. Alfred had to lift Ina into the dinghy then put a comforting arm around her shoulder. They waved to their family and friends gathered on the beach. It seemed everyone in the mission had taken the time to see them off, even a few mangy camp dogs barked incessantly in the background. Alfred spotted Lucy and Willy Hudson in the crowd and instantly felt the tears starting to form again. They had been his only family and had treated him like a son, guiding and supporting him through the milestones of life as he grew from a boy to a young man. They had found room in their hearts for him. As the tears fell and the tightness in his chest became noticeable, he knew he would miss them badly. Alfred and Ina clung to each other as they tried to savour the dying moments with their families.

Alfred lit his smoke and spared a thought for his sisters Kitty and Jane and wondered if he would return to see them again. They too had been raised with mission values at Mapoon, like himself, taken there as young children. Kitty had married a chap called Uiduldam and moved to Badu Island. Last he heard she was busy raising a family. She had called her first son Alfred after him, and he smiled appreciatively as he recalled the thought. Usually the girls married young men from the mission and settled at the outstation but Kitty's path in life was different. He wanted to be a part of their future but knew circumstances dictated differently. A new life for him, Ina and the baby was organised for them. A new life almost halfway around the continent.

Reverend Love had made the arrangements for them to leave Mapoon. Permission had to be granted by the state government and the mission authority for them to transfer to an interstate mission. Had Alfred and Ina decided to remain in Mapoon — assuming they had that choice — their opportunities would have been limited to continuing their current occupations at the mission or taking their chances in mainstream society. Employment opportunities outside the mission were subject to exploitation and abuse and they would have to live according to segregation practices in place for Aboriginal people.

When Ina and Alfred left Mapoon they never returned.

Arriving in Broome

It's strange that they were going to close the mission down when they couldn't get it going and it was him (Reverend Love) that came back and brought the mission up. Then after he left to go to Ernabella the mission seemed to go downhill again.

Laurelle

From Darwin, Alfred and Ina set sail for a town in the Kimberley rapidly earning a global reputation for its pearls. Broome had attracted a multitude of different races, and people from all walks of life went there expecting to strike it rich in the pearling industry.

They landed at the jetty on high tide and walked past a small cemetery overlooking Roebuck Bay before making their way to Streeters Jetty in Chinatown. As they walked through Chinatown they were struck by the tantalising smells, architecture and foreign languages that formed the ethnic melting pot Broome was becoming renowned for. There were Japanese, Kopeng, Malaysian, Chinese, Filipinos and other Asian races. There was also an edginess about the town, as a result of race riots in the early 1920s. They could feel it in the body language as they passed different ethnic groups. People stayed together, disappearing behind closed doors fearful they might be approached by a person deemed a mortal enemy. It was like a veil hanging over the town. It was a time when mysterious deaths occurred in a number of different situations; at sea while divers were trapped below, on luggers, on land, in the pearlers' camps or in dark alleys during the still of the night. Everyone kept within their own cultural group, not venturing beyond the safety of their own camp, fearful a walk down the street at night might result in a slit throat. Alfred noticed the tension, shivered, and rested in the knowledge he was taking Ina away from it.

The mission lugger, *Rolland*, lay anchored in Roebuck Bay. It would take them on the last leg of their journey to Kunmunya. The morning sickness that plagued Ina for most of the journey had subsided and she had perked up, regaining her appetite. Her mind was on looking for a familiar face. She walked with Alfred towards Streeters Jetty where they had made arrangements for Harry to meet them. Harry Shadforth was Ina's brother and had arrived at Kunmunya from Mapoon five years before with his wife, Mackie and two sons, Patrick aged seven and Percy aged three. Harry was the skipper of the *Rolland*. The vessel did regular trips to Broome for mail, freight and stores, servicing the government settlement at Walcott Inlet along the way and pastoralists and beachcombers residing in the area.

Ina spotted her brother and quickened her pace as she walked up to him, giving him a long hug then asking, 'How's Mackie and the children?' Harry held his sister at arm's length studying the changes that had turned her into a strikingly attractive woman. Only then did he reply, 'Mackie's well. She's pretty busy helping make dresses for the mission and teaching the women to crochet and embroider. As for Percy and Patrick, they're growing up since you last saw them, young lads, and there's Florence and Henry who you haven't seen.' The mention of the two older boys conjured up an image for Ina of the young Patrick. She had looked after him while Mackie was pregnant. Mackie was finding her pregnancy demanding so Patrick stayed with Ina in the girls' dormitory for a short time until she recovered. Needless to say he was thoroughly spoilt by the other girls and had developed the makings of a lovable scallywag. She knew he was about twelve years old and mentally pictured a clumsy lad all arms and legs waiting for adolescence to take its course.

Alfred was starting to feel he had made the right decision to move to the west. Seeing Ina laughing and enjoying the company of her brother seemed to make the journey worthwhile. She was very close to Harry and he had a gut feeling things would work out for them. He greeted Harry with a wide grin and warm handshake and together the men started loading their few belongings aboard the dinghy. Alfred was eager to finish the journey and settle Ina. She still had a lot to organise before the baby arrived. He was glad the fine weather could be expected to remain with them until the build-up to the wet started around October.

They piled into the dinghy and tried to catch up on the five years since they had seen each other. The conversation enthusiastically jumped from one subject to another. Alfred was keen to learn about the operation of the *Rolland*. 'I've got a pool of about eight men that I rotate around,' Harry told him. 'For a month I have four men as crew for the *Rolland* while the other four work around the mission, then I change them. That way they learn about sailing and running the mission. They're a good bunch and very loyal.' Alfred knew he would be working with Harry on the *Rolland* so he asked, 'How many other people along the coast do we pick up mail and stores for?'

'Well, there's Nicholas Kardamitz, a beachcomber, always visits the mission, often to attend church. They say he left Greece for murdering a chap. Nice bloke. If you ask me, he wouldn't harm a fly. Probably killed the bloke for having an affair with his wife. Then there's Haldane and Jack Cleverly living north at Scott Strait in Wunambal country, got a lot of Aboriginal people working for them. They use the mission as a place to drop off and collect freight and mail. They're in beachcombing. Willy Reid's got a good camp at Vansittart Bay with a small group of Aboriginal people. At Marie Springs there's Bob Thompson. He's got sheep. Then there's the likes of Fred Merry at Sale River growing peanuts and running sheep. Both Fred and Bob bring their wool to the mission on camels so we can bring it to Broome. Definitely no white women living up in those parts with those men. I forgot, at Munja there's Harold Reid. He's the superintendent for the Government Reserve. He looks after the Aboriginal people that stay there and keeps an eye on their movements. He often sends a runner over to the mission looking for natives who have run off with another woman or in trouble and the police are looking for them. Reid has to report the movement of natives to his boss in Perth. That's about it. Whenever they visit the mission they always bring some fresh dugong or turtle and we give them whatever fresh fruit and vegetables we have in season.'

After listening to Harry, Alfred felt he had a thumbnail sketch of the colourful characters living on the Kimberley coastline. He couldn't help but wonder what their attraction to this remote rugged land was. Were they running from the law, or their spouse and family, perhaps some wanted to strike it rich, or was it the boundless solitude?

Harry introduced Alfred and Ina to the crew; Freeny, Robert, Mundi and Goodman. Alfred and Ina were struck by their white teeth and wide grins that accentuated their wide nostrils. They had magnificent, gleaming black skin and a striking physique that made them tower over the Mapoon people. After the formalities were dispensed with, Alfred noticed Harry switch from English to their language, Worrorra, to give sailing instructions. Harry had a good grasp of Worrorra and with admiration in his voice Alfred said, 'How long have you been speaking the language?' Harry replied, 'Oh! I started learning pretty much after I arrived. You need it to speak to those who can't speak English.'

The journey from Broome to Kunmunya took two days. The weather was kind to them, providing a good steady wind to power the *Rolland*. The newcomers were completely taken by the beauty of the coast and the change from serene glassy water to dangerous whirlpools that Harry skilfully manoeuvred the lugger through, timing his movements precisely.

Alfred and Ina had come nearly halfway around the continent to their new home so they were pretty glad when the journey finally came to an end. Alfred inhaled the smell of mangroves, acacias and eucalypts while he slapped at the mosquitoes that started to settle on his back and bite him through his shirt. Harry steered the lugger into Nhorgor, the bay where the *Rolland* anchored. Alfred and Ina hopped into the dinghy and were ferried by the crew to dry land. 'We'll have to walk the three miles to the mission but Ina can travel on the cart. It's nothing flash but it will make the trek a little easier. The mission bought the old cart from Broome to help with carrying building materials when they moved from Port George IV to here. It's seen better days but it still goes and it's worth its weight in gold.' said Harry fondly. Alfred walked cautiously beside the cart then closed his eyes for a minute while he said a short prayer acknowledging their safe trip.

3

Kunmunya

Alfred was struck by the number of substantial buildings at the mission. The staff houses were built well off the ground and made from local hardwoods and basic construction materials transported from Broome on the lugger. They had been the original buildings from Port George IV and they were now showing signs of deterioration and in need of repairs.

Under the superintendent's house was a small area used as a classroom. It was quite unsuitable for educating children, being very dark and small, and it bordered on unsafe. It was built just over a decade before and was now unable to cater for the growing number of children.

Other buildings included the dispensary, the dormitory and church, all in a state of disrepair. There was no money available for maintenance, so the mission had to make do for a few more years.

The aspect was softened by the range of annuals the missionaries grew to make the place attractive and comfortable. They were avid gardeners keen to give everything a go. Iceland poppies and petunias were grown during the dry season when the climate was cooler. There were oleanders to give a spray of colour to the place as well as form a windbreak. Poincianas and lilac trees provided shade and more colour, red and purple. Alfred noticed a dead oleander burnt brown and lifeless next to the hospital, a remnant of a lightning strike the last wet season. The combined aroma of flowers and fresh bread gave the place an unusual homely smell.

As Alfred finished scanning the place he noticed everything was set in the forefront of a range that seemed to form a fortress around the mission. Suddenly he felt safe and immediately felt a sense of easiness wash over him knowing, he was in good hands.

'Good day, I'm George Beard and this is my wife Mrs Beard.' The booming welcome came at the same time as the warm handshake. 'Pleased to meet you. I'm Alfred Brown and this is my wife Ina,' replied Alfred. He felt comfortable with the Beards and learnt they had been there since 1920. Mrs Beard was the matron and looked after the welfare of the women while her husband took care of the agricultural and industrial concerns of the mission.

Together the two couples walked over to what Alfred rightly took as being the superintendent's house and met Mr and Mrs Holmes, who were helping out until the Reverend Love arrived. Mrs Holmes was the teacher while her husband attended to the accounts, religious affairs and medical needs of the Aboriginal people.

Alfred noticed on the fringe of the mission a collection of rather shabby huts. He later discovered that this was the village for the Aboriginal people, who lived separately from the mission staff. There were boys' and girls' dormitories, then three small-single room houses not much larger than garden sheds. A couple named Gertie and Stephen lived in the first one; May and William and their three children lived in the second house, while another couple by the name of Ernie and Ruby lived in the third one with their two children.

Further along there were crude dwellings made from bush timber, woollybutt bark, cypress pine and sheet iron. Beside these were makeshift humpies and camps.

Ernie's home, (l–r) Ernie's mother, Allan, Ruby and Elkin, Kunmunya, c. 1938–39. (Courtesy Ian Young.)

Alfred recalled hearing, 'The blacks love living by themselves. They can sing and dance without interrupting anyone. Besides, their relations from sister tribes, Ngarinyin and Wunambal people, can come and go as they please.'

Alfred and Ina became accustomed to the sound of the night sky laden with the singing and tapping of the corroboree. The men stamped their feet in unison on the cold pindan ground making an earthy percussion that resonated across the mission, while the women sang songs taught to them as young children by their mothers. The cacophony of sounds was a welcome lullaby each night.

Kunmunya boasted excellent race relations with the Worrorra people. Unlike other settlements in the Kimberley the staff had not encountered the physical conflict that can so easily lead to violence and fatalities. From the time he arrived, back at Kunmunya in early 1927, Reverend Love encouraged the Worrorra people to keep much of their traditional ways. His attitude towards cultural maintenance conflicted with the government's policy of complete assimilation.

Most non-Aboriginal people interacting with

Aboriginal people proceeded along the path of cultural genocide. Enforcing Western culture on Aboriginal people at all cost was accepted, encouraged and not questioned. Reverend Love encouraged the Worrorra people to retain as much of their culture as possible. He allowed the two mission cultures to emerge separately, respect each other and, where possible, mesh together. There were many ways of the Worrorra that conflicted with Christians beliefs and he resolved cultural clashes with an open mind.

Reverend J R B Love, with his son Bobby and a Worrorra infant, Kunmunya, c. 1929.

There were over three hundred Aboriginal people in touch with the mission, with an average attendance of eighty at church most Sundays.

Alfred was intrigued by a local custom he noticed very early after his arrival. It was the cultural behaviour known as rambadba, an avoidance obligation when a man comes in contact with his mother-in-law, her sisters and brothers. Alfred and Ina noticed both parties lowered their heads and covered the side of their faces and then proceeded in the opposite direction when they first sighted each other. Anything in the hand, a billycan, bag of flour, fire wood, would be raised to the side of the face to act as a shield. Rambadba is not as strict between two men as they are content to avoid each other. Where there was a mixing of men and women, buildings had a partition down the middle, as was the case with the church and the dining shed. In church the women sat on one side and the men on the other. The Shadforths and Browns did the same.

Alfred started work on the *Rolland* the day after his arrival. After he had been working for about a week Harry pulled him aside and said, 'We were going to leave the mission and return home to Mapoon. Mackie and I were feeling very homesick. We have been away from the family for a long time and missing everyone. But now that you and Ina are here we've decided to stay. When we saw you and Ina we felt much better, not so alone. We get on well with the missionaries, but they're not the same as family and they have different ways to "half-caste" people. I'm so glad to have you both here.'

The *Rolland* provide a communication link with Broome and a courier service for the various coastal settlements. Income generated from this service helped pay for the maintenance on the lugger and for Harry and Alfred's wages. But income was limited. The *Rolland* needed repairs and the mission badly needed a new and larger vessel to continue its service. There had been a drought the year before so cattle and crops didn't give very good returns for the mission that year. Fifteen children were attending school, but the money generated from the courier service was being spent on repairs to the lugger rather than on educational materials.

Ina settled into her new house and started teaching in the kindergarten almost immediately. Being pregnant she had to take it easy; however, she still found time to show the women how to sew, clean and cook. She explained to them, 'The secret to making a good sponge cake is to beat the egg white and sugar with a fork until it looks like this.' Ina would let them look into the bowl until their faces were inches from the mixture and wait for their nod

Mrs Love handing out dresses, Kunmunya, c. 1934.
(Photograph H R Balfour, courtesy Uniting Church of Australia.)

of approval as they each had a turn at licking the fork.

She sewed for the ladies and could whip up a dress in no time on the old treadle. One day while she was making a dress she had to chuckle to herself when she heard one of the staff comment, 'I've told Jeanie she's to wear a dress when she's working but she insists on taking it off and baring all, especially when visitors are here. If I've told her once, I've told her a hundred times.'

The missionaries tried, without too much success, to get the Aboriginal women to wear clothes while they were working around the mission. They were allowed to discard them when they returned to their camp or went hunting. It was pretty embarrassing when visitors arrived and women and men wandered around with just a hair belt on. The dresses Ina sewed were a very simple loose-fitting cotton design. They came to just below the knee with no sleeves, darts or waistline. Bright red was the favourite colour, so when material was ordered it was in various shades of red or other eye-catching colours. The women would rather go naked than wear a tight, dull-coloured dress that didn't have red in it. Ina lost count of the hundreds of bright red dresses she made.

She and Alfred were members of the staff and received a basic wage from the church. Most of their needs were provided for and they didn't need a lot of money. Alfred had to contribute a pound a month to a trust account which was controlled by the Chief Protector of Aborigines in Perth. This was compulsory for Aboriginal people earning a wage. The money was set aside to cover medical fees and the process was designed to foster good planning and finance skills. When they needed extra money, for a trip to Broome for example, Alfred wrote to the Chief Protector requesting a small sum from his trust account. Depositing and withdrawing funds had to be justified in writing to the Chief Protector and managed by Reverend Love. This was government policy.

Alfred's crew were treated differently as the mission did not have to pay them a regular wage. They were paid in food, tobacco and clothes; however, a visit to Broome meant a bonus of ten shillings. The Worrorra people had little understanding of the value of money. The women received a little pocket money from the staff but nothing regular or substantial. Some went out hunting for dingos, for which they got two pounds for each scalp, minus a handling fee. Turtle shell was sold through the mission store and fetched a small price. The concept of money was baffling to them. Alfred remembered a story Reverend Love told him that summed up their understanding of money. He said, 'I told them of Mr Hovenden's appointment at Moola Bulla and suggested that we also help. These Kunmunya blacks have almost no money to spend ... Yesterday at the beginning of our evening service ... I put a money box on the Communion table and invited anyone who wished to contribute to the Moola Bulla missionary's keep to put money in the offering box. A most interesting scene followed: a surprising number came forward. Men, women and children dropped their coins in the box. Apparently those who had money had, in true blackfellow fashion, shared it with their friends, and most of the friends wished to put their coin in the Mission box (they only had a little) and one nice little fellow, who had helped one of the men to get a dingo scalp and had received two shillings and six pence as his share, got some tea and sugar in the store, sent one shilling to his father who is in Broome native hospital, and put a silver coin in the box. I also noticed that a young girl, who is betrothed to the young man who got the dingo money, came forward with a gift. She had no money so I supposed her boy gave her some of his money to put in the box, and he gave of his own also.'

STARTING A FAMILY

> *The missionaries had their houses near ours. There was our house and opposite our house was the box heap where they stacked empty boxes and a meat house where they kept the salted meat. Then Shadforth's house with a fence separating us and the main buildings like the store, dispensary, bakehouse, school and church from the village. Mum had a chook run at the back of our house where she kept a few chooks, just enough to keep us in eggs. As kids we used to pluck their feathers and use them for decorations.*
>
> Laurelle

December was a time that tested the physical and mental endurance of those living in the Kimberley. By Christmas the build-up to the wet was well advanced and the constant oppressive heat made people do irrational things. It was bad enough to drive the sanest person insane and those with a good sense of humour and an open mind fared the wet season better than others. For this reason it was rightfully called the silly season as people did silly things. By December the humidity seemed to know no boundaries and the heat constantly sent the mercury to the top of the thermometer for weeks on end. At sunset lightning danced on the horizon, teasing everyone with its fireworks, only to disappear without a drop of rain. The rains seemed to hold off until around Christmas and when the monsoon finally broke it bucketed down. First the wind stirred the leaves and when the rustling became stronger you could smell the dust then feel the drop in temperature. The rain that followed was like manna from heaven, washing away the anxiety, layers of dust and the feeling of complete loneliness. The excitement didn't stop there. The next day everyone chatted about the onset of the wet season and the question on everyone's lips was whether it would be a big one.

It was smack bang in the middle of this type of weather, in mid December 1926, just before the monsoon broke, that Alfred and Ina had their first child, a son. It was a home birth. The closest hospital was in Broome, hundreds of miles away, and the weather was too risky. Besides it was the accepted practice for women living in remote settlements to have home births. Mrs Beard was the resident midwife, very experienced and capable. She set Ina at ease saying, 'I've delivered many babies safely including Mackie's children. All the women have their children on the mission. You'll be okay.' Ina was too tired to argue, the weather was making her irritable, so she rested and waited for her baby to arrive. Sure enough all went well and after smacking Ina's newborn baby on the backside, Mrs Beard declared, 'I'm going to name him Alwyn after my son.' And Alwyn he was called. He was a spritely baby who grew up in the company of his four cousins, Percy, Patrick, Florence and Henry, and many Worrorra children.

Each staff member had a house girl to assist with washing, cleaning and babysitting. It was part of the training process for the girls and a welcome relief for Ina who needed the extra help with Alwyn. It meant she could continue to teach at the kindergarten. House girls at Kunmunya included Dullan, Ruby, Vera, Daisy, Pearl, Gertie, Florrie, Amy and Hazel. They were compassionate women of strong character, very accommodating of the non-Aboriginal values that were starting to permeate their culture and tradition. They treated the families they worked for as an extension of their own and cared for the children like their own. The affection they gave the children knew no bounds. Dullan was Ina's house girl and each day she came up from the dormitory in the village to care for Alwyn in his own home. Before she returned to the dormitory each afternoon Ina gave her whatever food and clothing she could spare saying, 'You take this salt beef and flour for tea.' She knew what it was like to live in a dormitory. Extra food and clothes never went astray. Dullan took care of Ina's children for several years before going back to Sale River to be with her own people.

Shortly after Alwyn turned two years old Ina had a daughter. Once again Mrs Beard came to the rescue and Laurelle was born at Kunmunya on 6 February 1929. It was the middle of a good wet season. That year heavy rains washed away plagues of caterpillars, the creeks were breaking the banks and the results of the good wet season manifested months later in a successful crop for the mission.

Laurelle was only months old when Charles Kingford Smith crash-landed his plane on the mission reserve in

April 1929. A search party led by Mr Beard, Albert Barunga and another chap by the name of Wally went looking for them. They combed the mission reserve before finally finding them after twelve days at a location now named Coffee Royal, after a drink of brandy and coffee the rescued aviators had.

Alfred and Harry had a group of about ten Aboriginal men they trained to work as crew. The crew included Stephen, Mundi, Goodman, Freeny, Robert, Albert Montgomery, Micky Mulan and Jimmy Lullbunda. Later two other young chaps, Watty Ngerdu and Albert Barunga joined the team. The men rotated each month between working on the lugger and mustering cattle or doing general maintenance on the buildings around the mission.

Ina Brown with Laurelle, Kunmunya, 1929.

Mundi, a more elderly member of the team, appointed himself Alfred's guardian. He was a small chap and watched out for Alfred when they were at sea. On one occasion Alfred speared a turtle and jumped in after it not knowing a shark was close by. On sighting the shark Mundi hopped onto the railing ready to dive in to protect Alfred but held back when he saw the situation was under control. Alfred had seen the danger he was in and shoved the turtle at the shark. He was taken by the show of loyalty during the incident and knew he had a lifelong mate who would be there to look out for him.

It was around this time that the mission took ownership of a new lugger, the *Watt Leggatt*, named after two well-known members of the church. It was a handsome white boat that sat proudly on the water. Named by Lady Champion in Perth, it sailed under the guidance of Captain Bell from Fremantle to Broome. At Broome it was handed to Mr Beard and sailed by Harry Shadforth and his crew back to Kunmunya. Mr Beard's family were returning from holidays so they were on the maiden voyage from Broome to Kunmunya.

Several days after the brand spanking new lugger arrived at the mission Reverend Love decided to take everyone out on it for a picnic. During the picnic Reverend Love got up and announced, 'Well Alf, this is your boat.' Alfred was taken by surprise as he thought he would get the *Rolland* to work while Harry would skipper the *Watt Leggatt*. He was extremely proud and he skippered the *Watt Leggatt* for the next fourteen years with a flawless safety record.

The Watt Leggatt *in the creek at Kunmunya, c. 1934.*
(Photograph H R Balfour, courtesy Uniting Church of Australia.)

Early 1930s

We heard the word Depression, but we didn't know the full meaning of it. It wasn't until years after that, reading, by the stories you get in the book, it struck us how lucky we were. We grew our own vegies and all that, fish, turtle, oysters. We had everything provided by the Almighty. We didn't need money. It must have been awful for the people down south.

Alfred

Recognition of the work by Alfred and Ina was appearing in church correspondence in the eastern states. They had gained a reputation as committed, hardworking staff; practically indispensable to the mission. Reports and articles written by the church on Kunmunya constantly acknowledged their efforts, and visiting dignitaries commented on the enormous assistance they were to the mission. Kunmunya was their home and as their children were born there, the Worrorra people included them as part of their cultural group.

In January 1931, Kunmunya Mission was asked by the Aborigines Department to take out a permit to employ Alfred and Harry as the skippers of the *Watt Leggatt* and *Rolland*. Employers were required to have permits to employ Aboriginal people. In this way the department monitored the terms of employment and conditions of indigenous people in the work force. Employers paid a fee of five shillings for each permit.

Reverend Love did not take kindly to the request as he felt Alfred and Harry were staff and, as such, should not be subject to policies that discriminated them from other staff members. Alfred and Harry were in an unusual

Alfred Brown, skipper of the Watt Leggatt, *and his crew, c. 1934.*
(Photograph H R Balfour, courtesy Uniting Church of Australia.)

situation. In their capacity as captains of the luggers and their spouses' role as teachers, they were part of the mission staff and recognised and treated as such by the church. The Aborigines Act was wrought with anomalies and Love disagreed strongly with its application to Alfred and Harry and their families as natives. The solution was for them to apply to the Aborigines Department for exemption from the Act for them and their families.

Subsequently, Alfred wrote to the Aborigines Department asking for exemption so his family could access mainstream education, health and welfare benefits such as child endowment. Reverend Love supported his request, outlining very sound reasons for it. The Chief Protector of Aborigines wrote back stating he was reluctant to grant exemption because although Alfred and his family met all the requirements, they were living and working with traditional Aboriginal people. In the eyes of the department they had not made the transition to complete assimilation. This would involve leaving the mission and completely severing all ties with the Worrorra people before the Chief Protector would even consider exemption. Alfred's fight for exemption did not stop there.

On 27 October 1930, Ina and Alfred had another healthy son and called him Alfred. Decades later as an adult working at Derby he was known as Yogi by his mates. So as not to confuse him with his father he will be referred to here as Yogi. He was delivered under Mrs Beard's supervision by her eldest daughter Gladys, who took a shine to the baby. Gladys made it very clear to his parents that in the event he needed another home he was quite welcome under her roof. She would have liked to adopt him.

In September 1931, the Beards left Kunmunya after twelve years at the mission. The month before they left, Gladys married local pastoralist Fred Merry. It was the first non-Aboriginal wedding on the mission and cause for celebration by everyone. Alfred had the honour of being Fred's best man. Fred owned a sheep station at Sale River and was the mission's closest neighbour. Alfred got to know Fred when he called in to Munja to pick up his wool to take to Broome. They became pretty good mates. Gladys already got on very well with Ina, so everyone felt pretty comfortable with each other's company. After the wedding Gladys went to Sale River to live, taking Ina's house girl Dullan with her. Although Ina didn't want to see Dullan go she knew it was for the best, and said to her, 'Best you go and be with your people. Gladys will look after you.' Dullan was traditionally from Sale River and Ina knew Gladys would watch over her.

The Beards were replaced by Miss Giles and Mr MacDougall. Miss Giles had worked with Ina in the school at Mapoon, so her introduction to Kunmunya wasn't so daunting. Walter MacDougall was a red-haired Scot. In 1932 he and Gladys Giles married, and so the mission witnessed its second non-Aboriginal wedding.

Early in 1932 Alwyn had problems with his eyesight. Ina and Alfred were devastated by the long-term effects of the infection.

Alfred: *One of my sons lost — my elder son — lost an*

eye. I don't know what they called it, this disease of the eye. It came all the way from Meekatharra and down the coast. Trachoma. And he lost one of his eyes through that, living up north, no medical [attention]. And we were advised to clean his eyes, four, five or more times a day and put on Argyrol I think they called it. It is sort of like black. It broke my heart when he lost it, one of his eyes. But he is happy. You can imagine the feeling his mother and I had, after all we had done we could not save his eye.

In November 1932 Ina and Alfred had their fourth child, a girl they called Edith. Ina had to go to Broome to have her as Mrs Beard and Gladys were no longer around to deliver the baby. Ina was not permitted to have her baby in the hospital as she was under the Aborigines Act. Aborigines weren't allowed into hospitals. Esther Corpus, a close friend, delivered Edith. Esther was very experienced at delivering babies so Ina was back on her feet and ready to go back to Kunmunya within days.

During Alfred's freight trips to Broome Ina was kept pretty busy raising four children. With the help of the house women she was also able to continue teaching at the kindergarten. The harmonious working combination of the MacDougalls, Loves, Browns and Shadforths lasted for five years. It would be difficult to match their productivity and dedication to the church over that period of time.

Leprosy

Sore eyes, well we used to often get sore eyes but Reverend Love used to attend to that and we used to always line up for our medication in the morning to have ointment put in our eyes. First we had to wash our eyes with a solution and then he'd put ointment in our eyes. At night before everybody went home he'd line us up again and he'd do the same thing.

Laurelle

Each day Reverend Love ran a clinic for the aged and sick. It was common for him to strap broken bones, acquired more often from fights than from falls. During the tropical months it was prickly heat, boils and diarrhoea he dealt with. He was pretty good at extracting teeth, and treating sore eyes, and general chest infections, as well as aches and pains. Medical supplies were limited and antibiotics were unheard of. Diarrhoea was treated with cornflour. Eucalyptus oil was used for aches and pains while potassium iodine was used on sores, cuts and burns. Once he attended to a nasty camel bite. One of Fred Merry's camels bit one of his workers on his lower jaw and lip. Three teeth of the camel penetrated his face leaving ugly holes. He patched him up as best he could and sent him on his way with extra bandages and instructions for Merry to discipline unruly camels.

Workers and visitors having contact with the outside world frequently brought the common cold back with them, passing it on to the Aboriginal people who suffered badly from it. They had no immunity to the virus and often took months to recover. Reverend Love promoted good hygiene and encouraged prevention rather than cure. There were constant checks on living quarters, making sure they kept a healthy camp. It was not unusual to find a broken spear, discarded bark water containers, part of a carved pearl shell, chips of stone for making spear heads or axes. The rubbish was never a serious threat to their health and was completely benign. But it was the twin scourges of leprosy and venereal disease that the mission had no control over. The diseases didn't discriminate amongst age, gender, or location and seemed to spread like fire among Aboriginal people, taking the lives of many.

> Reverend Love: *The present doctor in Broome has interested himself in the Aborigines and finds that venereal disease is far more widely seriously prevalent among these people than we suspect. Leprosy is also a serious problem. These people are now in danger of extinction through syphilis and leprosy.*

It was thought leprosy was introduced to Aborigines through indentured Asian labour. The effect of leprosy on Aboriginal people was so widespread it forced the government to make amendments to the Health Act in 1932, giving government medical officers the right to medically and physically examine Aborigines. In 1931 the Cossack Leprosarium was closed and patients were sent to Darwin. The Derby Leprosarium opened in 1936.

In October 1935, Reverend Love hired out the *Watt Leggatt* to the Health Department. Alfred knew the coast like the back of his hand and was asked to take the Medical Inspector for Aborigines, Dr Davis, north to Drysdale River Mission. Dr Davis was to examine the Aboriginal people living in remote settlements and camps. The mission knew the importance of getting medical help to the people and assisted in every possible way. The visit included Scott Strait and Vansittart Bay, two popular ports where non-Aboriginal men had established makeshift camps in order to earn a living from beachcombing. They collected shells, bêche-de-mer, turtle shell and anything else that could be sold or traded. The beachcombers needed cheap labour and recruited local Aboriginal people, who were extremely vulnerable to the diseases that infiltrated the camps through visitors.

The party included Dr Davis, Constable Golston from Broome, Harold Reid, the government superintendent from Munja Station and Reverend Love. It was October and the first stop was Augustus Island for fresh water. The next day Alfred sailed north to where the Wunambal people lived, and anchored off Bigge Island. They were hoping to find a settlement run by a beachcomber called William Haldane. Reverend Love, Dr Davis and Constable Golston went ashore while Alfred stayed behind to keep an eye on the lugger and the tide. The land party eventually met up with Haldane and walked the three miles inland to his camp. Haldane hadn't planned on them meeting up with one of his Aboriginal workers who was in possession of his shotgun. Haldane had sent him hunting for kangaroos. Poor Haldane was immediately charged with allowing an Aboriginal person access to a firearm. Added to this was a second charge for employing Aborigines without permits when they found workers in his camp. They found six people in the camp, two had granuloma and one was so badly disfigured with leprosy that half his face was missing.

The next port of call was Vansittart Bay to visit a camp several miles inland occupied by Willy Reid. Reid had done a good job of clearing the land. The well-established trees and vegetable garden gave the place a very settled appearance against the makeshift camp. The doctor examined a dozen women and finding them in good health returned to the lugger. Willy promised to have the men from his bêche-de-mer camp available for examination on their return trip. The next stop was Drysdale River.

Alfred was pretty happy with the trip so far. They hadn't hit any bad weather and the lugger was making good time. All was going according to plan and he hoped it would stay that way. When they arrived at Drysdale a note was sent ahead to Father Thomas informing the mission of the medical visit. Father Thomas immediately acknowledged it and welcomed the party ashore. They stayed overnight at the mission, leaving Alfred on board. The doctor examined the people while Love took the opportunity to learn about the local Aboriginal language and dialect. After breakfast they returned to the lugger and with a strong headwind headed south for the return leg of the journey. As promised, they revisited Willy Reid's camp and Willy was charged for not having a permit to employ Aboriginal people. It seemed like a lot of revenue raising was going on during the trip.

On the trip home they faced strong winds and were forced to seek shelter in a nearby cove before arriving home in early November. After examining seventy-nine people the doctor found one positive for leprosy, thirteen had granuloma and one suffered from gonorrhoea. Five days later Constable Golston, Dr Davis and his patients were heading for Broome and Reid was returning to Munja. The patients were treated at the Broome

Alfred Brown (standing) and the crew aboard the Watt Leggatt, *c. 1939.*

Native Hospital and those suffering from leprosy went to Derby for further treatment.

Trips such as these left Alfred uneasy as he worried about the effect it could have on his family. He once said, 'I used to be scared in a way, because I was thinking about my children. I had to listen to the doctor's advice, he said, "Be careful, don't let them use your pannikin, or whatever you're drinking with, never let them use that," he said, so I took his advice.'

The medical trips Alfred did to isolated settlements and camps were few and far between. The next official one occurred in 1939, then in 1940. It was difficult to attract government medical officers to provide a regular health service so in most cases sick people simply died. It was common for sufferers to head for the bush when they heard the doctor was coming. They would rather die than face hospitalisation away from their people and country. They called leprosy the 'big sickness' and had witnessed too many of their people removed only to die a lonely death far from their country.

Leprosy was reaching endemic proportions in the Kimberley and Alfred played a very important role in taking medical help — when it was available — to the people. His comprehensive understanding of the sea and locality enabled him to take doctors safely to remote places accessible only by sea through dangerous waters. In spite of the health risks it posed to his family he continued to skipper the *Watt Leggatt* on these expeditions.

On occasions when people presented to the mission with leprosy Reverend Love would send them to Broome on the *Watt Leggatt* and Alfred would have to escort them to the hospital. According to Alfred, 'It was embarrassing to take them up to the hospital and then get scolded by the matron for taking them there.' Eventually Alfred got fed up with being scolded and retaliated saying, 'Well I'm working for a boss. Reverend Love tells me to take these people to hospital, so I have to do it, otherwise out I go. You're a government matron ... It's your duty to care for these people.' On the next trip when he was tired of arguing with the matron he took the patients to the police station for the police to sort out. The police sergeant said, 'What have you got there?' Alfred said, 'Oh some sick people from Munja.' 'Well take them up to the hospital,' said the sergeant. 'No,' answered Alfred, 'I'm leaving them here for you to deal with.' The sergeant asked, 'Why?' When Alfred told him about the difficult matron the sergeant said, 'Why didn't you tell me this before?' The sergeant had some firm words with the matron and Alfred had no further trouble.

4

Life on the Mission

Miss Giles had a chook run and we had to wash the waterbowl which was a huge clam shell and feed the chicks. We'd watch her tie up the outer leaves of the lettuce so the little chicks had to jump to reach the lettuce. We loved watching them and she'd say they needed to jump up to strengthen their little legs.

Laurelle

The agricultural part of the mission was usually left to the assistant superintendent, as he was generally trained or experienced in this area of work. Between 1932 and 1939 Mr MacDougall did a very great job trying to get the most out of the soil. Paddocks had to be hoed, fertilised and weeded in readiness to support a range of fresh vegetables and fruits.

The soil at the mission was fertile enough, however there was constant experimentation to improve the quality of produce by regularly analysing the soil and devising suitable techniques in drainage. There was total reliance on good annual rainfall to irrigate the crop as the mission did not have equipment to pump fresh water from the creek. The unpredictability of the rain taught the staff to appreciate every drop.

> Laurelle: *I remember when Mr MacDougall shot his fingers. We were in school but he was out with some men working the paddocks. We were in the classroom when we heard the boys yelling and screaming outside. They were calling for Mrs Mac so she rushed out, kids behind her, we all followed her up to the stockyards. Apparently he took his rifle out with him when he had a team ploughing the paddock. He thought he might get lucky and shoot a turkey. Instead he found a donkey with its foot stuck in a jam tin and drove the donkey home to the stockyards to remove the tin. As he went to drive the donkey into the yard his rifle fell and exploded. Mr Love heard the shot and raced over to find him with a badly damaged hand and splinters in his face. We had an airstrip there that we helped build but we had to get to work straightaway and clear it so they could get a plane to come and get him. They sent for the Flying Doctor from Wyndham. And the plane came and picked him up. He was okay after that, even though he was minus a couple of fingers. I think he lost a thumb and forefinger.*

Stock at the mission included goats, mules, donkeys, cattle and horses. Young heifers were brought from Fred Russ at Gibb River Station while the not-so-young ones were slaughtered for meat. This happened when the need arose and meat not consumed was salted and stored in the beef house. Fresh meat supplemented the supplies of dugong, turtle, fish and wild game. Mustering donkeys and cattle occurred several times a year.

The men plaited their own whips, repaired saddles and maintained their own gear, including relining work. The

Aboriginal men were well trained in stock work and even better at tracking stock when it went astray. The mission had two pet horses, Patch and Rosie, bought from Fred Merry. They were used as work horses when the kids weren't playing with them.

> Laurelle: *Early in the morning, just as dawn was breaking us kids went down to Mr Love's place to get the milk buckets to milk the goats. After milking the milkers, we took the milk back to Mr Love, who gave it out to everyone. We always seemed to get enough milk for everyone. While we were at school the shepherd took the goats out to graze and in the late afternoon they brought them back in. Last thing we did at night was separate the milkers from the kiddy goats. We had to give them rock salt, I think they called it saltpetre. It was purplish and we would get down and have a lick ourselves. I think in some instances we would push the goats aside and help ourselves to the salt. We all had our favourite little goats that we gave special names to. We knew them all, don't ask me how but we just did. There was this billy-goat we named Wattie and when we were separating the kiddies from their mums we kept one eye on Wattie so he wouldn't butt us. The kids would yell, 'Here comes Wattie,' and we'd scatter, climbing posts or rails, anything to get away from Wattie so he couldn't butt us. Sometimes Wattie was faster than us and he'd butt us so we ended up face down in the manure. Wattie had this goatee beard, long horns and he smelt horrible, absolutely foul. I've never known a billy-goat to stink as much as old Wattie. One day Percy got hold of this cigarette, I don't know where he got it from. He gave it to Wattie who proudly stood there and had a smoke. Smoke seemed to be coming out of his mouth and ears and he looked like a steam train. We said, 'Percy, don't do that you'll kill him.' But it was like water*

off a duck's back, Percy thought it was a great joke. Thinking back now, it did look funny. When the mission closed they killed old Wattie and ate him.

Donkeys were widely used for heavy pulling and lifting tasks around the mission. On one occasion they were used to lift the engine from the *Watt Leggatt*. They removed it and put it on a sledge which overbalanced and fell to the ground, missing the sea by inches. Alfred and Reverend Love, with about ten men and eight donkeys, pulled the engine over the steep part of the landing. After negotiating the landing the donkeys pulled the sledge a further three miles to the mission for repairs and maintenance. Donkeys were worth their weight in gold, pulling ploughs when the garden beds were ready for fallowing, dragging and carting gear around the mission, general transport and as a source of entertainment in organised races.

Laurelle: *Fridays was a working day for all the Aboriginal people. It was wood day. Everybody had to collect wood. There was a big cook house there where an old Aboriginal man named Cookamanjohn used to make enough bread for all the people. He had a pretty big kitchen where he cooked up a big stew. The people used to get their meals in a billy can and go off under the trees and eat. On Saturdays they would go to the store and get provisions like flour and sugar and tea and that would last them for the week. They'd get these blankets from the store. I used to like sitting on the woodheap with Cookamanjohn's fresh bread. I'd cut the crust off and sit on the woodheap and eat it with treacle.*

The school children had to work after school. When

school finished at twelve o'clock they went home for lunch and a short rest. After afternoon siesta Mr Love rang a big bell that was in the church, signalling it was time to go to work. Everyone

Worrorra women preparing the vegetable garden, Kunmunya, c. 1939.

gathered around the storeroom, usually half drowsy from sleep, and waited for Mr Love to delegate jobs. The men worked on repairing windmills, building, mending wheelbarrows and the cart, cleaning out septic tanks, painting the buildings, concrete work, building drains and repairing roads.

The children were given easy tasks and working in the vegetable garden was one which they happily accepted. Seedlings had to be watered and those ready for planting in garden beds had to be transplanted in the afternoon when it was cooler. There was a nursery under the elevated houses where seeds were sprouted and nurtured until they were hardened off ready for transplanting. Bananas ready for picking were chopped down by the older boys and the younger ones came along after to carry them back to the storehouse.

Laurelle was part of the crew that had to carry the bunches. She hated the sticky transparent sap that oozed from the stem and dribbled onto her arms. The sap always left brown patches on her arms and clothes that faded with time.

Laurelle: *The mission didn't use pesticides, we had to pick the bugs off the vegies ourselves and put them in buckets. Well, I didn't mind picking the beetles but I hated touching the grubs as there seemed to be hundreds of them crawling over the potatoes. When the bucket was full they seemed to crawl over each other and ooze over the edge. When the pumpkins and watermelons were in season we had to take them off one by one and how I hated it when they crawled all over my hand and up my arm. We had to burn them all. There were ladybirds, brown beetles, grubs. We seemed to have acres and acres of sweet potatoes so there were hundreds and hundreds of grubs to remove. They felt so slimy and soft and we had to grab them carefully so they wouldn't squash in our hands. How I hated that job; when I left the mission I never wanted to see another field of sweet potato again. After Reverend Love thought we'd worked enough you'd hear him whistle. You'd hear this piercing whistle he had and that was the signal to stop work. You never ignored his whistle and all the kids went up to him and then he'd say, 'Right come with me.' He'd give us a cake of soap and away we'd go down the creek, more like a river. There was always water there right towards the wet season. We used to just call it Kunmunya Creek. We would run down and have a good old swim and bath and get all the smell off us. He was thoughtful in that way. He'd say, 'Right go and have a swim,' and away we'd go. We seemed to do a lot of swimming at the mission, every day after we finished our jobs we'd go swimming.*

Collecting ant beds was another interesting job. The men chopped the ant beds down with axes and smashed them making it easy for the children to pick up the pieces as they followed behind. Gathering them piece by piece, they put them into hessian bags and carted them back to the mission ready for processing. The ant beds were crushed and mixed with water to make a paste that was spread to

Kunmunya Mission Station, c. 1934.
(Photograph H R Balfour, courtesy Uniting Church of Australia.)

form a floor, much the same way as a concrete is poured and formed. If the floor looked slightly dusty, a spray of water settled the powdery base. Most of the earlier houses had floors made from ant beds except for the main buildings like the church, dispensary and school, which had cement floors. The ant bed method was a cheap and functional way of laying flooring in the buildings.

Laurelle: *We had an airstrip at the mission. The men and women used to go and do their share of work, cut the trees down. It was more or less hand built. We had to help shift little rocks and pick up whatever trees and saplings the men chopped down. It wasn't hard work, we didn't have to do any hard labour or anything. Mr Love saw to that. It was the little things we had to do and we enjoyed it. Mr Love was in there amongst the workers, sleeves rolled up working away side by side with us digging up shrubs, cutting down saplings, dragging away debris and piling it up ready for burning. For a plane to come in was a big event. It didn't happen often. We were allowed to go and see the plane. Mr Love had a pedal set where he would radio for a plane, and it was only in emergency that he did. You could say the children built the airstrip. When a plane arrived we all stopped what we were doing to watch it. It was a special time when a plane landed at the mission.*

Working the peanut plantation was a team effort. The nuts were planted in December and relied on the wet season; if the rains were too heavy replanting had to be done. After a good night's rain it was common to see small frogs roosting on the peanut leaves the next morning. Keeping the camp dogs out was a problem; they often broke into the paddocks and dug up the plants. In May the peanuts were dug up, prepared and bagged, ready to send on the lugger to Broome. In addition to problems with flooding and stray dogs there was the worry of crows attacking the crop and eating the nuts. In spite of these problems the crop report for 1940–1941 showed the total yield of nuts was sixty-five bags at 4,228 pounds net.

Laurelle: *We had these little hessian bags that we tied around our waist and in them we carried the raw peanut that was shelled ready for planting. There would be a person walking in front of us making a hole about two inches deep with a stick. Then we followed and in each hole put a nut and covered it over with our toes. You could see a row of twelve women preparing the hole and behind them a row of twelve children planting. That's how we planted peanuts, of course we ate more nuts than we planted. Then we let the rains do their job and after the rains the men would dig up the peanut plants. The kids would go behind them and shake the plants that were full of about fifty or sixty peanuts per plant. We'd leave the nuts to dry for about one or two weeks. After this the men, women and children would stack them in a hay stack. When we stacked them the nuts faced inside with the bush facing outwards. They stayed there like that and when Reverend Love felt that the nuts were ready to break off from the bush we'd do that job. Next the nuts were sorted into sizes and variety. The men would bag them and sow the bags ready to go to Broome. Where they went to from Broome, I don't know, all I know is that Dad took them into Broome. We were never short of peanuts at the mission and we learnt to eat peanuts lots of different ways. Raw, roasted, steamed, fried.*

Occasional plagues of bush flies made working in the vegetable gardens almost impossible, driving everyone insane. Adults and children developed sore eyes and the donkeys ended up with infections from flies. Another problem was camp dogs eating the half-ripe pineapples. Poisoned bones were used as bait to kill them and as a reminder to the people to control their animals. There were times when the abundance of fruit got the better of the children and they had to suffer the consequences of their behaviour in the event they were caught stealing from the fruit and vegetable gardens.

Florence O'Donnell (nee Shadforth, Laurelle's cousin): *Between the superintendent's and assistant superintendent's house there was a big garden with everything in it. We'd pick three tomatoes, two would go into the bucket and the third we'd eat. There was another vegetable garden down the back of Love's place with this creek running from the top right down to the waterfall and on each bank they had bananas and there was a little bridge across, we all loved that little bridge, and we'd go over to the other side where all the cauliflower and carrots and that were growing. We were supposed to be weeding and we'd go along and pull up a few weeds and carrots as well. Then we'd pull the tops off the carrots, put it back in the same place then eat the carrots. We'd do the same with the cauliflower. I'm sure Mr Love knew what we were doing but he never said anything. The mission grew beautiful vegies. On Saturdays we'd pick bananas and watermelons. One day there was this huge melon and a group of us decided to pick it, thinking it wouldn't be missed. It was that big we couldn't pick it up so we had to roll it into the grass where we hid and broke it open with the tomahawks we were given to cut the bananas down with. The melon was perfect and when the blade touched the skin it just split open and we had a feed. We were having a great picnic when we heard footsteps so we sat quietly as the steps got closer and closer and stopped. When we looked down we saw two great big boots and we followed it up to see Mr MacDougall who was a very tall chap with red hair. He said, 'Yes I've caught you,' and we never said anything. 'So tell me, who is the child who picked the watermelon?' he said. Not wanting to dob, we didn't say anything. He frogmarched the four of us back to his house and gave us a lecture. He said, 'Now you've picked that watermelon, you've had your share now, for the next two weeks you'll go without fruit.' You see every Saturday we would all get a bunch of bananas, some watermelon and something else and the following week we would get different fruit. The thought of no fruit for two weeks was something to think about as we loved our fruit. I don't think we ever pinched a watermelon again.*

EDUCATION AT THE MISSION

> *Dad wouldn't tolerate any back answers from us. His word was law and the same applied with the Shadforths so there was no fooling around in school. The missionaries wouldn't tolerate the Aboriginal children fooling around. My brothers and sisters didn't dare misbehave at school because we knew if Dad found out we'd get a jolly good whack or two. Respect was something we learnt very early and didn't question.*
>
> Laurelle

In the mid 1930s education for indigenous children was the responsibility of the Aborigines Department as it was the legal guardian of Aboriginal and 'half-caste' children up to the age of sixteen years. The state government was legally responsible for the welfare of Aboriginal people and as such accountable for their education. The responsibility filtered down to missions, orphanages and government reserves. Education for Aboriginal children was very badly organised by the government, and those living in areas where strong non-Aboriginal parent groups operated suffered the most. The Education Act at the time gave parent groups the power to exclude from school children with contagious conditions such as ringworm and sore eyes. Aboriginal children could also be excluded in summer months if parent groups thought that their smell was causing illness in non-Aboriginal children. Parents in the south-west rural towns of Beverley, Quairading, Mt Barker and Katanning were completely excluding Aboriginal children from their schools. This practice continued until the early 1950s when the government became serious about addressing

Aboriginal education in state schools. Access and participation improved when the Education Department took on the responsibility for Aboriginal education.

When Laurelle started school in 1934 Kunmunya was expected to accept responsibility for the schooling of Aboriginal children in their care. The mission provided a good education under difficult conditions. In 1933 a generous parishioner in the eastern states donated the cost of a new school so Ernie, Jerry, two Worrorra men, and Reverend Love built one in readiness for the new year. The old school was a dark, dank and uninviting enclosure under Mr MacDougall's house and with growing numbers a larger well-lit room was essential. There was plenty of room in the new school, it was fresh, well-equipped and inviting to the children.

> Laurelle: *I went to school with people like Daisy Uttemorrah, Kudianna, Pudjawolla, Buruwolla, Rudniwalla, Hazel, Durawalla, David Mowaljarlie, Allan Mungulu, Donald Langi, Ian, Flora, Morlumbun and Jack Weira. There were about twenty-five including us and the Shadforths. Occasionally the Love children attended but most times Mrs Love used to teach them at home separately from us. I think it was because they had to eventually go to school in South Australia. We'd wear ordinary clothes to school, then we'd change when we went to play or work in the garden. Miss Giles came from Mapoon Mission to teach the Aboriginal children then she married the assistant superintendent, Mr MacDougall. She must have worked with Mum at Mapoon but I knew her as Mrs MacDougall.*

Mrs MacDougall was her teacher for most of the time Laurelle was at the mission. When she left in 1939, due to ill-health, Mrs Love's sister Miss Holinger replaced her. Later there was a succession of teachers including Mrs Holmes, Mrs Taylor and Mrs Paton. Schooling was taken seriously with annual examinations in early December. Students were assessed in reading, composition, handwriting, arithmetic, geography and drawing. The results ranged from encouraging, developing to excellent. Standards were important.

> Laurelle: *Mrs MacDougall had this old cow bell that she used to ring in the morning to start school at eight o'clock. I'm sure we did a little exercise in the morning then we went into the classroom and we had to open up with a prayer and hymn, that I do remember. Then we started our lessons. ABC was taught, counting was taught, and telling the time. We had a big wooden clock up on the wall that we learnt from. The clock didn't work and you used your finger to shift it to learn how to tell the time. It was made at the mission for the school. The schoolhouse was like a barn, made of local timber and ant bed floors with a couple of blackboards. Mrs MacDougall had this lovely big desk and we sat opposite her with the little ones in the front and the older ones to the back. Pencils, paper and exercise books were supplied by the mission and came from the church in Melbourne. There was one big long blackboard right in the middle. Mrs MacDougall would put the sums up for us and we had to write it in our book and at the end of the day she would correct it. We used to use nibs and ink and she wouldn't let us fill the inkwell because she knew we'd spill ink everywhere. Schooling was mainly reading, writing, spelling, dictation, composition, arithmetic and we had to learn the tables off by heart. We used to say them in a singsong manner, not like how it's done now, as the teaching is completely different. We used to do a lot of*

> word building and a lot of cutting out. We would get this card when we had our sewing period. We had to sew little animals on this card. They were drawn on with little dots where you had to put the needle in and out. That's what we did for sewing before we used material to sew on.

Reverend Love strongly supported the maintenance of Worrorra and other Aboriginal languages and dialects. He loathed the use of Pidgin, a contact language that was viewed as bad English. He encouraged the parents to speak Worrorra to their children and insisted the children switch to English at school. The language of instruction was English. Staff were expected to communicate in English and learn Worrorra to talk to the old people who couldn't speak English. This was a radical and inspirational attitude, given most people in contact with traditional Aboriginal people used Pidgin and not the Aboriginal language of that area to communicate.

> Laurelle: *At church we'd say prayers in Worrorra, the Our Father especially and Mr Love would say most of the mass in that language. Mr Love and Dad used to speak it with the crew and old people. Sometimes you'd hear the children speaking it, Mr Love used to encourage it. As a child I could speak Worrorra but I've forgotten most of it. Mr Love was a linguist and could speak Worrorra fluently to the people. He used to sit on the verandah in the afternoons with Heather Umbagai's grandfather, Albert Barunga and Wondoonmoi and another man translating the gospel. He could see us working in the garden, his verandah overlooked the mission and he'd keep an eye on us and translate as well. I'm sure it was the gospel they were working on. It was only men who taught him, never women.*

The education Laurelle received was vastly different to that available to her grandchildren today but in keeping with educational approaches elsewhere. The rote and drill method was the traditional way the three Rs were taught in all schools across the country at the time. The bright and colourful classrooms filled with stimulating charts and resources with teacher-directed learning in small groups are very recent initiatives in education. Although Laurelle went to school on an isolated mission the delivery of education wasn't much different elsewhere.

The translation team (l–r), Njimandum, Albert Barunga and Wondoomoil, with Reverend Love, 1929.
(Courtesy Mrs J R B Love.)

Laurelle: *We loved school and there were times when Mrs MacDougall let us walk around so long as we were good. She was very good, very patient, she didn't yell or scream at anyone. If you did anything wrong she'd call you in after school and she wouldn't chastise you in front of the class. She was a very good teacher. After school every day we would wipe the blackboard and stack the chairs and leave the room neat and tidy. The teaching's completely different now. I only had a mission education and that was only so you knew how to write and add up. We were taught how to write letters and things like that but I could no more put a good letter down on paper now. The words they have now are completely different. We had the ordinary everyday words that you used. Our schooling was nothing to be excited about, it was just to learn how to read and write and add up and things like that. Arithmetic was adding, subtracting, multiplying, division and that's all.*

Mrs MacDougall ran the Brownies and Guides for the girls and Cubs and Scouts for the boys. As she was their teacher it seemed like an extension of school and Laurelle found herself working her way up through the ranks starting with Brownies. You were doing pretty well if you got to be a leader in Guides, a position all the girls at Kunmunya aspired to. Her older brother Alwyn was in Scouts along with Henry and the Love boys.

Around twelve children met once a week on the front lawn of Mrs MacDougall's house. It was a time to honour the king, raise the Australian flag, salute leaders and participate in a range of activities from tying knots, sewing and playing games, to doing first aid. They always arrived keen and neatly dressed in uniform, complete with badges, hat and tie, but drew the line at footwear. Like most country kids they were exposed to good healthy fun and enjoyed the camaraderie more than the discipline.

Boy Scouts and Girl Guides meeting, on the lawn in front of the Reverend Love's house, Kunmunya, c. 1938–39. In the photograph are Alwyn Brown, Henry Shadforth, Bobby Love, Florence Shadforth, Daisy Uttermorrah, Elkin Umbagai and other Worrorra children.

When it was too hot to work it was picnic time. There was no need to carry water containers: when the children were thirsty they found a sandy spot near the river bank, dug a little well and waited for clear water to seep to the surface before bending down to drink from it. When a fire was required to boil the billy the women made a fire using liruk (firesticks). The liruk were two round sticks about two feet in length and made from a special type of wood. The friction created from rubbing the sticks together would ignite kindling to make a fire. The women always took their tomahawk and liruk on picnics and when they went hunting. After the fire was reduced to coals the women made damper while the children gathered around hungrily smelling the baking dough as it cooked.

> Laurelle: *One of my favourite spots was the waterfall. We used to get under the waterfall, you couldn't when it was flooding, it was too strong, but when it settled down and it would still be running we would crawl under the water and there were these rocks that we would slide down on a slippery slide and go down into the big pool. A few metres away there was this beautiful big boab tree that had nice clean sand around it and that was where we made our dinner camp. The waterfall was only a few kilometres from the mission; it didn't seem far to us and we didn't mind the walk. There were two magnificent goannas that lived there. We weren't allowed to throw anything at them. We knew Reverend Love would be extremely angry if he found out. Close by there were two springs that had Worrorra names. Argoo Wungootgari and Argoo Jullingari. Behind Reverend Love's place, away from the vegie garden, there was a hill and we'd walk up that hill and explore the caves that were there. We were warned about dingoes hanging around the caves but that didn't worry us, we knew every part of that hill.*

We'd walk along the top of the hill as it flattened out at the top.

Not all picnics were to the bush. One day they went on the *Watt Leggatt* when a new engine had to be tried out. Alfred took Mr Young and his family, the school children, the house women and a visitor, Dr Davis. They were all on board by 10.30am and an hour and a half later they were at old Port George IV, the early site of the mission. Only the stumps of the buildings, the remains of a fence and a white man's grave (said to be that of a policeman who went mad and took his own life) remained to show signs of previous habitation.

Laurelle: *We loved the wet season because it meant we could go looking for bush fruits to eat. There was mutkullom, a wild fruit about the size of a cherry that was green in colour and fell from the tree when ripe. Then there was gulgay and mudjawadda. A fruit like blackberry that grew on a bush was mudjawadda. The kids didn't like wild grapes because it burnt their tongue, leaving blue marks around their mouth as a tell-tale mark. Munjeewarri was a little round fruit like a bulb that was delicious and a favourite of everyone. I remember the bush fruits well. One of my favourites was mutkollum. They were like little apples. There were the wild lady apples which were a little bigger, they were like an apple and pink on one side. I liked the wild apple. They were big and sweet and grew up near the springs.*

When the Watt Leggatt *came in everybody had a holiday from school. The mission was about three miles from the landing. We'd all go down to the boat and stay with Dad and come back with him in the afternoon. It was great having Dad as the skipper as we got the day off school. All the Aboriginal people helped bring the stores up, the kids carried the lighter things. Larger stuff in boxes went in the cart, that's all we had to bring the real heavy stuff up in. It was hard because where the* Watt Leggatt *pulled up there was a nasty jump-up and they had to carry everything up this jump-up. They'd load the cart up and one of the men drove it up, it had three donkeys to pull it. The rest of us would walk back to the mission with a bag of flour or a bag of sugar or something we could manage. Everyone raced down when they heard the lugger was in, all the kids went down there, women, men and kids. The girls were with the women's group and the men went ahead. That was their culture. Their culture was never broken like that. They would get their stuff while the women stood aside. After the men were loaded up the women would come in and get loaded up with stores. Then they'd walk back in separate groups. All the time the men would remember which ones were their rambadba.*

The Aboriginal people were encouraged to take their children bush during the holidays. Wandering with their hunting dogs they went where they could find water and food. They walked through places like Marie Springs, Walcott Inlet, Sale River and Prince Regent.

When the adults and children went bush they discarded their clothes and replaced them with hair belts that had a tassel of spun hair hanging in the front. Kangaroo fur or human hair is spun to make the belts. The men often had a pearl shell hanging from the belt. Men were encouraged to keep their traditional head dress. This involved piling the hair skilfully on the back of the head and plastering it with clay, resulting in a very elaborate and distinguished appearance.

The boys learnt to spear fish, turtle and dugong as well as goanna and kangaroo, modelling their hunting techniques on their fathers and uncles. The girls dug for yams with a wondoon (yam stick) and learnt to chop down succulent bush honey and hunt small lizards. They learnt how and where to find bush medicines and clear fresh water. They watched their parents make a fire using liruk and how to cook the bush food gathered during the day. At night they listened wide-eyed to the stories of the Wandjina and watched the corroborees handed down through the generations over thousands of years. The only restriction on them, by the mission, was to have the children back for school.

Laurelle never went bush with the Worrorra people for extended periods of time such as this. It was through her daily interaction with them that she was fortunate to witness the full manifestation of their rich culture.

> *Laurelle: The young girls and little children used to wear tribal belts made of kangaroo hair and fur. I remember a couple of young girls, in particular Pudja, wearing only hair belts. I think that generation was the last to wear tribal belts. I didn't see too many women wearing them towards the end of our stay there. When the people went bush they'd always wear them. Reverend Love encouraged them to keep their culture. I know he didn't like it when the old men would take young women as their wives. I know that was hard for him to accept.*
>
> *After the flood and the wet season we'd pick up these stones, like shale, spearheads for the old men. Later on I found out it was a type of opal that washed down from the gully and finished at the creek bed. We also found quartz and amethyst but at the time we didn't think they were worth keeping. It was the same with little pearls that were*

found when we were out on the boats. It wasn't of any value to us, these stones were just something you came across every day of the week but they meant nothing to us. They were of no value at the mission. We'd give them to the old men and watch them make spearheads. Only the men made the spearhead and kept them in parcels of paperbark. The parcel doubled as a pillow and was called burung. We'd gather around one of the old men with our legs crossed looking like little buddhas, while he chipped away at the stone. If too much of the stone came off he'd say, 'Oh! Wauragi.' And we'd say, 'What's the matter, Goodman, what have you done?' And he'd say, 'Too much, take too much.' He'd think there for a little while, then he'd start again. All the time the old men were chipping away they'd be singing in their language.

Kathy's Arrival and the Cyclone of 1935

You could say Dad was one of the unsung heroes of the 1935 blow and he got no recognition for it.
Laurelle

In 1935 Laurelle experienced her first cyclone, an experience she vividly recalls today.

Alfred and his family had left the mission on the *Watt Leggatt* on 25 February of that year. The wet season was still upon them and Ina was ready to have their fifth child. He knew he had to have her in safe hands well before the baby was due in case the weather deteriorated or the baby determined its own arrival time. He had Ina in Broome in ample time and, after settling her and the younger children, returned to the mission, taking Alwyn with him. The mission was waiting for the mail and fresh food. He arrived back there on 16 March and set sail again on 21 March for Walcott Inlet, then Broome. On his way he sensed a cyclone brewing and anchored in the safety of the closest bay to sit it out.

The night before the cyclone Ina was still waiting for the baby to arrive. She was expecting Alfred and Alwyn to join them before the new addition to the family arrived. Ina and the children were staying with a very close family friend, Goodji D'Antoine. She lived in a quaint little house behind Sun Pictures in Chinatown. The clouds had started to build up and it had started to rain, not heavy, just regular light rain.

The night of the cyclone the wind howled ruthlessly through every conceivable space and crack in an effort to uproot and disfigure anything that stood in its path. There was very little rain; it wasn't pouring down in bucket loads, just steady rain, but it was the wind causing all the havoc. Coconut trees went down one after another with the occasional one flung into the nearest space like soiled clothes tossed flippantly into a laundry basket. Residents had made hasty attempts to protect the few windows they had with pieces of jarrah nailed across the glass, resembling a cross. There was no sign of humanity, only the occasional rubbish bin rolling around, posing a threat to any dog or cat daring to dart across the street. It was dark. Laurelle pressed her little face against a piece of unprotected window to take in the sights of the 1935 cyclone thinking how funny the trees and sheet iron looked as they danced to the tune of the gale force winds that ravaged Broome.

The corrugated sheets on the roof of Goodji's house started to loosen. They knew when the first sheet went then the rest would peel off like a ripe banana skin. In the lull of the cyclone, Laurelle's cousin Patrick Shadforth picked up Ina and carried her to Ahmat Bulldog's place. Ahmat was a Malay who lived very close to Goodji. The cyclone frightened and confused him. He didn't want too many people in his house, and the responsibility of a woman in her final stages of childbirth sent him into a panic. He tried to send them elsewhere, but Goodji, was a strong-willed person and proceeded to point out the error of his ways and threatened him. Ahmat succumbed and gave Ina a room. Patrick went back and fetched the rest of the family so they would all be safely together.

Patrick seemed to be hovering around Ina's room making sure she was safe. Ina was more worried about her other nephew, Percy, than she was of the arrival of her baby. She called Patrick into her room asking, 'Is Percy in yet?' Percy was out at sea on the *Coppia*. He said, 'No.' So she said, 'When it's safe, you go down to the jetty and see if you can find your brother.' She was very concerned for Percy and aware of the dangers of being stranded at sea during a serious blow.

In the middle of the cyclone Goodji delivered Ina's baby. In the howling wind and rain she was thinking, 'Any minute this roof is going to go and I haven't delivered this baby.' The baby was obliging and arrived safely. Ina named her Kathleen and the old people of Broome called her the 'willy willy girl.' At the time, cyclones didn't have names but if they had I'm sure she would have been named after it.

The effects of the cyclone were felt at Kunmunya. It caused extensive damage to livestock and property. The day before the blow the mission had heavy rain all day with gale force wind. The rain gauge showed three hundred and sixty points at 9.00am and a further four inches was measured later in the day. It rained and blew continually and the creeks broke their banks taking away the gate and two stretches of fence. The flood touched the fence by the girls' dormitory, covered the new peanut paddock, and practically all the back paddock and a good deal of corn was washed flat and carried away. Several milking cows were lost and others could be heard bellowing for their young calves, barely a week old. There were several newborn kids in the goat flock that were also lost along with the young calves.

In stormy weather and driving rains it was too dangerous to do any work or for anyone to go hunting. They settled on an evening meal of hot porridge for all hundred and eight present. By 28 March twelve inches of rain had fallen over the past three days. Harry returned on the *Rolland* the day after, reporting that the jib had been torn to pieces in the storm, otherwise all was well. Following the cyclone everyone was busy. Drains had to be dug to control the flow of water, fences had to be mended, vegetable gardens cleared and firewood collected. The mission was very lucky there was no loss of lives.

On Sunday 14 April the *Watt Leggatt* arrived back at Kunmunya late in the day to shouting and joy in the camp. They were happy the lugger and everyone aboard had survived the cyclone, including the new baby. The mission had almost run out of food, so it was celebration time when the fresh supplies arrived. Alfred, Ina and the family spent the night on the lugger and made their way up to the mission late the next day.

Compared to the damage caused by the cyclone to Broome, the mission came out relatively unscathed. In Broome it was reported that twenty luggers and one hundred and forty lives had been lost. A similar cyclone in 1887 claimed eighteen luggers with, coincidently, the loss of one hundred and forty lives. From newspaper reports it appears that the cyclone arrived with tropical suddenness as shipping movements and the falling barometric pressure suggested. The barometers dropped sharply on the afternoon of Tuesday 26 March and the pearling fleet made for shelter in Barred Creek. However, severe headwinds forced them to go about and put to sea in an effort to ride out the storm.

> Laurelle: *Well, Dad was at Walcott, Munja Station and they were on their way back to Broome. When he came out of the mouth of Walcott into Doubtful Bay, he noticed that the top of the cabin, inside the cabin, it was all just coated with flies. He said to one of the crew, 'I think we're in for bad weather.' He said, 'These flies, we don't usually get flies out at sea.' There wasn't any cloud, just a little bit, not much, nothing to worry about. The water was milky and he knew then that he would have to get to shelter quickly. He made straight for Barramundi Bay at Koolan Island as that was the closest bay and that's where he sat the cyclone out. Alwyn was with him all the time and they were quite sheltered there. Alwyn said there were trees and everything flying through the air but when Dad left next morning everything was calm. When he went through the Lacepedes he noticed masts sticking out of the water so he said to his crew, 'We'd better go and check that out, looks like one of the boats went down.' There were a couple I think that went down, I'm not sure how many. He picked up about seven survivors. He said to the survivors, 'Are there any more boats around here?' They said, 'No, we were the only ones.' So he took them into Broome and he got thanked for it. Now when the* Koolinda *went past the Lacepedes, must have been about a few days after, she noticed smoke so they went ashore and there were about*

three more survivors. I'm not sure of the exact number but I do know it was about three or four and the captain picked them up. I don't know whether he was going north or south but the Koolinda *got blessed by the Japanese emperor for this incident and the captain of the* Koolinda *got knighted for his efforts in picking up the survivors. But Dad, he got nothing, no recognition, nothing at all. Thinking back now, maybe they should have said something about the mission lugger, the* Watt Leggatt *picking up survivors but there was never any record or recognition of it and Dad's part in it. This was why I think the* Koolinda *was never bombed during the war because of being blessed by the Japanese emperor. A lot of people were saying, 'That's only hogwash, it was just luck,' but it wasn't hogwash.*

That was my experience in my first cyclone. But there were a lot of lives lost at sea during the 1935 cyclone. I guess it was just Dad's knowledge of the sea that kept him safe, otherwise he could have been caught out in the open near Collier Bay, but he knew what was happening and he read all the signs from the sea. It was interesting because Dad said the barometer never dropped before the cyclone to indicate bad weather. It was the look of the murky water and hundreds of flies in the cabin that made him suspicious.

It was reported that the *Koolinda* rescued eighteen crewmen from two luggers. The only formal acknowledgement of Alfred's rescue efforts during the 1935 blow was in the Presbyterian General Assembly minutes for 1936.

5

The Loss of Our Mother

I couldn't understand why Dad didn't take us back to Mapoon Mission. He had his reasons, I suppose. He didn't want to leave WA because Mum was buried out at Kunmunya. He never got over her death and I didn't know how to help him.

Laurelle

After Kathleen came along life resumed to normal. Ina was kept pretty busy with five children on her hands and Alfred away weeks at a time.

Occasionally she went on a trip to Broome with him if the family urgently needed to see the doctor or dentist. Alfred had made some genuine friends through work who invited him and Ina to stay with them when they visited Broome. Usually Alfred liked to stay on the boat but when Ina and the family joined him it was different. He came under the Act and was denied access to accommodation facilities such as hotels. Aboriginal people supported each other and offered their hospitality in situations like this. They lived together in segregated areas designated by the government and it was at such times they felt the full impact of the Act. On the mission everyone was equal.

When Ina was ready to have her last child, Alfred was still caught in the political battle of trying to obtain exemption status so his wife could have access to mainstream medical facilities. Alfred was contributing towards a health fund and had sufficient insurance to cover the cost but this didn't entitle his family to access a mainstream hospital. Only an exemption from the Aborigines Act could guarantee this and contributions towards a fund had no bearing at all.

Ina went to Broome towards the middle of April and Ivy, her last child, was born in early May 1937. Nellie Hunter delivered Ivy and after the birth she asked Dr Haynes to check on her. He thought Ina was fit to return to the mission but Nellie didn't want her to go back so soon after the birth. She pleaded with Alfred, 'You leave her here. You can take her back next trip, Alf.' Ina, not wanting to create a fuss, allowed Alfred to take her home to settle the new baby and see the children. Besides, Broome always made her feel uncomfortable with its segregated practices. Nellie sensed then that Ina hadn't fully recovered and was not ready to return. Years later she told Laurelle, 'When they took your mother and I saw her hop on the dinghy and go on board holding Ivy tightly in her arms, I said to Tommy, I don't think I'll be seeing my friend again.'

It was a Saturday that the *Watt Leggatt* arrived back at Kunmunya and being late in the evening Ina and Ivy spent the night on the boat. The next morning they made their way up to the mission on the cart, with Ina not feeling very well at all. She put it down to postnatal emotions playing havoc and felt it would settle down in a few days. Reverend Love was away on holidays and his replacement, Mr Taylor, was in charge. The MacDougalls were still on the mission. A day later Mr Taylor contacted the doctor by radio as he was concerned about Ina's swollen leg and constant nausea. The doctor said to watch her closely and make sure she was eating well; apart from that there was nothing to worry about. Several days later on the twentieth Ina seemed brighter and feeling much better but by 7.30pm Harry had to fetch Mr Taylor as she had taken a turn for the worse. When Mr Taylor arrived she was breathing very fast with great difficulty. Her pulse was very erratic and she said goodbye to everyone and passed away peacefully twenty minutes later, her breathing just becoming weaker and weaker until it failed altogether. Ina died that night leaving a totally devastated and confused family of four girls, two boys and a husband. They had been told she was getting better and there was no cause for concern. They couldn't understand what went wrong.

Laurelle: *The night Mum died, well the day before, we were cleaning the church with Mrs MacDougall and she said to me then, 'You'll be happy to know your mother will be up and about tomorrow,' and I was quite happy about that. I was excited to see Mum and the new baby. I was looking forward to helping her with Ivy. And we went off to sleep, then we were woken up by Mrs MacDougall and she said to me then, she said, 'I have to tell you and Alwyn your mother has gone to live with Jesus.' We knew straightaway what had happened then but it took a while to sink in. Alwyn never got over the death of Mum and he changed, it affected him badly, something in him seemed to fade away and he became withdrawn and developed a bad temper. He was very close to Mum and being the oldest he seemed closer to her. He went to stay with Mrs MacDougall as she understood him and could reach him. He never spoke about Mum, never said anything, just grieved by himself.*

Ina's death certificate showed the cause to be unknown, with anaemia due to hookworm a contributing factor. She was buried in the mission cemetery about a mile and a half from the landing. She was laid to rest among several other Aboriginal friends who chose Christian burials.

Laurelle: *We had to bury her the next day because they had no facilities to keep dead people, like freezers and things. The next day Mr Taylor was doing the coffin up, Kathy could hear this banging there and she was only about eighteen months old. She went up to the door and started hitting it calling out to Mum to open the door, thinking it was Mum making the noise. I didn't know what to do and I just stood there and froze. Florence rushed over and grabbed her and pulled her away from the door, trying to calm her. It was very hard for me, I just didn't know what to do. I remember Dad nearly passed out at Mum's funeral. Uncle Harry was holding Evelyn and struggling to support Dad as well. The Worrorra people were holding Kathy and Edith, they used to carry them on their shoulders like their own children. Ivy was being babysat at Reverend Taylor's house as Reverend Love was on holidays. I was clinging to Florence, totally confused. I'd been told my mother was getting better then all of a sudden she was dead.*

In June 1938 Alfred wrote yet again to the Native Welfare Department for an exemption. Reverend Love supported his application and in November 1938 he received his exemption papers after a debate that had taken seven years and seven months. It brought with it the freedom to manage his own destiny and that of his children but too late for medical help for Ina.

Alfred never returned to Mapoon and this may have been due to the exempted status he had fought so long and hard for. Returning to Mapoon would have meant he had to go through the trauma again as his exemption would not have been valid in Queensland.

Shortly after Ina died Alfred received pressure from the local protector living at Munja, who had heard about Ina, to send his children south to the Moore River Native Settlement. Alfred was distressed, insulted and appalled by the suggestion. He had heard terrible reports about Moore River mistreating inmates. He didn't want his children taken away from him. Memories of his childhood, growing up not knowing his parents, were still very vivid and painful. His children were fed, clothed, educated and cared for at no cost to the government, so what was the fuss about. He felt the government should have shown gratitude to the mission for the support they were giving him. His fears were put to rest when the church made it clear they would support him and not allow the government to interfere.

Alfred Brown and (l–r) Laurelle, Edith, Kathy and Yogi, Kunmunya, c. 1941.

Alfred never discussed his feelings with Laurelle on the way the government treated him, and it was many years later he told her about the pressure to send the children to Moore River.

Laurelle: *After Mum's death Dad tried not to change anything and I knew he was grieving a lot and that used to hurt me because I didn't know how to comfort him and Edie and Yogi and Kathy. We were too small to understand what was happening. Dad wasn't a person you could discuss things with and you weren't allowed to ask too many questions.*

When Dad was home, we'd go every Saturday afternoon and clean up around her grave. He'd carry Kathy on his shoulders and when Edie got tired he'd carry her too while Yogi, Alwyn and I walked. We'd put whatever flowers we could get on her grave. Sometimes it would be oleander, frangipani or bluebell creepers and we'd put them in a bottle of water. Ivy was too little to come so we'd leave her with the missionaries or the Aboriginal people. Kathy, Edie and Yogi would ask me, 'Why did Mum die?' and I couldn't explain to them why she'd died, I didn't know why myself. I was only eight.

I missed my mother badly. She died at a time when I was getting to know her and tell her things you can only share with a mum. There was something missing in our lives after she left, it was never the same. There seemed to be a hole in our lives. Sometimes when I'd see the kids doing the little things that are part of growing up I'd wonder what Mum would think if she were alive.

We found it hard to understand why our mother was taken from us. All the other children had their mothers. The missionaries' children had a mother and so did the Aboriginal children and the Shadforth's, everyone except us.

6

Raising Sisters and a Brother

Mission life is not a life I want for my own children. Your knowledge of anything was limited. To go to Broome was a big thing for us. To see all the shops and go to the pictures was a big treat. You need more than a mission education to survive today.

Laurelle

Alfred never remarried after the death of his wife. There was an occasion when he almost did, but decided against it when he saw the woman concerned hit her own daughter. The thought that she might treat his children in the same manner played on his mind and being the unselfish person he was, he terminated the friendship. Trying to be both mother and father to his children was very difficult but he drew the line at having his children suffer at the hands of a person he suspected might mistreat them.

Laurelle was eight years old when she started raising her siblings. She was expected to help care for her sisters Ivy, Kathy and Edie, and brother, Yogi. Her older brother Alwyn helped, but he was still having trouble coming to terms with the death of his mother. As the oldest girl, Laurelle was expected to cope with the daily demands of child rearing, sewing, cleaning and to a lesser extent cooking. As a child growing up she missed out on play; it was something the other kids did. She was busy making sure her sisters and brother were cared for.

> Laurelle: *I'd often wonder what Mum would say if she saw the little things the kids did. Like one day we were fishing up on the rocks and I was there and so was Edie and Alfred. Kathy was hurrying to get to the rocks to fish. She was responsible for bringing Ivy as I was busy carrying the gear. Kathy finished up dragging her and we could hear Ivy's voice saying, 'You knock me down I punch you up.' They eventually got to the rocks and started fishing but Ivy never stopped complaining about Kathy knocking her down. I used to wonder what she'd think of them growing up.*

To her sisters, Laurelle was the only mother they knew. When Alfred was away operating the mission lugger he called on an Aboriginal couple called Gertie and Stephen to be their guardians. Gertie had helped Ina around the house and, as the children were already very fond of her, it seemed natural to retain her services. Stephen often worked with him on the *Watt Leggatt* so when they were both away the responsibility was left to Laurelle and Gertie. There were the missionaries to go to in the event of an emergency so Alfred was able to leave on his trips knowing his children were safe, especially while Reverend Love and his wife were around.

> Laurelle: *I remember one night after tea when all the work was done, washing up and things like that. Dad was*

away. Us kids were talking outside near the fence. All of a sudden the place was lit up as if it was daylight and we were wondering what it was. Then all these pretty lights came on and the tail was amazing. My cousin Phyllis and I ran into the house. We said, 'Something terrible has happened as the place was lit up with pretty coloured lights.' We were told calmly, 'Yes, we know, we saw it, that's the end of a shooting star.' I never ever saw anything like that, I'd seen shooting stars before but nothing like the one Phyllis and I saw. Some time later a lot of people came out to the mission and looking back now I think it was in search for this meteorite that would have hit close to the mission. Whatever it was it certainly frightened me and my cousin.

There was another time when Dad was away. Yogi and I were teasing each other and mucking around, I was getting the better of him. We were out on a picnic. I was giving him just as much cheek as he was giving me but then he started to tease me, saying, 'You're going to marry Dougie. You're going to marry Dougie D'Antoine.' He kept on and on until I picked up the closest thing, which happened to be a boomerang, and let fly, hitting him on the neck. It left a permanent mark on one side of his neck. Later Edie was to give him an identical mark on the other side from a boomerang too. Apparently they were both stalking this plover and Alfred had a ging. He was lying on the ground lining up the plover, ready to let fly when Edie threw this boomerang. She was trying to hit the bird but instead, hit Alfred on the side of the neck. Alfred ended up with two identical boomerang marks on his neck, one on either side, both given to him by his sisters. He never teased me again and stopped stalking birds.

Straight after Ina's death Mrs Taylor cared for Ivy as

Mrs Love was away on holidays. In the afternoons, after school, Laurelle went down to Mrs Taylor's house to help bath Ivy before feeding her. Mrs Taylor had a baby a few months older than Ivy called Anne and needed the extra help with the two babies. Part of the routine was to exercise the babies, making sure their little arms and legs became strong and healthy. Once Ivy was bathed and fed for the evening Laurelle returned home.

When Ivy was about five months she was allowed to go home with Laurelle for a couple of hours in the afternoon. Mrs Love had returned and was caring for Ivy so it was more to give her a break as she had her own children to care for. By now she was quite a heavy baby so Laurelle had to heave her onto her hip and wobble off with Ivy clinging to her like a baby koala. There was no such thing as a pram on the mission, babies were carried everywhere. Laurelle didn't mind babysitting because it meant she didn't have to work in the vegetable garden and pick those dreadful grubs off the potatoes.

> Laurelle: *I'd help Gertie feed Yogi, Edie and Kathy, then put them to bed. I used to sit down with Gertie and sew their clothes. Alfred's clothes first, he was terrible for ripping his clothes, especially his pants. He seemed to be forever tearing his pants in the backside. I knew how to sew; how I learnt, I don't know, maybe Gertie taught me, I just learnt. Dad had most of our clothes made in Broome by Aunty Nellie, Goodji and Aunty Gypsy and I'd do the patching. We didn't have many clothes, we didn't need it. We had special outfits for Sunday for church, a special outfit for school and the rest were house clothes.*

Stephen was a strong black man with a striking physique, typical of the Aboriginal men of that area.

Gertie was an intelligent, well-built woman, commanding respect like most Worrorra women of her standing. They were traditional people, seasoned by their passage through the initiations of their rich mythology and law, custodians of the land and culture. Unlike many of their counterparts throughout the Kimberley, their contact with the white man was peaceful and they were spared witnessing the violent dispossession that frequently came with contact. The mission staff relied on Gertie and Stephen as mediators between the two cultures.

> Laurelle: *When Dad was away Gertie and Stephen came and stayed in our simple house. It was a small house made of corrugated iron and painted with a whitewash, the same powdered ochre Aboriginal people use to decorate their body for traditional ceremonies. The design was extremely basic with one large room and a verandah at the entrance going the full length of the house. We all slept in the single room and later Dad brought us a big double bed from Broome. We loved that big bed, it was so comfortable. Unlike houses today we had a combustion stove outside on the verandah that was packed with ant bed, locking it in place. As the cooking was done outside, the verandah served as the kitchen with the Coolgardie safe in the bathroom at the other end. We used it to keep perishables cool in, consumables like tinned butter, jam, vegetables and even sugar and flour, more to keep the ants out than anything else. It was like a big box with fly wire around it and a big tray up top with water in. It was kept cool with wet hessian draped over it. It sat on legs off the ground in a big tray with water in, which had to be changed daily, keeping it fresh so ants wouldn't crawl up. If you left the water for about a week or two a thick scum would form on*

it and the ants would march right over it and up into the food. It wasn't anything flash, but it was practical and served a purpose. Water was carted from a hand-pumped well and poured into large galvanised washing tubs about the size of a forty-four gallon drum sawed longwise in half. It was always a challenge to see how many kids fitted into the tub. The toilet and laundry area was outside and shared with the Shadforths. Later they added an extra room and more verandah space, almost doubling the size of the living area.

One day Kathy decided to give Ivy a bath and in doing so felt she should wash her hair. By now Ivy was a few years old and living at home with us. Kathy got a dipper full of hot water from the copper and poured it over Ivy's head while she was sitting in the tub. Ivy's scream attracted Gertie who raced her down to Mrs Love who administered first aid. When I came home from school Ivy's head was bandaged up. I asked what had happened and Gertie told me. Ivy had to go to the dispensary every day to have her bandages changed. It was then that Dad decided to send her to Broome to live with Aunty Gypsy Hunter who was also looking after Alwyn at the time.

When the children suffered their usual bouts of childhood illnesses Gertie was always there for them. They went off to school in the morning and when they returned Gertie had lunch cooked, the house was clean and the washing done. Laurelle felt at ease with her. Although she never replaced her mother Laurelle had a rapport with her that was built on trust and respect. When Gertie and Stephen went bush the children longed for them to return. Their temporary guardians were lazy and Laurelle did not feel comfortable with them.

> Laurelle: *I remember when I had a bad toothache Gertie said, 'We got no medicine but you put this little bit of nickynicky on your teeth.' So she'd break off a little bit of the tobacco and gave it to me to put on my toothache and that seemed to take the pain away. When we had whooping cough at the mission she'd tell us we weren't to eat any peanuts at all. The peanuts made us cough, as they would tickle our throat as we swallowed them and she didn't want us coughing too much. It was little things like that which made life easy for us.*

CHRISTMAS AT THE MISSION

As a child growing up in the mission Christmas was synonymous with the wet season. You waited for the wet and Christmas to come together. At Kunmunya the tyranny of distance, isolation and weather seemed to bring people together to celebrate the meaning of Christmas in the simplest way possible. There were always visitors, church, good food and entertainment. But after 1937 Christmas was different for Laurelle.

> Laurelle: *I used to look forward to Christmas but after Mum died it didn't seem to be the same. Dad tried not to change things but the feeling just wasn't there.*

Their nearest neighbour, Bob Thompson, rode over for the day. He lived at Marie Springs where he grew peanuts and farmed sheep. He wasn't put off with the day's ride on horseback to get to the mission, in fact it was his idea of a good Christmas. It was the company, the laughter of the children and adult conversation that made the journey worthwhile. He always brought a few camels to take back any cargo and mail waiting for him.

The kids called him Uncle Bob and Christmas couldn't start without him so as soon as the children spotted the dust from his horse and camels in the distance, they'd race off to meet him. The children only gave him a few minutes to clean up before dragging him off to church. They were pretty excited and wanted to get the show on the road. The church held about one hundred people and on Christmas Day it was always full to capacity. Aboriginal people seemed to come from far and wide to celebrate the day and included people from the sister tribes, Ngarinyin and Wunambal.

Alfred Brown (left) and Bob Thompson (right) with crew members aboard the Watt Leggatt, c. 1936.
(Battye 53004P.)

After church, around mid morning, Bob helped the missionaries distribute presents to everyone. The missionaries stood in a line with a box of gifts in front of them and as the people passed they were given a present from each staff member, so by the time they got to the end they had a few gifts. The gifts came in large boxes from South Australia, Victoria and Western Australia. They were donated by the Presbyterian Church and contained an assortment of toys, clothes, books, shoes, scarves, and so on. The boxes were shipped up well before Christmas and the staff sorted through them matching up clothes and gifts for the Aboriginal people and anticipated visitors. Everyone in the mission from the oldest to the youngest member received a gift; no one went without. Even latecomers who arrived the following day received a gift.

At lunchtime the Shadforths, Browns and of course Uncle Bob met at the Loves' place for Christmas lunch. It was always a baked meal followed by traditional Christmas pudding full of sixpences and threepenny bits. Naturally the kids ate too much, just to get the extra pocket money rather than to satisfy their appetite. In 1941 this tradition was broken. The hot meal was replaced by salads and jelly, made possible by the arrival of two Electrolux fridges at the mission two months earlier. It took two teams of six men to carry the fridges from the landing to the mission. The introduction of the fridges revolutionised eating habits at the mission.

In Christmas 1937 there were a hundred and ninety-two Aboriginal people present. This included people from Marie Springs, Munja and Sale River. A day or two previously Mr MacDougall told some of the men that he only had trousers for the local Worrorra men. Christmas visitors could have tobacco. A local man called Martin assured him that the visitors wanted 'chented choap' (scented soap). The old men routinely bought washing soap with their scant savings for the purpose of sticking up their hair; but scented soap was something special, worth walking sixty miles for. The weather was fine that day and the people consumed nine four-gallon pots of porridge for breakfast. When the gifts were handed out the men received trousers or shorts, a shirt, scented soap, a pipe and tobacco and lollies, two bags of flour and half a bullock to share. The women received dresses, combs, mirrors, needles, cottons, scented soap and lollies, two bags of flour and, like the men, half a bullock to share.

In 1941 the Browns spent their last Christmas at the mission. It started with a memorable Christmas party before school finished. There was a Christmas tree made from a native pine by one of the mission staff, Mr Paton, decorated with homemade ornaments. In the afternoon Mr Paton acted as Father Christmas, complete with a suit made by his wife from odds and ends. He handed out lollies to the children but the highlight of the celebration was eating cold jelly for the first time. The children ate the jelly very tentatively at first, comparing it to bush food as each spoonful stimulated their tastebuds.

After church, the giving of gifts and lunch there was a fine display of traditional sports starting at 3.00pm. The men's firelighting race with liruk involved lighting a fire using friction between two sticks. One stick has several shallow hollows and the other a pointed end. The hollowed stick is placed on the ground with the pointed one slotted into the hollow and rubbed vigorously. The action causes a drilling effect and the wood shaving is ignited by the friction. In twenty seconds an Aboriginal chap by the name of Jimmy Montgomery had lit his fire, with smoke at five seconds. In the women's competition Eileen Edwards managed a fire in two minutes four seconds. Then there was the spear throwing competition with Jimmy winning again. He threw his spear a hundred and twenty-six yards, as measured with a tape. The final feat was throwing a spear at a target. A kangaroo was drawn on a piece of sack and accuracy was achieved at thirty yards. Christmas Day that year was an entertaining and festive event and was finally brought to an end with the distribution of a further three bags of flour to the community.

At night, after the festivities, the insects made their presence felt. They seemed to come out in full force when it rained. Often there were at least twenty different flying varieties: moths and flying insects of all colours and descriptions, from the size of a full stop to stick insects measuring seven inches long: no matter what angle a stick insect was placed in, it would stand perfectly still and looked exactly like a small piece of stick. There were beautiful and numerous butterflies, and many of them built their little silver cocoons on the oleanders. Strangest of all the insects were the fireflies. Slightly smaller than the ordinary housefly, they emitted a brilliant flash of light every two or three seconds. It was a treat to watch them on a dark night flitting about in the sky. If a bug got in your ear you poured oil in your ear so it could float to the top. The insects both interested and annoyed the staff.

Laurelle: *The Aboriginal people seemed to come from far and wide to join in Christmas and the mission never turned them away, feeding them and making them feel welcome. There was always plenty of bread, fresh meat, black tea and sugar for them. We had sports in the afternoon. The race I liked the most was when the missionaries would line up these presents at the finishing line and you'd hear the men discussing which ones they wanted and before they started they'd wish each other good luck. When the men ran it sounded like cattle stampeding, they were very good runners. The men and women always had separate races. The children used to have sack races and running and three-legged races. Gee it was fun and everyone joined in and celebrated together. It didn't seem to cost us any money and we appreciated the simple gifts that came in the big Christmas boxes from the Board of Mission.*

Scarlet Fever

Dad nursed me throughout the illness and I think I was in and out of consciousness for about a week. During this time I took a bad turn and there was nothing Dad could do.

Laurelle

During the lay-up season Alfred was home for longer than usual. The lay-up season was from around November to May when the cyclonic weather was a danger to all who sailed. Trips between Broome and Kunmunya almost ceased and everyone braced themselves for the wet season. Laurelle enjoyed this time of the year as it allowed the family to spend time together. Alwyn, who was going to high school in Broome, was home on Christmas vacation and Alfred enjoyed having the time with his children. About three miles away from the mission was Nhorgor, the landing where Alfred and Harry moored the *Watt Leggatt* and the *Rolland*. During the lay-up season the mission luggers were anchored there so the annual maintenance and repairs could be carried out. Each morning after breakfast Alfred and the children walked the three miles to Nhorgor and they entertained themselves in the water or on the beach while he serviced the *Watt Leggatt*.

Laurelle: *We had a large area of lawn at the front of our place and Dad used these wool shears to cut the lawn with. Then he would lay his sails out so he could patch them up. He would get this twine and run it through beeswax so it would slip through the canvas when he was sewing. He had a great big sail needle and a palm he used to push the needle through with. Dad always made sure he kept his sails in good working condition as he didn't want to be caught out at sea with bad sails.*

It was during the lay-up season that Laurelle was stung by a bluebottle and was fortunate to live through the ordeal. The quick thinking and courageous efforts of her friend Paddy Morlumbun saved her life.

She was about nine years old. The two mission luggers were anchored at the landing as Alfred and Harry were carrying out maintenance. It was full tide and the children were in the water swimming and frolicking around the luggers, duck diving and generally having a good time.

Laurelle, Paddy and the older children were swimming from lugger to lugger. They dived off the *Rolland* and swam to the *Watt Leggatt* then turned around and repeated the game. The luggers were anchored in relatively shallow water free from rips and currents, and besides they were seasoned swimmers. Being only a young girl Laurelle was wearing a pair of bloomers with nothing covering her chest. She had just jumped off the *Rolland* when she felt something brush against her chest and sting her, rendering her totally helpless in seconds. She screamed in agony and this attracted the attention of Harry, who dived in clothes, hat, pipe and all. During the time it took him to reach her, Paddy managed to keep her head above the water, which was not easy as Laurelle was thrashing and clawing at him. When Harry had her safely on deck he rubbed cream of tartar on her to kill the stingers. She had thick red marks on her chest for years after. The memory of the agonising pain was not something she forgot easily and the scars took years to fade It took a lot of courage for her to enter the water again.

Another harrowing time for Alfred was when Laurelle fell sick with scarlet fever. The closest hospital was days away by boat. Medical supplies were limited and all he could do was sit with her and pray she'd make it.

Laurelle: *There was the lay-up season when Dad was home, I'm not sure of the year. I had been feeling sick for about a week. Gertie and Stephen still looked after us while Dad was away. When he was home they went back to their camp and Pearl, an Aboriginal woman, would do the housework and be there for us after school while Dad worked at the landing on the boat. On this particular day Dad was down at the landing and old Pearl was at home doing the housework. When I arrived back from school that afternoon I said, 'I feel sick Pearl.' Between the time she put me to bed and Dad arriving home my health had deteriorated. Before I passed out I can vaguely remember Dad walking through the door with Pearl saying, 'I think we're going to lose this girl.' By now Pearl had become distressed and worried. She was doing all she could do. She had a wet towel that she kept sponging me with. I kept moving in and out of consciousness but I can remember my sisters Edie and Kathy hanging around my bed showing me their dolls and asking me to nurse them. They didn't understand how sick I was and Dad never stopped them, maybe he felt that this would help me through my illness. Later they were warned to stay away from me as it was thought that my condition was contagious. I turned out to be sick with scarlet fever. I can remember before I became sick the skin would peel off my head. Not knowing what was happening, I'd pull layers of skin from my head and as this occurred there was a foul smell, obviously coming from the infected skin. Naturally I was self-conscious so I wore this navy blue rag hat that Dad had given me. I wouldn't take the hat off even in school. It was several days after this I fell ill with scarlet fever. My friends and cousins weren't permitted to visit me for fear of an epidemic on the mission. Fortunately I was the only person that contracted scarlet fever. As part of the treatment Dad had to rub this ointment all over me and he'd apply it with a spatula. I'd protest, complaining how much it hurt me so Dad would rub it on with his hands and that seemed to feel better.*

Dad nursed me through the illness and I think I was in and out of consciousness for about a week. During this time I took a bad turn and there was nothing Dad could do. He couldn't go for help as the missionaries lived some distance away and he was frightened of losing me and sending my older brother Alwyn was out of the question as he too was ill in bed with a rather large gum boil. Being the middle of the night my younger brother and sisters were asleep so Dad had to sit by my bed feeling completely helpless. That was the night I was expected to die and I remember an experience I'll never forget. I can recall these people going up this golden staircase with beautiful music playing in the background. Everyone was dressed in white man gowns and I kept telling Dad, 'I like the music, the music is nice.' At that stage both Dad and myself must have fallen asleep and I awoke some time later to tell Dad, 'I feel terribly sick, I want to spew.' He was that exhausted from nursing me he said, 'Can you get up and hang over the window?' When I hung over the window this bloke was standing there and he was holding a staff in his hand and he said to me, 'You'll be all right.' Thinking nothing of this as I was sick, I went to bed and woke up in the morning feeling very weak but much better. When I recounted the incident to Dad the next morning he said, 'What did this man look like?' I showed him a picture from the Bible and he said, 'But that's Christ.' As a result of this incident I feel strongly that there is life after death. Dad must have spent endless hours nursing me. When I drifted in and out of consciousness he always seemed to be there. I don't think he ever left my bedside during the whole time I was ill with scarlet fever.

Mary Pascoe Island

Dad always put us kids first. He made sure we were safe.

Laurelle

Nineteen thirty-nine was a very unsettling year for Alfred and the family. Ina had been gone for two years. Each time Alfred left on a trip to Broome he worried about his children and relied on Gertie, Stephen and Laurelle to look after them.

The incident where Kathy burnt Ivy left Alfred questioning the stress he was putting on Laurelle and Gertie. He had friends in Liveringa Station and in Broome who offered their support with the family. He contacted Nellie and Tommy D'Antoine in Liveringa and made arrangements for Kathy and Edith to stay with them. On a trip into Broome he spoke to another loyal friend, Gypsy Hunter, and arranged for Ivy and Alwyn to stay with her on the hill overlooking Roebuck Bay. This left Laurelle and Yogi at the mission. He felt he could ask Harry and Mackie to care for two children during his trips away. Their two older boys, Percy and Patrick, were young men and working in Broome. Living conditions were a little cramped at times but that didn't seem to worry the children. Feeding two extra children also wasn't a problem given most of the food was either grown or caught from the sea.

More importantly for Alfred than the incident with Kathy burning Ivy was the constant fear of the Aborigines Department taking his children from him. The local protector was close by at Munja Aboriginal Reserve and it was within his rights to enquire about the welfare of the children, especially now Alfred was a widower. He and his family were exempted from the Act but that was of little comfort to him. On his trips to Broome he heard stories of local parents having their children removed from them. His own removal was still fresh in his memory and he did not want that for his children. Reverend Love was there to protect his family and that comforted him but he knew that if the government wanted to take his children they would and that frightened him immensely. Exemptions were easily revoked and the government could do as it pleased in this matter.

Laurelle and Yogi remained at the mission and lived with Harry and Mackie during Alfred's trips away. This suited the children as Harry often took them on trips to the bêche-de-mer camps provided they did not miss out on too much school. Like Alfred, Harry valued education

Edie, Laurelle, Yogi and Kathy, Kunmunya, c. 1941.

and insisted the children attend. Laurelle was not going to miss out on all the fun, especially as she now had plenty of spare time on her hands without Edith, Kathy and Ivy to watch over. On the morning of the trips Harry woke them up very early and after a bite to eat, more asleep than wake, they boarded the *Rolland*. Harry had four reliable men as his crew so the safety of the family wasn't a problem. When he located a bed of bêche-de-mer he anchored the *Rolland* and sent the dinghies to collect the sea slug. The crew went in one dinghy and Harry took the children in the other. The children were excited by the prospect of spotting the first sea slug. The water was crystal clear so you could reach down and pluck the speared slug from the sea.

> Florence O'Donnell: *Another time we were on the boat and we ran out of water. We used to go to Augustus Island and fill up with fresh water as there was plenty there. Dad said, 'We might not be able to get fresh water for two days.' So we had no water and all we had was a tub full of turtle eggs. Dad said, 'We'll need to suck the turtle eggs when we get thirsty.' We had no water so we had no choice. This kept us going for two days otherwise we would have perished. To get water we had to go to Camden Harbour. There was beautiful spring water coming out of the sand and when the tide comes in it covers it.*

The sea slugs were taken to Mary Pascoe Island, now known as Sheep Island. Harry used the island as a base for processing the bêche-de-mer which was scrubbed, cleaned and boiled in big iron washing tubs. Overnight it cooled, then the workers sliced the slug through the middle, cleaned it and staked it out flat to stop it from curling during the drying and smoking process. They used bamboo skewers to keep them flat and placed them on wire racks ready for smoking. When the smoking was finished, and the bêche-de-mer completely dry, Harry packed the processed slugs in hessian bags ready for the trip back to the mission. He'd sew the bags up with a large bag needle using coarse string, then heave them in the dinghy making sure the bags didn't get wet. It only took one wet slug to send the whole bag mildewy and useless so Harry made sure he was the only person handling the bags.

Left to right: Daisy Uttemorrah, Florence Shadforth, Elkin Umbagai, Kunmunya, c. 1938–39.

While Harry and his crew were busy processing the sea slugs the kids visited the grave of Mary Pascoe. She was a young pioneer who was part of the 1864 Camden Harbour expedition that came from Victoria. She died months after they arrived. The kids were intrigued by the lonely grave and every time they were at Sheep Island they felt compelled to visit it. Laurelle and her younger cousin Amy took the time to clean it up, decorating it with wildflowers and seashells. Amy in particular was fascinated with it; she'd sit cross-legged on the ground beside the headstone for hours singing hymns and paying her respects to Mary Pascoe.

Florence: *One night we were at Augustus Island and the tide was against us and took us right over the rocks and* coral and the boat was balancing on its side and Dad said, 'You kids better get off.' So we got off and went onto the island. He didn't want us staying on the lugger because if the tide came over it might tip. We all got off and there was no place for us to sleep so we all slept on the rocks and it was uncomfortable. Dad had to stay on the boat in case something happened to the lugger.

Another day the kids decided to take to sea. There were the four of them, Phyllis, Laurelle, Henry and Alwyn, who was home on school holidays. They got in the dinghy and almost sailed out to sea, not realising the tide was taking them.

Florence: *I yelled out to Dad and told him what they had done. They weren't too far away, but far enough. He went out in another dinghy and brought them back and they got told off for going out to sea without thinking. As if that wasn't enough, that night we decided to go and sleep on a big canvas on the beach under the stars. It was high tide of course so the tide came in and the next thing we knew Dad came along and said, 'Get up you kids, you'll be floating away. The tide's in and it's all under the canvas.' So we all got up and shifted the canvas to higher ground and proceeded to go back to sleep. We thought it was great fun, we didn't think there was anything to worry about.*

The extra responsibilities placed on Laurelle since her mother's death had turned her into a mature person. She was starting to see her life on the mission differently and became aware of the different cultures there. She started to become very conscious of the purpose of the mission and the role of everyone. It was around this time that she witnessed the marriage of a young Worrorra woman she respected and admired. It was a significant event for Laurelle not only because Elkin was her friend, but because it made her aware that the Aboriginal people she was raised with were changing. They were starting to integrate Christian rituals into their culture.

> Laurelle: *I knew Elkin very well, she was much older than me but she was a good friend. She was a house girl for Mrs Love, so when she got married Mrs Love went to a lot of trouble to make her wedding special. Mrs Love made her a lovely wedding dress and made sure Andy looked smart. I remember he wore a suit and these shoes with elastic sides. They looked so different dressed up. It was the first full Christian wedding for a young Aboriginal couple. Mrs Love made this beautiful wedding cake, it was chocolate with their names written in this white icing, we couldn't wait to hoe into it, it looked absolutely delicious. It was a lovely wedding, then Elkin had to go to Munja with him. It was their culture that the women follow their husbands. Andy must have been Ngarinyin because Dad took them on the* Watt Leggatt *to Munja where Elkin worked for the manager's wife, Mrs Reid. Munja was a government settlement and Elkin didn't want to go, but it was their culture. Anyhow Andy died and she returned to the mission just before we left and she married Sam Umbagai and had quite a few children to him.*

7

Last Years at Kunmunya

When the Shadforths and Loves left there was only us, the Aboriginal people and the Holmes left at Kunmunya.

Laurelle

By the end of 1939 the family was back together at Kunmunya. Alfred had missed them and felt in his heart there must be a better way than having them spread across three locations. Circumstances for Alfred and Harry were starting to change. Their children were older and they had to send them to Broome for further schooling. Florence, Henry and Alwyn were already in Broome attending high school, returning to the mission for the Christmas holidays in December. Harry felt that with half his family away he may as well join them, and in August 1940 the Shadforths left Kunmunya to live in Broome after nearly twenty years service to the mission by Harry and Mackie.

> Laurelle: *When Uncle Harry and Aunty Mackie and them got on the boat for Broome, I was old enough to*

really feel it. I used to follow him around and he'd call me 'girlie.' He said, 'I have to go but you can always come to Broome and visit me.' I didn't want them to leave but it was something they had to do. They had worked so hard for the mission. I suppose it was a new chapter in their lives, the kids were growing older and Kunmunya didn't have much to offer. I just couldn't imagine Kunmunya without them. I know Dad missed not having Uncle Harry around.

Just when life seemed to be settling down again the Loves decided it was time to move on too. After thirteen years at Kunmunya they made plans to leave in October 1940 for Ernabella Mission in South Australia. Reverend Love felt Kunmunya had turned into a stable mission and would continue to do well under the leadership of an experienced superintendent. He felt it was time to channel his efforts into Ernabella which was in the same state Kunmunya had been in when he arrived back in 1927. He also had his family to consider as the older ones were schooling in South Australia and his wife Margaret wanted to be close to them.

At eleven, Laurelle was

Reverend and Mrs Love with their children, Margaret (seated) and Bobby, Kunmunya, c. 1939.
(Battye 53002.)

Alfred Brown in the foreground, with members of the Love family aboard the Watt Leggatt, *c. 1938–39.*

starting to feel she was being deserted. Approaching adolescence she required the support and guidance of trusting women. With Mrs Love, Auntie Mackie and Florence gone she only had Gertie to turn to when her father was away. She suddenly felt very vulnerable, lonely and afraid.

Laurelle: *Reverend Love didn't like leaving the mission, but it was something the church asked him to do and he took his vows so when the church asked him to go to Ernabella to get that back on track he had to go. He felt the mission was doing well and the missionaries would keep it going and that the Aboriginal people at Ernabella needed him more. We were all standing on the bank when they boarded the* Watt Leggatt *and they were all sitting on the cabin looking back at us. We were waving to them and you could see they didn't want to go. Their children Bobbie, Margaret and Johnny were already over in South Australia. They only had Joseph as he was the last baby. We never referred to him as Reverend Love, it was always 'jijey' to us, which means father and 'amakunya' was Mrs Love. Margaret, John and Joseph Love had Aboriginal names. The other missionaries were never given Aboriginal names. The Worrorra thought they were special. It's a pity there weren't more missionaries like them. If they had more people like them at places like*

Moore River there wouldn't be all this hatred. When I read about how the Aboriginal people were treated at Moore River I thank God we had Reverend Love at Kunmunya. You ask the Aboriginal people at Mowanjum what Reverend Love and Mrs Love were like and they'll tell you they loved them and that's because they were treated fairly, never ill treated but respected.

THE DEATH OF STEPHEN

On 4 February 1941 Stephen was killed as a result of a tribal dispute. Stephen had been the Brown children's friend and guardian for several years, making him a special person in Laurelle's life. She found his death difficult to come to terms with because of the way it happened. In Aboriginal law if two men are fighting you leave them alone, but he was killed from behind by a third man. He had a nasty blow behind the ear, one on the cheekbone and some terrible gashes on the back of his head; probably his neck was broken. Alfred was totally devastated when he heard the news of Stephen's death. It was like losing a member of the family. He was killed two days before Laurelle's twelfth birthday.

Mr Love had been gone from the mission four months. His replacement, Mr Holmes, was unable to prevent Stephen's death. This was the first killing for ten years and one of the most miserable in the history of the tribe. It started as an argument between Stephen and another chap. A few words were exchanged, then Stephen was attacked. Stephen started to get the better of him when the other man's brother joined in to defend him, clubbing Stephen from the back. The whole ordeal was over very quickly and by the time the missionaries arrived Stephen was dead. The death had to be reported to the Department of Native Affairs, who requested a full inquiry. The department was the guardian of Aboriginal people and it was department policy to investigate a reported murder. In the eyes of the department the incident did not look good; it suggested the mission was not capable of caring for the people.

> Laurelle: *If Reverend Love was there this would not have happened. It was sad and it was like losing your own father. We'd just lost a mother and we'd accepted Gertie and Stephen as our parents and then this thing happened. The Shadforths and Loves had gone and we felt afraid of what would happen to us. Gertie was devastated, her spirit seemed to go with him because she was never the same happy person again.*

Stephen was given a Christian service followed by a native burial which was done entirely by Wunambal people. Full traditional practices were followed and his body was placed on a platform about six feet above the ground and covered with leaves and branches, then heavier logs. Generally this is followed by the placing of stones at intervals of two or three feet in a circle under the body. The stones are placed there by the men and when the body starts to decompose the fluid drops on the stones. The first stone that is marked is matched to the man who is deemed the murderer, who then faces a tribal death. In Stephen's case this probably didn't happen as there were witnesses to the event.

The inquiry that followed Stephen's funeral was held in Broome and it was a distressing time for everyone at Kunmunya. Mr Holmes and other people from the mission were summoned to appear in court. The experience of testifying and appearing in court must have been frightening and confusing to the Aboriginal people. They would have felt bewildered and confused with the smell, sight and sound of the courthouse. Alfred took them to Broome on the *Watt Leggatt*, making it difficult to put the ordeal behind him and concentrate on the future. It took several months to sentence the men responsible; they each received five years imprisonment. The counsel for the defence stated that the killing could have been prevented had senior staff acted in a responsible manner to address the cause of the conflict.

> Laurelle: *I remember one afternoon when Alwyn was home on school holidays from Broome, we followed Stephen to watch him throw his boomerangs. His daughter Jean was with us, she was like a sister to us. He'd say, 'Now you stand near me.' We'd all huddle around him and he used to throw his boomerangs. He'd say to us, 'Now I want you to watch this, this boomerang is going to come back to me and I'm going to knock it down with my other boomerang and I'll make it land at my feet,' and that's exactly what would happen. Then he'd say, 'Now you watch this one and I'm gunna grab it with my hand,' and that is exactly what would happen. It would come back to him and it would come around to him very very slowly and he'd grab it with his hand. It was amazing what he could do with boomerangs, I've never seen a person do what he used to do. He used to have his woomeras. We'd sit down on the dirt in front of him and watch him make his woomeras and do his spear up and that sort of thing. I can't remember the tree he would use to make his spears from but it would have to have been some type of hard bush wood. He used to shape the spear,*

the handle part he used to put that through fire, bending and twisting it till it was the right shape. When he was making his woomera he had this certain wax and he had to have the sinew from a kangaroo tail. When you cut a kangaroo tail off you just pull the sinew out and it would come out like long strings. It would have to be dried. He'd put the wax on and tie it up with the sinew to make sure it was secure. He'd use the sinew from a kangaroo tail for a lot of things and the wax came from spinifex. He was very skilled at what he did and we'd watch him for hours while he worked. His knowledge of these things was incredible. He was a very good hunter and a strong tribal person.

The remainder of the year slipped by with its usual calendar of events, visitors and ups and downs. Compared with the departure of the Shadforths and Loves, and the death of Stephen, these events had minimal impact on Laurelle. December that year was Laurelle's last Christmas at the mission.

Laurelle: *In 1942 we left Kunmunya, I was thirteen. The next time I saw Gertie was in the early 1980s at Mowanjum. She cried when I saw her. We cried together. Stephen and Gertie were very good people, caring people who cared for us after Mum's death. You could trust them with your life. So many, many years had passed. The last I heard she'd died. They were very intelligent people.*

In late 1940 the first signs of the war started to become a reality in the mission. The mission took command of a wireless transmitter and receiver. It was given to them by the Naval Department to report coastal movements of ships and planes in the area. Unusual or suspicious sightings on land or sea had to be reported immediately to the department.

Living on the Watt Leggatt

They were sailors in those days, I suppose being brought up on the sea, they understood the sea, they could read the tides, reefs, the colour of the water and winds. We got to know the coastline between Kunmunya and Broome very well, making many trips with Dad until Broome was bombed in 1942.

Laurelle

Nineteen forty-one was a soul-searching year for Alfred. He was feeling restless and a sense of having outgrown the mission seemed to infiltrate him. The Shadforths had left, Stephen's death had unsettled him and the staff had changed completely. The missionaries who replaced Reverend Love didn't seem to be as committed. Although Alfred respected the new superintendent, Mr Holmes, he didn't have the same rapport with him that he had with Reverend Love. Something was missing and Alfred had a gut feeling things would never be the same.

The war was starting to rear its ugly head and although it didn't directly affect them they knew it was a reality in other parts of the world. Alfred listened to news updates on the radio when he was in Broome. The town was full of talk about the war and was studiously followed through the radio and newspaper.

Alfred had an overwhelming desire to have his children by his side. He was reluctant now to leave them on the mission when he was away. He worried that the government superintendent from Munja might visit one day and take them from him. If they learnt he had friends taking care of them this would give them grounds for removing them. Mr Holmes was still developing an understanding of government policies and Alfred didn't feel he would be helpful should the government decide to intervene. He was at the mercy of the Aborigines Act with his fair-skinned children and no Reverend Love to protect them. With thoughts of the war ticking away at the back of his mind he decided to take his children to sea with him where they would be totally under his control.

> Alfred: *I think the coast we sailed is one of the most treacherous in Australia, apart from the Barrier Reef. The most interesting place was the Prince Regent, at the entrance especially. You get some beautiful islands there, Coronation Island, Port Lincoln, Cape Wellington, Mount Trafalgar, Mount Waterloo, St Andrew's Island in St George's Basin. That's what makes it so interesting. You've got to know the coast, the tides and the way it runs all different ways. See, it splits up, you know, in groups and meets on the other side. It took me about three years to know this and know the coast so well. On the treacherous channels I used to make a point to go through in the day time at low tide so I could pinpoint the reefs and take my bearings. I did that and after that I could go through blindfolded. The most treacherous place was Walcott Inlet. I sat there for three hours watching the tide and the whirlpools, timing it with a clock so as I knew when to go in because some of those whirlies you can see them going back three feet down. I learnt to escape the whirlies because we only had a windjammer. After that we got a little fourteen horsepower auxiliary to take us through. We*

were depending on wind in those days and it was no fun, believe me.

The kids lived on dugong, turtle, fish and oysters. Alfred was a pretty good cook, nothing flash. He did all the cooking and if they ran out of bread he'd make damper and, if that was eaten, puftaloons, which were eaten with jam or golden syrup.

He was very strict when it came to doing the children's school work, making sure a few hours a day were set aside with the books.

The *Watt Leggatt* had four bunks where the children slept while the crew had swags on the deck. It was their job to keep their quarters clean, or face a scathing reprimand from their father. Dishes had to be washed and the cabin kept spotless along with the ablution area. Cleaning the portholes was one of their favourite jobs. Alfred handed out Brasso and clean rags and after showing them what to do, set them to work, expecting nothing short of a thorough job. For obvious reasons, the area around the barometer and compass was out of bounds to all except Alfred and his senior crew. High standards were observed by the skipper who always led by example. Maintaining the lugger and equipment was always a priority for Alfred, who believed

Alfred Brown with a dugong.
(Battye 53003P.)

prevention was better than cure. Any spare time Laurelle had was spent on mending the family's clothes before they were beyond repair. The salt water was hard on clothes. At an early age she learnt the meaning of several of her father's quotes: 'If a job's worth doing it's worth doing well,' and 'A stitch in time saves nine.'

Alfred's first port of call sailing south was Walcott Inlet. He was met by Reid, the manager of Munja, which was the large government settlement caring for the welfare of Aboriginal people. He picked up the south-bound mail and Fred Merry's cargo, wool and peanuts, which he brought down on camels from Sale River. Alfred steered the *Watt Leggatt* to the bank and set down wide pieces of timber to connect the boat to the shore so the wool could be rolled on board. On the return trip he dropped off stores and mail for Fred and the people at Munja. The mission charged a small fee for this service, just enough to cover costs. Before the lay-up season Alf dropped off extra stores and supplies to see Fred, and other residents living along the coast, through the wet season.

> Laurelle: *We called Fred Merry 'Uncle Fred' and we liked his company. One particular night he'd had had a few drinks and was slightly tipsy. Dad was in his cabin having a well-earned sleep after putting in an extra long day when Uncle Fred yelled out, 'Alf, Alf, come here quickly, I want to show you something.' Dad scrambled out of bed more asleep than awake, thinking something drastic had happened, only to see these smelly camels strung out along the bank. In a slurred voice Uncle Fred said, 'Don't they look beautiful Alf? Aren't they the most beautiful animals you've ever seen?' Well! Dad nearly hit the roof, he was not happy when he looked in the direction Uncle Fred was talking about, only to see these very, very*

ugly camels. It was several days later before Dad saw the funny side and forgave him. I never knew a man who loved his camels as much as Uncle Fred. He had an Afghan chap by the name of Joey to help look after them.

A round trip from Kunmunya to Broome and back took Alfred and his crew about seventeen days in good weather and longer if conditions deteriorated or they had to wait in Broome for the mail.

If the weather was fine Laurelle and her brother and sisters sat outside on the cabin roof singing hymns — they were the only songs they knew — and the crew would join in. And it was through singing jingles and reciting chants that Laurelle taught her young sisters, Ivy in particular, the basics of literacy. If the weather was bad they were banished to the cabin until the wind died down.

> Laurelle: *I can remember Dad saying, 'Get down in that cabin, quickly,' and we'd peep through the portholes watching the whirlpools. Yogi would say, 'We've got the backwash now, we're going to go to the other side now,' and you'd think you were going to smash into the rocks on the other side but the backwash would swing you free. We loved the smell and feel of the sea. I tell you what, they were sailors in those days.*

When the crew wanted turtle eggs Alfred called into Slate Island. If they fancied birds' eggs, they stopped at Bird Island, aptly named after the thousands of birds that made their home there. They'd anchor off shore and everyone except two crew members would visit the island to gather eggs. Alfred always insisted the children wear a hat as it was common for the birds flying over to drop their eggs and other refuse. The foul smell was not very pleasant and the thought of this was enough to make the children keep their hats firmly on their heads. When they had gathered enough eggs they returned to the lugger to cook them. Alfred had modified a petrol drum to make a simple stove. It had bars through the middle to hold pots and billies to cook with. The drum sat on several sheets of tin tacked to the deck. A fire was lit under the bars and the pots and pans sat on top of it. Although it was a primitive apparatus which doubled as a barbecue and grill to cook turtle, dugong, fish and other seafood, it was very functional and safe.

> Laurelle: *Albert Barunga was a crew member that used to be on the* Watt Leggatt *when we were there. I'll never forget the walloping I got from him for swinging on this empty kerosene box. I was swinging backwards and forwards and Dad was in having a sleep and Albert was in charge of us and this was outside Carnot Bay. I kept swinging and swinging and he said, 'Look you're gunna go over.' I didn't take any notice and I kept swinging and over I went. He grabbed me by the leg and he pulled me back up and he walloped me. It wasn't so much the hiding I got from him, I was scared he'd tell Dad, but he didn't tell Dad what happened. Maybe later on he did but he was in charge of us and it was up to him to punish us because Dad never took any nonsense from us. He couldn't afford to while we were at sea. We had to do what we were told and if he put a person in charge we had to do what they told us and it was just my stupidity and stubbornness that I wouldn't listen to him.*

Montgomery Reef was another port of call to spear dugong. Sometimes Alfred or his crew jumped off the jib boom of the *Watt Leggatt* with a harpoon to spear dugongs. They often strayed from the herd and ventured within spearing distance of the boat. Other times they would hunt for dugongs in a dinghy. They were always successful with their catch and fresh grilled rib bones would be on the menu for tea that evening. Alfred salted the leftovers for consumption during the remainder of the journey. On the return trip a dugong would be speared, salted and stored in recycled kerosene tins to take back to the mission.

> Laurelle: *There was another time when Dad was in the creek looking for some fish for lunch and we were sitting on the deck with the rest of the crew. I was busy concentrating on sewing Edie's dress while Kathy and Ivy were arguing in the background. Ivy was swinging on a deckchair while Kathy was fishing. I could hear Kathy tell Ivy not to rock too far, or else she would fall in the water. Ivy decided not to take Kathy's advice and continued to argue with her older sister. Several minutes later Ivy leant too far back in her chair and promptly fell in the water. I quickly dropped my sewing and jumped overboard to grab Ivy and managed to lift her up to the crew then scramble back on board. The rescue incident must have taken seconds as I quickly reacted and before I knew it I had Ivy by the scruff of her neck passing her up to one of the crew. Ivy then blamed everyone else except herself for what happened. She said that we should have been looking after her and made all the excuses under the sun. By the time Dad arrived back everything was back to normal. Ivy never disobeyed Kathy after that.*

Hidden Island was a favourite place of Laurelle's. It had a beautiful white beach that seemed to stretch for miles. The sand made a crunchy sound as you ran on it, making an ideal place for the children to entertain themselves while the crew collected firewood. After the confines of the lugger, they appreciated the space to run around in and the freedom to explore the many surprises and peculiarities the island had to offer.

Alfred called into Augustus Island to get fresh spring water. The water was carted in big kerosene tins and poured into a large water tank that sat at the back behind the stern mast. Every available container was filled with fresh water. On the return trip, if Alfred was running short of water, he'd call into Silvergull Creek. At Augustus the children had to assist with cleaning the *Watt Leggatt*, filling the water tank and washing their clothes. There were jobs to do and everyone from the youngest to the oldest pitched in and helped.

> Laurelle: *We called into Cockatoo Island. Koolan hadn't started till after the war. But on Cockatoo they had this big shed down on the water's edge, just up on the rocky part, then you'd walk straight onto the beach. There was Tom and Mr and Mrs Starkies' house and one house for the workers, the men. They were beautiful big houses up on stilts with verandahs right around. Several times when we were on the boats we used to go and check out the houses and they were beautiful. I remember when we used to go on the boat with Dad we would call in to Cockatoo to see if there was any mail to be picked up and Mrs Starkie would always come down to the beach to meet us. She was a very pretty woman always dressed nicely. I can't remember much about her husband but I can remember her shoulder-length curly hair. She'd always come down and bring lollies and biscuits for us kids. There was George Balsom, Maurie Donovan, they were always there, I can't think of the other blokes, and*

one Christmas time I can remember getting an umbrella from them. They used to buy us Brown kids toys, something nice for Christmas. Koolan didn't open up until after the war, 'cause that was all Australian Iron and Steel then, BHP came in later. When I think back we were pretty lucky to live on the Watt Leggatt *with Dad. We had a great life, all of us at sea.*

Just after passing Cape Leveque Alfred threw in a tow line. He tied it to the rigging with a slip knot a few metres away, so that it unwound easily when a fish hooked itself. Only enough fish to eat was caught; there weren't facilities on board to store fish and Alfred hated wasting food. Fresh fish fillets grilled on the open barbecue seemed to be the standard meal the last night on board.

Their arrival in Broome was timed with high tide. Alfred anchored the *Watt Leggatt* in Roebuck Bay then took the children ashore in a dinghy to Streeters Jetty. This was a wooden structure about half a mile long with a track to push a trolley along. The master pearlers used the trolley to unload pearl shell. The place was a haven for pearlers, beachcombers and sailors. Ethnicity knew no boundaries as there were the smells and sounds of Malays, Japanese, Koepangs, Filipinos, Aborigines, Chinese and other races that were attracted to Broome.

After Alfred supervised his crew unloading the cargo, he visited the mission agent, a chap by the name of MacNee who managed all correspondence and cargo for the mission. After a yarn about the war and a cup of tea, Alfred shopped and attended to other duties that were by now second nature to him. It was only after he had completed these errands and the lugger was packed for the return trip, that he allowed himself to relax and attend to his personal business.

Alfred slept on board while the children stayed with Tommy and Nellie D'Antoine. He never left the lugger unattended during the night. A storm could develop suddenly and cause extensive damage, a risk he didn't want to take; besides, there was also the chance it could be ransacked. The children welcomed the firm ground beneath their feet and friends to play with, a relief from the restrictions and sway of the lugger. Tommy and Nellie had children of their own and they all got on pretty well together. Visiting Broome was a big treat for them so they took the opportunity to window shop, see a movie and take in the peculiarities of the pearling town and its cosmopolitan population.

> Alfred: *We always looked forward to the south-east. That was a good land breeze and we'd hug the coast a lot. The worst time was going back to Broome in the westerlies, that was rough. But then we had a lot of anchorages. But whether it was night or day, I had to push through because I sailed according to a schedule. Had to be there at a certain time in Broome, load up and leave Broome at a certain time to catch the tides at Walcott Inlet. We not only took cargo for Walcott Inlet, there's Mount Barnett, and Mount House too. To get to Walcott Inlet, it took about forty-eight hours to get there, sometimes a little over. At Munja Station you've got to get there at the top tide of the 'springs.' At the station there was no water there in the 'neaps' which meant that I had to land the stores about five miles down the river. They used to send a six ton wagon to pick it up there on a donkey team. So it suited them better if I could go right to the station.*

> Laurelle: *Dad loved the sea and knew a lot about it. He travelled a lot at night using the stars as his compass.*

During the day they weren't that far off land, they could see the land, they could recognise the land and he had a compass. Dad could read and write but some of the other beachcombers, they couldn't read and write and during the night when they were sailing they relied on the stars. Although Dad had a compass he relied more on his enormous knowledge of the sea. I remember we were on the boat when a cockeye bob struck and there was Dad and a bloke by the name of Pablo Acosta, a friend of his. I suppose you'd call a cockeye bob a tropical storm or something like that. It comes up and hits fast and clears off but can do a lot of damage. Dad made us go down to the cabin and took the stairs away so we couldn't come up. All we could do was look through the portholes. The waves seemed to be breaking over the deck and the seas were rough and Dad with his crew and Pablo, they came through it quite good.

8

The War Years

On 8 December 1941 radio contact with Wyndham revealed Japan had struck Pearl Harbor. The mission was asked to make radio contact twice a day to inform authorities of unusual aircraft activities over the mission.

About eighteen days later Alfred was given a letter in Broome to deliver to the Japanese crew working on Streeter's pearl lugger *Peggy B99*. The lugger was stationed at Hall Point, not far from Kunmunya. The mission was the closest contact point to the lugger so the request to deliver the letter was not unreasonable. He took the letter to them and as they couldn't read English he read it for them. The letter informed them they were at war with Australia and had to return to the port of Broome. They seemed quite bewildered by the news. As pearl divers they had no understanding of the directive to report to authorities. In a few minutes their status had changed from competent pearl workers to enemy of the country. Alfred wished he could say something to make them feel easy but there was nothing he could do. He was only doing his job. A sick feeling washed over him as he realised the war was starting to become a reality and he would have to start thinking of the safety of his children.

The following year on 18 February 1942 a four-engine flying boat flew low over the mission heading northwards. It was a monoplane similar to a 'Short Empire.' It bore no national marking, only a combination of letters under its wing, and the mission staff were not sure whether it was an enemy reconnaissance plane or not.

The next day the mission heard the news that Darwin had been bombed for the first time.

On 20 February Alfred left on his usual trip to Walcott Inlet to collect the mail and freight and then go on to Broome. He took his children with him, but he did not know it was to be his last trip on the *Watt Leggatt* and that he would never return to Kunmunya.

THE WAR IN BROOME

> *When the Japs raided Broome it was terrible. It was terrible to see the people, they didn't have a chance ... swimming ashore, some getting shot, and on the flying boats and all. The Dutch had come down from the Balikpapans and the Dutch East Indies. They were shot. It was terrible.*
>
> Alfred

Japanese and Germans living in Broome were interned during the war. A group of Japanese people had developed a market place aptly named Japanese Gardens a few kilometres out of Broome. They made a living from selling fresh vegetables and when the war broke out they were interned. Their place was left abandoned, becoming a haven for squatters. Many other Broome residents with Japanese links were treated like traitors and interned. They were stripped of personal belongings and assets and sent to a prisoner of war camp interstate and were never compensated when they returned to Broome after the war. This had an enormous impact on many who had developed a generation of links with local Broome people. Their families still carry the scars of their internment today.

> Alfred: *Jimmy Chi got caught in those — see, his mother was Japanese and his father was Chinese but the authorities didn't take that into consideration. Seeing he had a Japanese mother he was sent to a concentration camp down south somewhere. He was a businessman, he owned a restaurant and of course when the war broke out he lost it all.*

It was March 1942 and Alfred went to Broome with the intention of sending his daughters to the local Catholic school. Alwyn, his oldest son, was already in Broome working at the bakery and Laurelle, at thirteen, was ready for high school. Alfred wanted to keep the family together in a time of crisis. The war was upon them and Broome was already feeling the ramifications. Alfred knew the Catholic Sisters in Broome quite well; he often delivered them fresh peanuts from the mission harvest. On a previous trip he had discussed his plans with Sister Raymond. She recognised the dilemma he faced and encouraged him to enrol his children in the convent school where they would be safe, leaving him free to continue his work with the mission.

Yogi had gone to Melbourne four months earlier with Mr and Mrs Holmes. George Holmes had expressed concern to the Board of Missions regarding the future of Alfred's family. He felt the mission had very little to offer the children as they grew older and that they needed to be integrated into mainstream society. Broome was even less desirable due to its prevalent attitudes towards and treatment of Aboriginal people. Holmes' opinion was that since they were light-skinned they could blend in with children in a Presbyterian home down south where they would be protected from segregationist practices. He argued that the children were three-eighths Aboriginal and would breed out their colour if married to Europeans. He even sent a photograph to verify his argument and took Yogi to Melbourne to meet the board in person.

Yogi (left) in Melbourne, with John Graham, 1941.

The attitude of George Holmes reflected the government policy of the time on biological absorption. The aim of the policy was to absorb Aboriginal people into the general community: by marrying into white society they would breed out their colour and take on the aspirations of the dominant race. Unlike Reverend Love, Mr Holmes did not share his thoughts with Alfred and felt it his duty to act on the matter.

When Alfred arrived in Broome the town was in a state of disarray. The army had taken complete control. Luggers operating from Broome were commandeered by the army and many were burnt to prevent them falling into the hands of the Japanese. This was the case with the lugger of a friend of his, Ginger D'Antoine. Ginger was the son of Frenchy D'Antoine, who had come to Broome from the Seychelles at the turn of the century in search of a new life. He had several children to a Djau woman, of whom Ginger was one. Frenchy had built up a beachcombing business and his son had followed in his footsteps. Ginger was doing quite well from beachcombing, but now all that was going up in flames as he watched the army burn his lugger, the *Blanche*. He stood helplessly watching as his blazing lugger slowly, ever so slowly disappeared before him, feeling his livelihood slip away with each plank that crumbled and fell. He too was never compensated.

> Laurelle: *The day before Broome was raided Dad brought us into town, along with Mrs Woods and her daughter. We picked them up at Cape Leveque. He had heard they were flying people out on planes but all the people had gone and there were no more planes coming in to take people out. Anyhow that night Pat, my cousin, took us out to Japanese Garden in a little old car he had. Dad had loaded the* **Watt Leggatt** *up early and we were to sail back to the mission at night and hide in the creeks during the day. Dad didn't want to sail during the day because of enemy aircraft. I know he had a terrible row with the mission agent, MacNee, about sailing back to the mission. Patrick's wife Dot, and Florence and all them were coming with us back to the mission. Instead of that at about nine o'clock in the morning the Japanese planes came over and machine-gunned all the planes and the Dutch flying boats that were all there. I was wearing a white skirt and pink blouse with white polka dots and sitting out the back on a wooden garden seat. Dot was pottering around the kitchen. We'd had breakfast and the washing up was*

completed. I was sitting down with Florence while Ivy, Kathy, Edie and Amy were playing.

I'm sure Uncle Harry, Auntie Mackie, Henry, Richard and Evelyn were on a station out of Derby — Liveringa I think — when the town was bombed. Anyhow Florence was hand sewing a dress for Phyllis and we were sitting down talking to her. Planes flew over and Phyllis said, 'More Americans.' Florence said, 'Gee they're going awfully fast for American or Australian planes.' The next thing you heard were machine-guns, then we heard Dot yelling and screaming, 'Get in the thick bushes so they can't see you. Broome's being raided.' She was worried the pilots would see my white skirt so she told me to get under the shade of the blackberry tree. We didn't know if they were going to drop bombs or what. The only thought on our mind was to get as far away from the house as possible in case they bombed the house. You could hear the planes very clearly and I remembered being told at the mission not to look up at them as they flew over, they'd see the white of your eyes. Thinking back now it seemed funny. I was throwing kids over the fence and dragging Ivy into the bush. Everyone just scrambled for the cover of the bush. A goat started bleating and someone yelled, 'Shut that bloody nanny goat up, the Japanese pilots might hear it.' Then a baby started crying and someone yelled, 'Stop that baby from crying, give it nanya, they can hear us.' Someone gave us torn pieces of sheet and told use 'Here use this, they could gas us.' We really didn't know what to do or to expect, it was turmoil, people, kids and animals were scattering everywhere. Dot seemed to be the only one who knew what to do.

Just when Alfred thought he had arrangements in place with Sister Raymond he had to rapidly change them.

Prior to the raid he had felt the safest thing to do was to return to the mission and take the Shadforths with him. Sailing by night and hiding in the creeks during the day should have allowed him to dodge the Japanese planes and possible enemy attack, however this didn't happen as the raid put an end to that. With the scene of the carnage created by the attack on Broome fresh in his mind, Alfred appealed to the mission agent, MacNee, for help to get his daughters out. Trying to reason with MacNee proved frustrating and he gave up, saying, 'I've got my girls out there, my children. They're motherless. I've got to get to them.' As he walked out he handed MacNee the keys to the *Watt Leggatt* saying, 'It's loaded, cabin's locked up, with mail and everything. My children come first.'

He walked out the door angry, confused and scared, trying to hide his emotions. He wanted to be strong when he approached his crew Mundi, Goodman, Pompey and Wattie. They didn't understand the peril of war and Alfred could sense panic in their eyes and voices. They were determined to walk back to the security of their country and people. To make the walk overland back to Kunmunya would be an incredible feat, and Alfred tried to persuade the elders to let him take the youngest crew member with him but they did not agree. He was worried young Wattie wouldn't complete the journey. Alfred knew they would have no problems finding water so he gave them plenty of food and advised them of the dangers of war. Not knowing when he would see them again, he said goodbye and watched them fade out of sight.

The army were busy evacuating the township. It was absolute bedlam. People were looting business houses and anything lying around. Unknown to Alfred, his children were taken by Reggie Fisher and Joey D'Antoine on a crowded Bell Brothers' truck to an area just out of

Broome where everybody was gathering. When Alfred tried to find his family he was told, 'You'd better go out there. Your kids aren't at Japanese Garden, they're at the turn-off to Beagle Bay.' Alfred was starting to panic and headed straight out with Pat Shadforth in a little old bomb of a car.

> Laurelle: *We were in a hurry to get where everyone was congregating at the turn-off to Beagle Bay. Before we left the Japanese Garden there was this Chinese bloke and his friend, an Aboriginal chap. They were hastily packing their belongings to leave Broome. In their rush to pile their horse and cart with cargo well over load control limits they forgot to harness the horse to the cart. When they got on and gave the horse one almighty hit with the whip, off it galloped okay, but left them behind, sitting in the cart looking quite angry at each other. Both were blaming each other in their own language in a fit of rage but it looked funny to us. It sounded so funny listening to them argue in different languages, fuming away throwing their hands up in the air as they growled at each other. We didn't stop to see if they caught the horse because we were in a rush ourselves. I didn't see them at the turn-off because there was a huge crowd at the turn-off.*

It wasn't until after Alfred found his children that he was able to think rationally again and together they hopped on the back of Stan Vincent's butcher's truck, with Patrick and his family abandoning the little old car in a dishevelled heap in the scrub.

As they were crossing Engadine Plains a man ran out towards a little bush that was close to the marsh. Patrick yelled out, 'Hey Donald, what are you running from?' He said, 'Oh! It's you Pat, I thought you were a bloody Jap plane.' The children were fascinated by the look of distress on his face and tugged at each other's sleeve saying, 'Donald! What's his surname, Donald what?' and Florence turned around and said, 'Donald Duck.' She said that more to shut them up, but they thought her answer was funny and burst out laughing. At the time the comment eased the tension everyone, including the kids, was feeling. The name stuck and the children nicknamed him 'Donald Duck.' Later they learnt his name was Donald Munroe, but he took his chances with the nickname and hopped on board for a lift south. Along the way he entertained the kids showing them how to make soap from native trees.

Thus, Alfred and his children found themselves on Stan Vincent's butcher's truck heading south, making their way to Anna Plains. Other evacuees had hitched a ride with Stan so the truck was heavily laden with distraught people, hastily gathered luggage and frightened pets. Alfred didn't have any plans beyond reaching Anna Plains. With the war in full swing he was operating in survival mode, facing each decision as it presented; he knew it was impossible to plan ahead. At one stage a plane headed straight for the road and Stan spun the wheel and headed for the safety of the bush. Edith went flying off the truck, clutching the family dog, Rusty. Fortunately the soft sand cushioned her fall and she landed safely with a death grip on Rusty. Florence quickly jumped off the truck, hitched up her dress and ran to rescue her, heaving her and Rusty back on the truck within seconds. Fortunately nothing became of what they thought was a Japanese plan about to open fire on them.

Being a remote settlement did not make Kunmunya immune from the perils of war. The Youngs and the

Patons were refusing to abandon the mission and evacuate. The Patons had just returned to the mission, and didn't want to be sent away again because of a war; they were prepared to take their chances. The situation with the Youngs was different; they had a young child, Ian, to consider. Strange planes flying over the mission at ungodly hours of the morning started to make them nervous. Even the Aboriginal people scattered when they heard planes circling overhead. It was decided that Mr Young would stay while Mrs Young and Ian left the Kimberley via Derby.

The superintendent, George Holmes, returned to the mission after his holidays. He had left Yogi in the care of the the Presbyterian Church's Byford Home, an orphanage in the foothills south of Perth. Holmes was caught in the chaos of those early days of the war but managed to make his way back after the bombing of Broome to find the mission without a lugger. George was not happy with Alfred's decision to put the welfare of his children first, reporting that it was selfish and thoughtless of him to behave in such a way. In Holmes' opinion, Alfred should have ignored the ultimatum given by the army, sneaked the lugger out of Roebuck Bay and taken his chances, risking the lives of his children and all on board.

THE DROVING ROAD TO MEEKATHARRA

Camping along the way to Anna Plains proved very difficult. You weren't allowed to light a fire. When anyone tried, they were howled down by yelling voices, 'Put that bloody fire out, the Japs might see it.' At meal times food just seemed to appear out of nowhere, cold and uninteresting. Then there were the mosquitoes that attacked at sunset. It seemed like there were millions of them and there was nothing you could do. Repellent wasn't available and you couldn't light a fire to smoke them out; you just had to grin and bear it, swiping them away hoping infection wouldn't eventuate.

It rained frequently and a scout was sent ahead to check the road conditions. It seemed even the gods were against them. When asked, 'What's our position?' Alfred replied, 'You got Jesus Christ stopping you with rain from the south and the bloody Japs from the north. This is where we'll have to stay for a few days.'

When Alfred and his family finally arrived at Anna Plains, a cattle station south of Broome, it was packed with evacuees. They were distressed and confused, sleeping in cars and trucks loaded to the hilt with belongings hastily packed after the raid. It seemed like hundreds of people had gathered there, some on their way south and others not knowing whether to sit out the aftermath of the raid and wait till things settled before returning to Broome. Alfred and his family were part of the group that didn't know their next move.

A man called George Betts was taking cattle overland from Anna Plains to Meekatharra where they would be sent by train to the abattoirs in Perth. He knew Patrick Shadforth and noticed he was part of the war-torn group assembled at Anna Plains. George went up to him and said, 'Why don't you come with me as a drover, while I take these cattle to Meekatharra? I could use some extra help.' Patrick said, 'Well I can't go, I've got all my sisters, wife, cousins and Uncle Alfred. I can't just walk out on them.' Taking his reply as an opportunity to recruit workers, George Betts replied, 'Bring the whole lot with you, I could use some able-bodied workers. Bring the kids too.' So, the next thing they knew they were working for George and on the droving road heading south, their short-term plans giving them a sense of direction and lifting their spirits.

Alwyn, who was sixteen by now, returned to Broome with Aubrey Davy. Aubrey had asked permission from Alfred to take Alwyn with him, and Alfred gave his blessing provided Aubrey looked after him, which he did. Alwyn worked for Aubrey for a short time before moving to Lombadina Mission where he stayed with his cousin Percy.

George Betts employed several people who had fled Broome. As well as Patrick and his family, there were Goodji D'Antoine and her five children, Douglas, Adrian, Lexie, Peggy and Aubrey and her nephew Joey. Billy Watson was another character on the droving road. He'd come down from Beagle Bay to Broome with Goodji at the first sign of Japanese attacks. When they got there she bought an old T-model Ford and as she didn't have a licence, persuaded Billy to drive it south for her and be George's general handyman for the trip. George had his son and several other drovers with him, so in total he had a formidable team including two trucks, horses and about twelve hundred head of cattle.

Billy tried to teach Alfred to drive, an experience he initially baulked at. After sailing a lugger for many years he found the new skill of driving a truck very difficult to master. One day Goodji allowed Alfred to drive her truck. He went from one side of the road to the other, narrowly missing the trees that hugged the edges. In the end Goodji's patience got the better of her and she shoved him over saying, 'You can't drive at all Alf, move over and I'll drive this car.' But Goodji wasn't much better. Between them they just managed to keep most of the wheels on the track and maintain pace with the rest of the convoy. When the old truck refused to go up the sand hills Billy got in and reversed it up. The kids thought it was hilarious, cheering Bill along and grabbing the sides to help push it up. Goodji's truck finally gave up, collapsing in a rusty heap of steel and wood. The wooden spokes had completely fallen out of the wheels and Goodji had no choice but to abandon it on the side of the road.

The wet season was still hovering, in fact it seemed like it was at its peak, bucketing down, turning the dirt road into huge muddy veins of slush and mud. The creeks and river beds were filled with water and debris, making the crossings difficult and dangerous. The only way to stop bogging the trucks was to get out and lay sheets of tin in front of the wheels, drive forward several metres then take the sheets from the back wheels and repeat the process. It was very slow and tedious, but the children thought the whole ordeal was great fun, feeling the mud ooze through their fingers as they freed the tin and dragged it to the front for the adults to secure in place. Their faces were covered with mud that was flicked up as the wheels spun to get traction. Everyone looked forward to a relaxing bath at the end of the day to clean the dirt and grime before a meal of corned beef and damper.

One crossing was so bad to negotiate it was aptly named the Ugly Crossing and took a full day to cross. It was at the Oakover River, another tediously slow crossing, where Laurelle saw her first green budgerigar. Not knowing what the bird was, she consulted the oracle, George. He was a full bottle on the bird life and flora. George was very patient with the children and took the time to explain things, knowing the native plants and animals were new experiences for them.

Laurelle: *We used to go out and dig up the spinifex and turn it upside down so that the spikes were upside down. We didn't have any sheets so we put canvas on the top, then a blanket. To stop the wind we chopped the small trees down and faced the leaves towards the head of the bed to keep the wind down. We made the swags for all the stockmen. We tried to make their bedding as comfortable as possible. We used to do their washing. When we came to a creek or billabong we did a big wash. Patrick's wife Dot cooked for us and Dad, and Goodji cooked for George Betts and the drovers. We ate a lot of stew, salt beef and bread. We didn't eat anything fancy, no butter. There was no such thing as lollies or chocolates. It was wartime and you couldn't get those things.*

One night the constant rain forced Alfred to make a bed for the girls under George Betts' truck, which was high off the ground. He made a trench around the truck hoping the water would be trapped in the moat and not seep through their bedding. His theory didn't hold water however, and the girls started to get wet. In the middle of the night Laurelle could hear Edie telling Kathy, 'Well if you just keep laying on one side and keep your top part dry it won't be too bad, you won't feel so cold.' The night was very long and uncomfortable with bouts of numbness taking over.

Laurelle was aware that when cows calved along the road the calves were killed. It was too demanding on the drovers to move cattle and care for the calves. In spite of this rule Laurelle and the other children managed to sneak a calf on their truck thinking if they tucked it under the bedding no one would notice. The noise eventually attracted the attention of George as he walked past. 'What's this?' he said. There was guilt written all over their faces and George didn't have the heart to put it down. He told them they could keep the calf provided they take total responsibility for it. Needless to say the children were happy to comply and the calf escaped death.

During his trip south Alfred was subject to surveillance by the Department of Native Affairs. Although he was exempted it did not stop them tracking his movements. The mission wanted to know his whereabouts, and invite him to return as the skipper of the *Watt Leggatt*. Mr Holmes was starting to realise Alfred was practically indispensable. They were having difficulty finding a skilled and reliable person to operate and maintain the mission lugger. Holmes wrote to the commissioner of the Aborigines Department who contacted the native protector at Port Hedland in an effort to locate Alfred. The local protector was Constable Chipperfield, who was only too pleased to reply to the request, informing Holmes that Alfred had been sighted at Wallal. Due to communication problems, however, the police could not make personal contact to pass on the request.

Alfred and his family did not have to worry too much about money on the trip. George Betts was a fair boss, providing meals and other consumable items such as bath soap, washing powder and toothpaste, and deducting the cost from their wages. Along the way they met a man called Claude Eets who was selling clothes and had a reasonable supply for sale. Being wartime you needed coupons to buy them. Knowing they had been on the road for some time and wouldn't have any, he allowed them to purchase some clothes which they persuaded George to pay for, promising to repay him. Everyone took the opportunity to replace their dull threadbare clothes with bright fashionable garments. They last saw Claude heading north in an old car that was destined to meet the same fate as Goodji's T-model Ford.

> Laurelle: *During the war you were given coupons. Being wartime you couldn't buy anything. You used coupons for clothing, tea, sugar, meat, petrol. People got coupons for different things and they had to last for twelve months and if you used it up then you went without. We didn't get any until we got to Byford. We only had coupons for clothing and Dad got them from Matron Cairns at the Home. The Home supplied all our food so we didn't need ones for food. I suppose nowadays you'd call them vouchers.*

About halfway through the trip they met up with a family called the Brockmans. They were another droving team making their way to Meekatharra. They stopped long enough for Patrick to give two young Brockman boys a haircut. There was a middle-aged woman and a young girl driving a horse-drawn cart. Laurelle said to Dot, 'Who are they?' and Dot replied, 'Oh! that's the boys' mother and sisters. Their job is to go ahead of the droving team and set up camp and prepare meals.'

As they travelled further south the weather became very cold. Not being prepared, they found it difficult to get warm, the cold seemed to cut through to their bones. The weather didn't stop one of the young members of their team, Aubrey Greatorex, from finding the coldest pool to swim in. When he was noticed missing all they had to do was look for the closest waterhole with frost on the surface and sure enough Aubrey would be found paddling contentedly in it. Amazingly enough he never caught a cold, let alone pneumonia.

Laurelle: *Joey D'Antoine was travelling with us. He was Goodji's nephew and was the horse tailer. He was still learning to ride a horse so he wasn't a very good rider. One day we were watching him and holding our breath thinking, 'Oh! he's going to go over, Oops,' then he'd get his balance and go a few metres then start to wobble in the saddle and we'd hold our breath yet again waiting for him to fall off. This went on for some time then some cattle broke away and he was told to go after them. Suddenly the horse turned and Joey went one way and the horse went the other. Joey was then demoted to caring for the horses and told to leave the mustering to the skilled stockmen. He had to look after the old and sick cows, the slower type more suited to Joe's ability.*

Another incident concerning Joey was his first meeting with a camel. One day he came flying out of the bush, obviously frightened and confused. He stopped and started to pant as he wiped his brow nervously with a white handkerchief. Then he gasped, 'I saw something terrible back there, some kind of terrible ugly animal. I've never seen this kind of animal before.' We said, 'What did it look like?' He said, 'Well it had a big hump.' Recognising the animal from our days at Kunmunya we all burst out laughing. He didn't see the humour and angrily said, 'What's so funny about that, what are you people laughing about? It must be some sort of a devil!' Someone said, 'That's only a bloody stinking camel, Joey, haven't you seen one before?' 'Well if it's a camel, I'm not going near them again,' he said firmly. Poor chap, he hadn't seen a camel before and was not happy that we laughed at his ignorance.

Meekatharra to Perth

In 1941 further legislative restrictions were introduced to prevent Aboriginal people living in the north moving south of latitude twenty degrees without a permit. This imaginary line was commonly known as the Leprosy Line. It was a measure to control the spread of leprosy within the state and contain it within the Kimberley. If Aborigines wanted to cross the line they had to have written permission from the Commissioner of Native Welfare. Temporary permits were issued to drovers and those seeking specialist medical attention and legal assistance. This piece of legislation was abolished in 1972 along with other restrictive punitive policies dealing with the treatment of Aborigines. Although Alfred was under the surveillance of the Native Welfare Department they couldn't stop him crossing the Leprosy Line. He took his family across with the knowledge that they were all exempted and did not need a permit. By now he was simply tired of the suffocating tentacles of the department squeezing his every effort of independence. It did not seem to matter he and his family were exempted from the Act.

At Meekatharra Goodji managed to rent a two bedroom house, and Alfred and his four girls boarded there.

Most of the droving team went their own way. Patrick and Dot found work on a station just out of Meekatharra for a short time, taking Florence, Phyllis and Amy with them. They eventually returned to the Kimberley after Broome began to recover from the war. George Betts returned with his droving team to Anna Plains.

The effects of the war in the Kimberley seemed to be fading and Alfred had to start thinking of a future for his family. As soon as the opportunity arose he contacted the Byford Home to see how his son Yogi was. Yogi had been there since his trip to Melbourne with Mr Holmes the previous December. Alfred contacted Reverend Tulloch, the moderator for the church, and when he learnt of their situation, insisted Alfred and the girls catch the next train to Perth and stay at Byford.

Goodji put Alfred and his girls on the train for Perth. She had mixed feelings about seeing them go. They were great mates but she knew Alfred and the girls were better off at Byford than returning to the mission or Broome. She didn't know how long it would be before she saw them again.

Goodji and her oldest daughter Lexie had started a laundry business in the town and were gaining a good reputation as hard workers. They had the laundry contract for the three hotels in Meekatharra and had no immediate plans to return to Broome. Goodji sent Alfred and the girls on their way armed with homemade biscuits and plenty of food for the trip.

The journey took three days and the frequent stops along the way allowed them to take in the changing country and weather. The trip was a new experience; they had never travelled on a train, let alone this far south, and the memory of the experience remained with them well after they arrived in Perth.

> Laurelle: *It was the second time I'd seen oranges on a tree. I was used to seeing them in the shops. On the train trip we passed these lovely green lush looking trees. I'd first seen them at Peak Hill but the ones here at Northam were beautiful big oranges, they looked so luscious. I suppose it was because we were looking down at them from the train. I never knew country like this existed*

because at Kunmunya when it was dry it was very dry. There was all this lush looking country.

Alfred and his daughters arrived in Perth around October 1942 and were met by the secretary of Byford Home, Miss Matthews, and Yogi. The train trip from Meekatharra had played havoc with their biological clocks so by the time the girls arrived in Perth they were pretty tired and weary but happy to see their brother. It was their first trip to the city and they were completely stunned by it.

Laurelle had seen snippets of city life on newsreel at Broome picture theatre, but it was nothing compared to the real thing. Her first impression of the city was one of shock. She was overcome by the enormity and vibrance of the shops, traffic, food, houses and other elements of city life.

Laurelle: *When we got to Perth I couldn't take my eyes off the buildings, I'd never seen anything so big. It was a real eye opener. When we arrived, Miss Matthews greeted us then she took us outside to her car. Yogi was standing by her car and I got the shock of my life to see him standing there all dressed up. He was wearing a grey suit, white man shirt, tie, patent shoes and long socks. I'd never seen him like that. At Kunmunya I was forever patching his pants and as for shoes, there was no need for them at the mission, I'd never seen him in shoes. He seemed so sophisticated. I remember Edie saying to me, 'He's talking like a white man.' My sisters were all huddled around me, I guess they were frightened too and by Yogi's standard of dress we were feeling pretty shabby. It was a shock to walk out of the station and be hit by big skyscrapers like Boans, Bairds, Moores, Aherns, Bonmarche, Foy and Gibsons.*

9

The Byford Home

When they were driving us up to the Home, the hustle and bustle and smells were very noticeable. The different smells of fresh bread, fish shops and fruit stalls were so strong. It was beautiful driving out to Byford and it was really good when we started to go up the hill. Everything was woodlands and it reminded me of the mission, but this vegetation was thick, lush and green. The thickness and greenness of the bush struck me. Along the roadside there were crepe myrtles, leschenaultia and other native plants. Every now and then we'd come across a stream meandering along with the road. The country was so very different.

Laurelle

Arrangements had been made for Alfred to work as the handyman at Byford Home. For a short time he stayed in a small cottage away from the main home, slightly isolated from everyone. The cold seemed to seep in through every available crack and permeable surface so Matron Cairns made him move to a comfortable room at the rear of the main building.

> Laurelle: *The culture was very different. When we were at Kunmunya, even though it was an Aboriginal mission, we lived separately from the Aboriginal people. We were allowed to go with them on day trips. We would go hunting and swimming under the waterfalls and creek, collect bush fruits and mix with the children and people. They treated us like their own children. We had a lot of freedom there. The lifestyle at Byford was different and we weren't allowed the same freedom we had at Kunmunya, we seemed to be restricted. The weather was different. I really felt the cold and so did Dad.*
>
> *We were the only Aboriginal children at the Home but we were treated the same as any other child there. The kids didn't treat us any differently. They respected Dad. Even the staff respected him. There was nothing, nothing at all about the colour of your skin or your Aboriginality or anything like that, none of that there. I suppose you could say it was a culture shock for me. I can remember when I first saw the Home it was so huge to me it seemed like a palace. The houses we lived in at the mission were so small, and the buildings here were so big and grand. When I first walked into the place, I'm sure I would have got lost in it. I can even remember the thick brown carpet that had specks of white in it. The first question I asked myself was, 'How do they keep this place clean and shiny?' I quickly found out, we were expected to clean it ourselves. I couldn't get over how young the kids were, they were only preschool age and all white kids and they didn't seem to have any family. They came from broken homes, and there were part orphans, and war legacy children. They seemed helpless and lonely, at least we had our father with us. Later I*

found out we were expected to help and care for them too.

As in Kunmunya, Presbyterian values prevailed at Byford and there were striking parallels between the two places, especially in the enforcement of work. In place of weeding the struggling vegetable garden and milking the smelly goats were the endless floorboards and dormitories to clean, dining room to set and clear, clothes to wash, infants to care for and many other jobs. Saturday was spent cleaning and polishing the Home from top to bottom and if it failed to meet the matron's regimental expectations, it had to be redone without sulking or throwing a temper tantrum. You quickly learnt to do a thorough job first off and make sure the yardstick she used of seeing her reflection in the polished surface was met before you called for her approval. The most painstaking job was polishing the dining room floor. Getting down on hands and knees on a hard unforgiving surface applying oil and polish that stained clothes and skin was not Laurelle's favourite job. It evoked the same dread as picking those dreadful grubs off the vegetables at the mission. But she knew there was no escaping institutional routines, so she learnt to roll up her sleeves and polished the boards till they shone.

Laurelle took comfort in the knowledge they could go swimming later. The children had a homemade dam they had shaped from a stream at the bottom of the hill. Frolicking in the pool reminded her of Kunmunya Creek back at the mission, and basking in the memory seemed to wash away the Byford blues.

There was always plenty of fresh fruit and vegetables to eat. They grew roughly the same type of vegetables they were used to at the mission except they grew them all year round instead of seasonally and they were greener, bigger and fresher. There was porridge, bread and jam and cream for breakfast, which was washed down with a cup of cocoa drunk slowly in the quadrangle. They liked the quadrangle, it was a place where they could savour the morning warmth of the sun on their skin and quickly discovered the spots that received maximum heat.

The Home had a dairy that was leased to one of the local chaps and as part of the deal, he kept the Home supplied with fresh milk and cream, a treat the Brown children quickly acquired a taste for. They had an endless supply of fresh milk and although they had goats' milk at the mission, it seemed flavourless and stale compared to this.

The supply of fruit seemed endless, and you didn't have to steal it. The Home had orchards of almonds, plums and peaches and other stone fruits. These were supplemented by fruit that the local farmers couldn't sell and donated to the Home. The farmers would ring the matron and if the farm was close Alfred bundled the children on a horse-drawn cart and went to pick up the fruit. If the farm was at a distance he'd take the truck, piling the kids in the back. By now Alfred was getting quite good at driving, even venturing into the city.

The fresh fruit, vegetables and dairy products seemed like manna from heaven to Laurelle and her family who quickly acquired a taste for stone fruit and cream.

> Laurelle: *The kids at the Home loved Dad and they always asked him to fix things. One day Bobby Matthews went up to Dad and said, 'Mr Brown, can you fix this for me?' and Dad said, 'Well, I'll try,' and when Dad looked down Bobby had this broken marble in his little hands. Dad fixed it with glue and he said to Bobby, 'I don't know*

how long it's going to last.' People were still feeling the effects of the war so nothing was thrown away, not even a broken marble. Bobby was happy with his glued marble.

Another time Dad went into Perth with a lot of loose change and went to Charlie Carters. He said, 'I've got sixty kids at the Home, can I get threepence worth of lollies made up in sixty different bags. I can't take lollies back for my own kids and not take any for the others.' Sure enough they did as he asked and he came back with all these little bags for the children with threepence worth of lollies in each. The kids thought it was great. Dad was always thoughtful like that.

At the Home there was a little boy called John Smith. He had had a cousin there too, then she left. He was one of the many children that were taken in by the Home because of family circumstances. Postwar many families experienced financial difficulties; parents didn't have permanent jobs so the children came to the Home until their parents could afford to at least feed them. John was very young, about one or two years old, and wasn't there very long. He took a liking to Edith. She took him under her wing, bathing, feeding and dressing him. She treated him like a baby brother, fussing over him, putting his hair into curls and pampering him, giving him the love and affection he needed.

Each year the Home entered a wildflower competition that involved picking a range of wildflowers. The children scoured the countryside looking for orchids, smoke bush, kangaroo paw, leschenaultias and many more wildflowers. Laurelle was amazed at the picturesque countryside dotted with neat farms, horses and fat cattle. It was a far cry from the turbulent seas and dry hills of Kunmunya.

The day after picking the flowers were sent to the main Presbyterian office in Perth, where they were arranged then entered into the floral exhibition. The Home won the floral arrangement competition for three consecutive years. Following the judging Matron would call the children into the dining room and say, 'Well children, I've got some lovely news for you. This is for you. The cup is yours.' She held up a large silver trophy shaped like a soup tureen and very intricately worked. When Laurelle saw it her jaw dropped, thinking, 'How long is it going to take to dust and polish the trophy?' She knew it would be her job.

Laurelle: *At the Home we went to school in this little old farm house where we were taught English and maths. We loved school and played the odd prank or two. We had this teacher, we'd pronounce his name by joining the two words Sir and Raymond together so it sounded like Sirraymond. He had a motor bike he rode to school. Anyhow at the Home we used to receive these big tea chests full of biscuits and my friend Shirley Stewart and I had to put them into biscuit tins. When we had finished putting them into tins there were all these biscuit crumbs at the bottom of the box. We'd go off to school eating these crumbs, leaving the remains for the boys. Unknown to us, the boys would stuff the crumbs into the exhaust pipe of Sirraymond's motor bike. When he took off after school biscuit crumbs were flying everywhere. He didn't know until he got on his bike and took off. He never growled at us and took the pranks as they came, knowing it was one of the small joys the kids got at the Home. He finished up coming to school on a push bike and I'm sure we spent more time outside riding his bike than inside learning.*

TECHNICAL SCHOOL

After finishing at the primary school in Byford, at the beginning of 1943 Laurelle went to the city to further her education at a technical school in St George's Terrace. It was generally accepted that young girls would specialise in domestic subjects such as dressmaking and cooking rather than pursue a professional career. During her second year, her friend, Shirley Stewart joined her. Apart from herself and Shirley, the other students came from the metropolitan area. Travelling on the train with Shirley felt safer. Being a relatively shy person Laurelle appreciated the moral support in a daunting environment. The city was a frightening and lonely place compared to the simple life at Kunmunya.

Waking up before dawn to catch the 6.00am train to Perth every Monday was far from exciting. Laurelle loathed the cold dark mornings in the middle of the year that always started with drizzling rain and hail. It was the cold she hated the most; the dark did not bother her, it was tolerable compared with the cold. Alfred took her the three miles to the train station on a horse and cart. She prayed the wind wouldn't find them; it seemed to halve the temperature and make the trip to the train station twice as long. When the Home got a truck it was not so bad as she managed to board the train with dry clothes and hair. In the summers she enjoyed travelling. It was a stark contrast to the winter that heralded the cold and darkness. During summer there was still plenty of sunlight left to spend outdoors with her family.

Monday was dressmaking classes with Miss Annert and Tuesday was cooking with Miss Missingham. The church supplied accommodation for Laurelle in the city and after school on Tuesday she caught the munitions train back home. It left Perth about four o'clock in the afternoon, arriving in Byford by five to pick up the munitions workers. There was a large ammunition factory at Byford that manufactured bullets and other war products, providing employment for city people who commuted every day.

> Laurelle: *We had this young boy, John, he was partly crippled and he was to attend this Christmas party for children like him. I brought him down on the train with me and when he saw those people who came to meet him he started screaming and kept calling me nurse, he was screaming, 'Nurse, nurse, don't leave me.' I felt terrible leaving him and they tried to explain to him that I would pick him up. I didn't want to leave him but I had to go to school. Anyhow they managed to drag him away and take him in the bus. After school I waited for him at the station and as soon as he saw me he raced up and grabbed me and I said, 'We're going home now John.' He was quite happy to see me and we went back to the Home together.*

Another time she had charge of a little boy who was returning to the Home, his name was Bobby Henderson. They got on the goods train which was such a length that when it pulled up way down the other end of Byford Station and Laurelle and Bobby went to get off a lady said, 'Oh! no the carriage will pull up closer.' But instead of that it went on to Mundijong.

Laurelle and Bobby had to catch the goods train coming back the other way and it was dark and chilly when they eventually arrived at Byford. They had no choice but to walk the three miles to the Home. Bobby was only five so when he got tired Laurelle had to carry him. She piggybacked him to the closest farmhouse and by the time she got there she was feeling pretty tired. She explained to the owners what had happened so they let her leave her case and gave her a hurricane lamp. By now they were feeling tired, cold and hungry. Laurelle knew her father would be along shortly looking for them. They walked on for another half an hour when she sighted lights coming down the hill. Sure enough it was Alfred and Miss Tonkin. Miss Tonkin was in charge at the Home.

It was around this time Laurelle had her first dealings with the Native Affairs Department. When Aborigines reached fourteen years of age they had to apply for individual status or revert to coming under the Aborigines Act. Laurelle wrote to the department saying,

> *I have now reached the age of fourteen years, I wish to make application to you to be declared exempt from the provision of the Act relating to natives. I am living in Byford Home belonging to the Presbyterian Church and am employed there as an Assistant. I am also studying at the Technical School in Perth, where I am learning Cookery and Dressmaking. Please find enclosed the testimonial from friends who know me.*

References from reputable citizens of good standing in the community had to accompany her application so Matron Cairns wrote a letter supporting her request. All correspondence relating to this issue had to go through the Reverend B W Morey, the superintendent of the Byford Home, totally bypassing the people it concerned, Laurelle and her father. Surprisingly Laurelle's exemption papers came through in 1943, giving her access to a range of civil rights enjoyed by other Australians.

Laurelle: *When I went to get my exemption I remember sitting in a lounge type room and Edie was with me. Dad did all the talking while we waited outside. Then I had to go in personally to the commissioner's office to receive my papers. It was a little grey book that was replaced by citizenship rights that I got in Broome years later, after I was married. With exemption papers, the Department could take them off you if they wanted to, but later when the citizenship rights came in they couldn't take it away. Anyhow, when I got back to the Home Dad said, 'Here's your exemption, you have to look after it.' And I said, 'What's this all about?' and he said, 'Aboriginal people have got to have exemption.' That was all Dad said and he didn't explain anything and he wasn't the type of person you could keep asking questions of. It wouldn't have been so bad if I knew why I had to have them, I didn't understand why we had to be treated differently. When I was attending the technical school I had to carry my papers around with me. I remember seeing other Aboriginal people being stopped and having to show their permit but I was never asked by authorities if I had them, I guess it was because I looked like another white person.*

At Byford racism was never an issue for Alfred and the family, but it did rear its ugly head one day when he visited the city. Alfred had been issued with his exemption papers in the Kimberley and was not familiar with their application in the city. Aboriginal people not exempted and under the Act needed permission to enter the city. It was not until 1948 that metropolitan restrictions were lifted. Being exempted, he had no need to have a permit to enter the city but needed to carry his papers to prove his status.

The policemen in the Kimberley knew his status and he

was completely taken by surprise when stopped in Perth by a young constable and asked, 'How long are you in for?' Alfred said, 'I've just come to pick up some stuff and I'm leaving this afternoon.' The constable said, 'Where's your permit?' Looking puzzled, Alfred said, 'What permit?' The policeman replied, 'Aboriginal people that come into town have to have a permit to come into Perth.' Confused and vulnerable, Alfred started to defend himself when another policeman named Laurie O'Neil, a detective Alfred knew from Broome, said 'Are you having problems Alf?' Laurie flashed his badge at the young policeman and said, 'Leave this bloke alone, he's all right. He's from the Kimberley and he works at the Home. Take the number of the truck and when you see it in town don't stop it and don't question why he's here.' Alfred was fortunate that Laurie came along, he knew him as a passenger on the *Watt Leggatt*.

Alfred was quite shaken by the incident but never had any further problems when he visited the city. When he recounted the incident to Matron Cairns she was far from impressed. 'You mean to tell me that they stopped you because of the colour of your skin?' she said.

In 1944 the state government introduced the Natives (Citizenship Rights) Act. Aboriginal people could apply for these rights through the magistrate, who had the power to approve, suspend and cancel them. Citizenship rights replaced exemption papers and gave Aboriginal people the civil rights enjoyed by non-Aboriginal people. It was similar to a passport, with a photograph to verify identification, and it had to be carried by the recipient and presented on demand. As with the conditions of exemption, Aboriginal people had to cease all association with their traditional lifestyle and assimilate into

Alfred Brown's Certificate of Citizenship.
(Courtesy Donella Brown.)

mainstream society. Holders of citizenship rights were subject to constant police surveillance to ensure they were living in a 'civilised' manner. It was not until 1971 that the Citizenship Rights Act became redundant and finally repealed, making Aboriginal people no longer subject to draconian welfare surveillance.

> Laurelle: *With citizenship it was difficult for them to take it away from you once you got it, whereas with exemption they could take it off you the minute you did anything wrong. I had to apply for it then. I had to go to court to see the magistrate to get it. I went there at about ten o'clock, I know it was in the morning and the kids were at school. A friend of mine had told me, 'When you go to see them, you*

tell them you want it to have the same privileges as white people.' I felt nervous and frightened as I'd never been in a courthouse before. I didn't understand why I had to do this, it was something you just did. When my name was called I went in to see the magistrate and sitting next to him was the JP, Jock Costello, who Doug worked for. As he knew me I didn't have any trouble getting my citizenship. When I went next door to the clerk of courts to have the paperwork completed the clerk there said, 'Why do you have to get a citizenship? You look to me like you don't need one. You look white.' I said, 'I'm classed as an Aboriginal so I have to have one.' You see, there were some Aboriginal people who were very fair and passed as white. Dad always told us to be proud of who we are. The clerk and I laughed over the whole ordeal and I was glad it was all over and ended on a happy note. When equal civil rights came in and Aboriginal people were free, I threw mine out. I didn't want anything to remind me of those days. I even threw my exemption papers away.

LAURELLE AND DOUGLAS

At sixteen years of age Laurelle was an attractive young woman. A young family friend named Douglas D'Antoine was taking an interest in her. His father, Ginger, had had his own lugger, the *Blanche*, and beachcombed along the Kimberley coastline. He and Alfred would meet on Alfred's trips to Broome on the *Watt Leggatt*. Both men often took their children with them on the luggers so both families knew each other quite well. Douglas' mother was Goodji D'Antoine, who was also close to the Brown family, having safely delivered Kathy in the middle of the 1935 cyclone. And, of course, both families had travelled to Meekatharra together after the bombing of Broome.

So, Douglas was no stranger to the family and had continued to write to Laurelle after the two families separated in Meekatharra in 1942. His letters frequently reached her second-hand after Miss Tonkin had opened and read them. It was an administration policy: however, when Alfred did the mail run he intercepted them, so occasionally a few came directly to Laurelle's hands.

Doug worked for Allied Works and managed to visit Perth once a year. Taking a truck to Perth for servicing gave him the opportunity to visit Laurelle at Byford. When he visited he took gifts for everyone.

> Laurelle: *The kids at the Home used to love it when Doug visited. He used to bring them chocolates and cigarettes for Dad, who would share them with his mates. Old Stan North used to say to Dad, 'When is that son-in-law of yours coming back?' He was waiting for cigarettes. Doug would bring them American cigarettes like Lucky Strike, Camel, Philip Morris. The only thing they could get from Michaelidis in Perth was Luxor, poor quality tobacco. They were lucky when they got Woodbines. You see, before Doug came they had to go to Perth and stand in line for hours to get their rations of inferior tobacco. Old Stan would tell Alfred, 'I'm going to Perth now, it's my turn to stand in line for tobacco.' How they hated the cheap tobacco.*

On a trip to Perth to visit Laurelle at Byford Douglas told her of the rescue effort of his older brother Charlie during the raid in Broome in March 1942. During the war Charlie had the job of cleaning the seaplanes when they were moored in Roebuck Bay. The day before the raid on Broome, the *Nicol Bay*, a refueling vessel, came in loaded up with high octane fuel. The skipper, Harold Matheson, and Tommy Spencer were responsible for seeing to the refueling of the planes. After they moored the *Nicol Bay* safely in the creek they decided to spend the rest of the night at the Roebuck Hotel. The next morning they had to wait for the tide to come in to take the *Nicol Bay* out to the planes waiting to be refuelled. There was a large sand bar separating the *Nicol Bay* from the planes so they had to wait for the tide to come in and cover it. While they were waiting the Japanese struck and caught everyone totally by surprise. Charlie was already on board one of the planes. He had gone out earlier in the morning on a dinghy to clean the planes and do his job. While he was inside cleaning he heard these planes arrive and thought nothing of it. Then he heard the machine-guns firing but it did not register with Charlie it was the Japanese. It simply did not occur to him that Broome was being raided. Nobody expected it to happen.

Next thing, Charlie heard a woman screaming and yelling for help while the plane behind her went up in flames. Next minute he heard the Japanese planes fly over again so he dived in the water and swam over to help this lady and her child, who were very distressed when Charlie got to them. There were planes flying everywhere and the woman and her child were clinging to Charlie as he was trying to keep them out of danger. When he turned around the plane that he had been cleaning was hit and burst into flames. Charlie's thought was, 'Maybe it was a good thing this woman screamed for help otherwise I would have been killed when the plane was hit.'

Douglas was in Chinatown at his mother's house behind the Sun Pictures. He heard the machine-gun and raced to the jetty knowing Charlie was on board cleaning the planes and possibly in danger. When he arrived at the jetty people stopped him from going out to Charlie, saying it was too dangerous to row out in a dinghy. By this time the Japanese had shot all the planes anchored in the bay, attacked a few planes at the airport, then left. During the raid the *Nicol Bay* remained anchored in the creek waiting for the tide. It was not until after the Japanese planes had gone that it had enough water to leave the creek and went to rescue the survivors, including Charlie and the Dutch lady and her child.

Charlie felt as though he had been in the water caring for the lady and her child for hours when in fact it was probably only thirty or forty minutes. There were people everywhere in the water swimming, screaming, panicking, some just floating and many dead. There was nothing Charlie could do as his hands were full rescuing the Dutch lady and her child. Later the Dutch government gave him a certificate and a medal officially recognising his bravery. He also received an invitation to the Netherlands so he could be personally recognised for his rescue effort.

10

Back to the Kimberley

Alwyn was the only family member remaining in the Kimberley. Alfred wasn't happy, but Alwyn was a young adult and there was very little he could do but trust he would be properly cared for.

After returning to Broome Alwyn made his way up to Beagle Bay and stayed with his cousin Percy for a short time. Then he moved to Derby, eventually getting employment with Ronny Ah Chee and later staying with them. The Ah Chees owned the local bakery and Alwyn acquired the skill of baking the magnificent bread the family was renowned for. When Alfred heard his son was in Derby working and staying with Ronny he felt satisfied that he had found a family where he was safe.

In early 1946 Laurelle, Alfred and the rest of the family returned to Broome to a changed situation. Although the town was still experiencing the after-effects of the war, class distinction seemed to have crumbled, along with the structures that had reinforced it. They stayed with Laurelle's cousin, Pat Shadforth.

Not long after returning to Broome Laurelle and Doug got engaged. Doug didn't drink, he worked hard and gave Alfred no reason to doubt his ability to be a good husband. How could he say no to a man who kept him supplied with good quality cigarettes during the war?

They were advised to go to Derby to get married; both parents felt it was in their best interest to do so. Doug's father said, 'Best you go to Derby and get married. You get married in Broome and you'll have all the riffraff hanging around looking for a free feed and things.'

Listening to their advice, the whole family went to Derby to make arrangements for the marriage. Doug's older brother Charlie owned a car so they all piled in, leaving in the early hours of the morning. The trip took them a full day. Laurelle squeezed in the front with Doug and Charlie, nursing Ivy on her lap, while Alfred, Edie, Kathy and Yogi sat in the back.

It was still the wet season and the road wasn't sealed, so it was very boggy. The car slid from side to side, with little traction, and seemed to cover twice the distance, frequently getting bogged. They took a short cut near Nobby's Well and Charlie had to walk in front to pick out the road that was overgrown with kangaroo grass and low hanging tree branches. Doug drove Charlie's car, an old blue Chev, which wasn't the fastest thing on earth, but it soldiered on. At about eight o'clock that night they arrived safely in the outskirts of Derby, totally exhausted. They camped the night there before going into town the next morning.

Derby 1946

Derby was a small town consisting of two streets and numerous bush tracks. Loch was the main street with Clarendon running parallel to it. The town provided services and facilities for outlying cattle and sheep stations such as Yeeda, Meda, Noonkanbah and Liveringa. A railway track ran from the jetty to the goods shed where the Black Swan Company is today. A local Derby identity named Georgie Ah Chee was the train driver transporting goods and people between the town and jetty. A wooden cattle race went to the jetty and was used regularly to load cattle on ships going south to the abattoirs. The shops included Watties, Bill Ayling and Goldsborough Mort. The local butcher shop, owned by Vic Haymes, was on Loch Street.

The only building that now remains in its original location is the Derby Pictures. The Post Office was between the pictures and the butcher's shop. Telegrams sent through the Post Office were personally delivered by telegram boys and girls on bicycles. The town boasted two pubs. The Port Hotel, where the Chinese restaurant now stands, was burnt down shortly after Laurelle left Derby in 1947. The Club Hotel was on Clarendon Street and was eventually replaced by the Spinifex many years later. The Ah Chees owned the bakery and produced fresh bread each day, making home deliveries in a little van. Phones were only found in businesses and were not yet household luxuries. The town hall diagonally opposite the pictures was run by the Roads Board, and hosted dances and weddings and doubled as a church for the town's Catholic population.

Trucks carrying bales of wool from sheep stations left a film of dust over the small town. When the trucks came through town everyone stopped work and lined the streets to watch and discuss the event. Stockmen drove cattle from outlying stations to Myalls Bore where they rested them before herding them in sections across the marsh into the cattle race leading to the jetty. As the cattle moved across the marsh you could hear the hundreds of plodding hooves on the crumbly dry mud. As they moved across the outskirts of the town you could smell the combined odour of manure and dust. Like the trucks, they left a thin coat of dust behind them.

Lou Kent owned the power station and supplied the town with electricity, which was expensive. He also ran a trucking business carting wool from the sheep stations. Laurelle's brother Alwyn now worked as a truck driver for him. There was a garage as you came into town where the Boab Inn stands now. Several years later, the local taxi driver, Jimmy Ah Chee, opened another one in Clarendon Street.

There was a small hospital with one ward and a sleep-out. There were no vets or dentists so the local doctor also attended to the oral well-being of the local people and the general health of their pets and any stray animal he took pity on. His name was Doctor Hertz and he was the proud owner of a red jeep the locals aptly named blood and guts. He transferred to Carnarvon where he drowned at the blow holes as a result of a fishing accident.

Aboriginal people requiring medical attention went to the Native Hospital on the outskirts of town. Opened in 1926, it also served as a holding place for Aboriginal patients suffering from leprosy. In 1934 it held forty-six patients, some waiting over a year for transportation to Darwin. It later became an aged persons' home called Numbala Nunga.

Another very important medical facility was the Leprosarium built about twenty-five kilometres out of town on the Gibb River road.

In all Derby was a friendly place to live in and there was plenty of work for those seeking it.

Laurelle: *Derby had terrible dust storms. You had to race around and close the shutters when you knew one was approaching. The worst time was during the build up to the wet in December. At night you'd be lying in bed sweating and it was bad enough not even having a fan then the dust storms would appear out of nowhere. The dust would find its way into everything and you couldn't sleep so you got up and shook the sheets then had a shower otherwise you'd feel grit on the sheets. That was one good thing you could look forward to was a good shower, unlike Broome where the water was that hard not even the soap would lather. Then the next morning you'd be busy shaking the dust from the bedclothes and wiping the tops of tables, fridges, cupboards and other surfaces. It seemed to permeate everything, even the walls had to be wiped as they were made of corrugated iron and the dust gathered in the grooves, staining your clothes as you leant against it.*

MARRIAGE AND STARTING A FAMILY

It was not until 1963 that marriage restrictions on Aboriginal people were lifted allowing them to marry whoever they pleased. Laurelle and Douglas had to have permission to marry from the Commissioner of Native Affairs. Added to this was the confusion that Laurelle was exempted from the Act but Douglas wasn't. Father Albert, a Catholic priest, wrote to the Commissioner on 8 April 1946 seeking approval for their marriage. He wrote:

Douglas Phillipe Dantoine, son of Richard and Amy Dantoine, now residing at Derby N. W.A. wishes to get married to Laurelle Andrewina Brown, daughter of Alfred

Brown and Andrewina, nee Shadforth. Douglas believes he is not under the law, but he has no exemption papers, it may not be true and I ask here with your permission to marry Douglas in the week after Easter. Laurelle claims to be free and to have exemption papers, though she will not show them to me as they are still in Broome, her former residence. If for this purpose, special forms are to be used, please send me a few. I am the first resident priest at Derby. I am here four weeks. I was at Wandering last year as you perhaps may still remember. Hoping you are well. I remain with kind regards.

Father Albert Scherzinger P.P.M.

After getting the necessary consent and completing the essential paperwork, Father Albert married Laurelle and Douglas. The wedding was held in front of family and friends on 30 April 1946 in a little presbytery near Ah Chee's bakery. The presbytery was an ordinary house which doubled as accommodation for the Catholic nuns. Laurelle was told many years later that theirs was the first Catholic wedding in the presbytery. Marriage in the Catholic Church was the beginning of a move away from the Presbyterian religion Laurelle knew so well.

Both families witnessed the event, except Alwyn who was in bed sick with the flu. Henry D'Antoine was the best man and Edith the bridesmaid. Being a small town everyone pitched in and helped with the catering, generally making it a community event. They held the reception at Nellie D'Antoine's place.

Fresh flowers failed to arrive on time and although Laurelle was disappointed the usual country hospitality prevailed and Daisy Hunter went over and got Elsie Maxted to make up a bouquet. The two-tiered wedding cake came from a shop in Geraldton; it was lovely, and arrived COD through Rowell's. To this day Laurelle doesn't know who paid for it, it certainly wasn't her. The only thing missing was a photographer, but they were as rare as hen's teeth in Derby.

There was one funny part in the ceremony when Father Albert asked Doug, 'Do you take this Laurelle Andrewina Brown to be your lawful wedded wife?' Being nervous Doug temporarily forgot his rehearsed line and said, ' I will,' and Father leant over and slowly said in a German accent, 'Doug, you're supposed to say, I do.' Needless to say, Doug said the right words and all went well.

After their marriage Douglas worked for the Main Roads Department. He had a good reputation as a reliable steady worker, one he had acquired at Allied Works. Working with mates like Bill Marvin and George MacDonald he drove trucks, graders and other plant equipment. At one stage he was a truck driver for Bob Maxted who was a contractor for Main Roads in Derby.

Private accommodation was not readily available in Derby so Laurelle and Doug lived with his relations Nellie and Tommy who had a three bedroom house with plenty of verandah space. They weren't the only ones short of accommodation. Doug's cousin Henry, his wife Ada, and their four small children squeezed in too. They were in Derby because Henry was building a dinghy for Bob Maxted. There wasn't much space in the little house and what little privacy Laurelle and Doug had was interrupted by the arrival of a baby.

In 1947 in January, a month before Laurelle turned eighteen, she had her first child, Richard. They called him Dickie and he was the first of ten healthy children. It seemed Dickie had more aunts, uncles, grandparents and cousins than any other baby in Derby.

Laurelle: *When I had my first baby you could apply for a child allowance to buy baby clothes and I think I had to go through the Native Department for that too. Having Dickie was a turning point in my life. When I had Dickie I knew nothing about having babies. I didn't know your membrane broke and when my membrane broke I was sitting in the pictures with Doug. I thought I'd wet myself so we came back home. Thinking nothing of it, I changed and went to sleep. I didn't tell anyone. If I had told Aunty Nellie or Ada, they would have known straightaway. I guess I was a little shy and frightened at the time. It wasn't the done thing to have discussions on pregnancy and childbirth. Not having a mother, I felt slightly confused and lonely. Anyhow, the pain started and I told Doug it was time to go to hospital. They got Jimmy Ah Chee, he was living across the road, he had a taxi, so he drove me to the hospital. When I arrived Doctor Hertz said, 'When did your waters break?' and I said, 'When I was at the pictures.' He hit the roof and said, 'Why didn't you come up straightaway, you told me you knew all about having babies.'*

Dickie was born the next day. In those days husbands weren't allowed in the labour ward when the women were having their babies, so Doug stayed home.

When I became pregnant, I didn't tell anyone, even though I knew. You never spoke about those things, even with my best friend Shirley at the Home, we never spoke about those sort of things. Nowadays girls discuss all those sort of things with each other. Not having a mother, well that was harder. When I started to get big, Aunty asked me, 'Are you going to have a baby?' and things like that. Then Doctor Hertz saw me down the street when I was well and truly pregnant and he said, 'I think you had better come and have an examination.' I was coming out of the post office, I didn't feel embarrassed by then, I felt good that they took an interest. When I went to see him he sat me down and said, 'Do you know anything about having a baby?' and I said, 'Yeah,' but I didn't know anything about pregnancy and childbirth. Sure, I'd raised my brother and sister but that was different to having your own.

When Dickie was born there were only three patients in the hospital. In those days having a baby in Derby was a big event and everyone wanted to know what you had and how big your baby was and if everyone was okay. There weren't many babies born each year, I think Dickie was the first for 1947. People were interested, they weren't stickybeaks or anything, they just cared. Ethel Buckle was out at the station at the time and she was always asking the truckies as they passed by, 'Has Laurelle had her baby yet?' Derby was so small that even people in the outback were thrilled to find out what babies the women had and what was going on in Derby. I remember the staff taking bets and here I was thinking to myself, 'I'm in pain and they're taking bets on how much my baby's going to weigh and if it's a boy or girl.' Anyhow it turned out to be a boy and weighed seven pounds ten.

They telephoned Edie, who was working at Wattie's Store and told her the news, so she raced home and told Doug. When Edie told him he had a son, he started to cry. Then there was postnatal treatment because in those days after I'd had Dickie they had to bind your stomach and breasts to cope with milk fever and make sure your body kept in shape. It was January and no air conditioning so you can imagine how uncomfortable it was. The staff used to take Dickie for walks around the hospital. It was nothing to see Dr Hertz walking around the hospital with Dickie over his shoulders, patting his back while he did his rounds.

Then there was this incident with the grasshopper. One

night when Dickie must have been about two days old, this night sister said, 'Would you like to have your baby in with you?' I said, 'Yes,' so she brought him into my room in a bassinet and he had a net over him. This grasshopper got in and there was Dickie crying and I was crying. You see I was crying because I couldn't get this grasshopper out of the bassinet and I started to panic. Sister Stevenson, I think that was her name, she rushed in and said, 'What's the matter?' and I said, 'There's a grasshopper in the bassinet and it won't come out.' She whipped the net off and got rid of the grasshopper in no time flat. Later I felt silly, but I was only seventeen and knew absolutely nothing. Dr Hertz said to me, 'When you go home and want to know anything remember you just have to ask.' I felt good knowing that there were people who cared.

Going Our own Ways

Alfred was working on the Derby wharf as a lumper unloading the boats and doing general labouring jobs on the state ships when the *Watt Leggatt* came in getting stores and freight. The crew heard he was in town and went around to see him. David Mowaljarlie, Allan Mungulu and Sammy Woologoodja approached Alfred asking, 'When are you going to return to the mission? We still need a good skipper for the *Watt Leggatt*. It would be like the good old days. We could be your crew again.' Alfred's reply was, 'I'd return only if they'd let me have the *Watt Leggatt* in Derby during the lay-up season. Laurelle and Doug are here with their family and I want to see my grandchildren grow up. The mission won't allow it, otherwise I'd jump at the opportunity.'

One of the crew continued the conversation, informing Alfred about what had happened since he left. 'The *Watt Leggatt* was impounded along with other luggers in Roebuck Bay during the war. A lot of the luggers were burnt by the army, but they missed the *Watt Leggatt*. After the bombing Chris Hunter sailed it back with Mr Holmes to the mission.'

Alfred was pleased to see them all looking so well and invited them to visit him when they were in town next. He had already heard that the *Watt Leggatt* had returned safely to Kunmunya but hearing the news from his old crew made him feel easier. The war had forced him into leaving the lugger not knowing its destiny and hearing of its safe return put his mind at rest.

Eight months after Laurelle married, Alwyn followed suit, marrying Tilly Puertollano. Tilly was one of the town's telegram girls and it was while she was making one of her deliveries on her bike that Alwyn introduced her to Laurelle. Tilly lived in town with her parents Alf and Pat Puertollano. Alwyn had left the bakery and was now driving trucks for Albert Archer. After the marriage they settled happily in Derby.

Ivy, Edith and Kathy lived with Doug and Laurelle, and were finding it difficult to take to the Derby lifestyle. Byford had become their home and they wanted to return. They found the heat oppressive, the food different and living conditions cramped. Even though there were a lot of children at the Home they managed to have their own personal space. The girls were going to school in Derby but the standard of education didn't go beyond primary level. The town seemed dusty and a far cry from the green of Byford. Alfred sensed this and was not taken by surprise when they asked to return to Byford.

He contacted the superintendent at the Home who

said, 'Send them down, first available plane.' Although he didn't want to send them south he knew there was nothing for them in Derby and it was unfair for Laurelle to continue taking care of them, especially as she had a new baby and husband to care for.

Edith would be seeking employment in the next year or two and career prospects were limited in Derby. The knowledge of them being thousands of miles away upset Alfred, but he knew they were better off there with plenty of opportunities. At the Home they came under the care of the church and were safe from the Native Welfare.

Laurelle: *When Dad put the girls on the plane I thought he was going to collapse. He was terribly upset as it was the first time the children were so far away from him. He'd done so well to keep us all together after Mum died, not even the war could separate us. Yogi followed the girls to Perth several weeks later. Dad wrote to the Home to see if they could get him a job. Next thing I knew he was on the plane south then working for a firm called Plastics. He was boarding with a family called Kirkby, they must have had something to do with the Home. That only left Dad, Alwyn and myself in Derby.*

ALFRED AND THE YAMPI LASS

After his three youngest daughters went south 1947, Alfred got a job with BHP as a deckhand on the *Yampi Lass*, a company boat that serviced Koolan and Cockatoo Islands. BHP was mining iron ore on the islands. The boat did a weekly trip to Derby for stores and it was an opportunity for the islanders to visit the mainland to shop, see the doctor or just have a break.

At the time there was not a plane service so BHP depended on the *Yampi Lass* as it was a vital link between the islands and Derby, especially in emergencies when people had to get to the closest hospital. The company had a staging house opposite the post office which the islanders used for accommodation on their trips to Derby. The house was cleaned and cared for by a well-known Derbyite called Jessie Colman who was well-respected by the islanders. Her hospitality extended well beyond house cleaning; she took the time to drive them shopping, visit a friend or go to the hospital, nothing was too demanding for Jessie.

Alfred worked on the *Yampi Lass* for twenty-seven years. He started as a deckhand and at retirement was the skipper. During his time he had some interesting passengers including the directors of BHP, Lord Casey, Essington Lewis and Mr Darling. It was Alfred's job to take them fishing after the formalities of their trip were dispensed with.

Essington Lewis was a regular passenger. Alfred liked him and took him fishing a lot. He was very sick when he made his last trip and Alfred rigged up a deckchair and after making him comfortable told the crew, 'Don't disturb him, let him have some rest.' When he left he dropped twenty pounds into Alfred's hand as he shook it saying, 'Buy yourself something.' He made a point of shaking the hand of all the crew members when he left. 'I want to thank you for the friendship you have given me all these years,' he said and Alfred replied, 'Sir, the boot is on the other foot.' He never returned, and he died the following year.

Over the years Alfred got to know many of the families who went to work at Koolan and Cockatoo Islands. Wes and Hazel Oakes first met him in December 1949 when they went to the island to work. They had a very young family and on their first trip from Derby to Cockatoo, Alfred made their journey as comfortable as possible, knowing they were probably feeling a little homesick and having difficulty coming to terms with the heat, flies and dust. On another occasion Wes had to climb down the side of an ore ship by means of a rope ladder to the *Yampi Lass* moored alongside. He wasn't exactly happy and not feeling very comfortable until he heard Alfred's voice and felt his firm hands guiding his feet. Alfred was thoughtful like that.

Alfred also took BHP geologists prospecting for bauxite along the coast to Wyndham. These trips were a bit more complicated and required planning. Before the trip Alfred and the captain, Barney, flew along the coast in the company's plane, the *Scottish Pioneer*, looking for suitable places to make fuel dumps. The dumps had to be approximately one hundred kilometres apart. They stopped at Kalumburu and had lunch with Father Perez, then flew back to Koolan along the coast, confirming the places they had already picked out. Back at Koolan they loaded the drums of fuel on the *Yampi Lass* and made the fuel drops. The exploration trip took twelve days and each day they stopped at a spot a hundred kilometres further north. Each day the *Yampi Lass* was met by a helicopter which took the geologists inland to conduct exploration assessments and tests for bauxite. Alfred never did say where they found deposits of bauxite.

> Alfred: *I remember one trip I did while I was working on the islands. They wanted to see if the north was worth defending. They sent, from down south, the army, the navy and the air force ... There was a squadron leader*

from the air force, an army general, and a Captain Howden ... I remember on one occasion we'd come along, we were going through a small passage, a narrow passage, called Gagg Pass. And we had a glass window at the back of the wheelhouse and we had the army general and the captain, Captain Howden, lying down there and it was towards morning. Captain Howden looked through the wheelhouse and the skipper was asleep on the couch. And he came and he could see the boat going from one side to the other and I was battling with the wheel to counteract the tide movements. Being a seaman he came over and he said, 'Can't you keep a straight course?' I said, 'With all due respect to you, Captain, and your rank, take the wheel.' 'Oh, can I?' he said. 'Yes,' I replied. Well, he took over. One minute we was going one direction, the next the other. And he looked at me and said, 'We're never too old to learn, Alf.' ... The tide through a narrow entrance was causing this. Then I said to him, 'Captain, you run a big ship. She's deep in the water. This is only a small craft. She only draws six foot of water, and the tide just swings her like a cork.' He said, 'Yes, I realise that now. Carry on.' I said 'Aye, aye sir!' That was a great experience.

11

Broome

Douglas had always been interested in boat building so when an offer to join a boat building company in Broome arose, he seized the opportunity to combine his interest with employment prospects. Douglas and Laurelle had started their family so steady employment was essential to feed and clothe everyone.

Henry D'Antoine, Doug's cousin, had lobbed into Derby looking for bush timber for boat building. Natural shaped timber from white gum and bush cadjebut was used to make the ribs and stems of luggers. Henry was involved in the maintenance side of things and not directly responsible for building. He had a truck, so Streeter and Male contracted him to look for solid local timber. He had an eye for good timber that produced fine luggers. He told Doug, 'Why don't you come to Broome to work with us and Uncle Jack? He needs young blokes to help him build the luggers. He could use you in the yard to help. Besides, you'd be back with the family. I'm sure you and Laurelle and the baby could find somewhere to live. Maybe with your mother.' No sooner was the invitation given than Doug and Laurelle were on the road to Broome. Laurelle knew Doug would be much happier working on the luggers close to the sea.

It was difficult for Aboriginal people to get accommodation in Broome. The Native Welfare Department controlled where they lived and although Laurelle was exempted, Douglas was not, and she had to live according to his status. Douglas' mother Goodji still lived with her family in the little corrugated iron house in Chinatown behind the Sun Pictures.

A lot of Aboriginal people lived grouped together on reserves dotted around the town — Morgan's Camp, around Streeters, behind Kennedy's in Indian territory or just out of town at a place called Two Mile. State housing didn't exist and owning a house was beyond the financial means of most people.

Chinatown was an interesting conglomeration of shops built close together, exotic smells, gambling houses and a culturally diverse population. Unaweis was a typical Chinese shop that sold anything from Bex powder to designer label towels, tucked away in dusty boxes shoved haphazardly under the counter. If you wanted decent long soup you went to Tang Wei's; he made his own noodles on a macaroni-making machine and was renowned throughout Broome for it. Arthur Tack specialised in drapery products that he proudly displayed in glass cabinets; his shop had a pungent smell from the naphthalene flakes he liberally sprinkled around. Then there was Ellis', Streeter and Male's, and Kennedy's. The butcher's shop was owned by Sam Male but run by a local by the name of Eddie Roe. Ma Kim also had a restaurant that sold great Chinese food. Each morning the smell of fresh bread wafted through the town.

Once a week during the dry, Bob Laurence personally delivered fresh tomatoes, carrots, cabbage, beans and other seasonal vegetables. A week's supply of vegetables for an average family cost no more than a pound. Bob was a big burly looking chap who had one leg shorter than the other. He drove an old battered ute, was a member of the Buffs Lodge and played a saxophone that had a dead key. He was fondly called 'Uncle Bob' by the Chinatown kids.

> Alfred: *In Broome before the war there was class distinction. Not only colour distinction between the pearling masters, but the class. If you were a poor white man you couldn't drink in the same bar as the master pearlers in those days. There were special bars. There was the bushman's pub, they called it the Roebuck and it was run by a fellow called Billy Ward. So long as you were clean, with a good shirt, you didn't have to put a tie or coat on. The others, the Continental and Governor Broome, you had to have a tie and coat.*

Douglas worked for Sam Male, under the supervision of Jack Hunter, building luggers for the pearling industry. Jack was his uncle and came from a family highly experienced in boat building.

The machinery used to build luggers was very simple, it wasn't until many years later that sophisticated tools such as planing machines were introduced. Shaping the timber for the keel was done using an adze and axe. Electric drills didn't exist; the workers used brace and bits. Everything was done manually and was labour intensive, so the men put in a good ten hours a day.

Douglas enjoyed his work and took pride in it, spending many hours down at the boatshed building majestic luggers that are still operating today.

Laurelle: *He was working for Streeter and Male. Doug's uncle, Jack Hunter, was in the process of finishing the* Irene Castle. *She was a boat that was built from natural timber. Doug helped build the next lugger, I think it was the* Trixon, *the last one built of natural timber. After that Arthur Ruston came up to build for Morgan and he introduced laminated boats. Arthur worked with Doug on one of the luggers, giving him suggestions on using lamination. This process was much quicker than building natural timber boats. The time to produce a lugger was nearly halved so they started using lamination.*

Doug built quite a few luggers for Streeters. There was the Phyllis *that was named after Sam Male's wife but was later renamed. Then there was the* Skelton *later in years to come that was sent up to Thursday Island with Ron Shipway. He was shares with Male, actually by then it was only Male, but everyone knew it as Streeter and Male. Then there was the* Centurion *and* Cornelius. *Last heard of, the* Cornelius *was advertised in this trader boat magazine, sailing the Whitsunday Passage. There's the one they've got in the Maritime Museum in Fremantle, the* Ansell, *that was built for survey purposes for the mining people and when they finished, it was left on the beach at Port Hedland so the museum took over ownership. There was also the* EWS *and the* SPS. *Doug built about eleven or twelve luggers for Streeter. The* Trixton *is in the Maritime Museum's yard now.*

Laurelle and Douglas lived with his mother Goodji and his younger brother Aubrey and sister Peggy. Goodji was making a living selling homemade ice-cream and lemon drinks made from a concoction of crushed ice, freshly squeezed lemons and a sugar-flavoured syrup. Ice was bought from local suppliers and Goodji used an antiquated manually operated churn that stood about one metre high and worked like an upside-down carpenter's wooden plane, crushing the ice as she pushed it back and forth. You had to use gloves or a tea towel to handle the ice or your hands and fingers got too cold to get a good run. Goodji made a small profit from her confectionery stall. She was very shrewd when it came to money, cunningly doubling it, on most occasions, on the card table of Deps gambling house.

After a few months Laurelle and Douglas moved from Chinatown and rented the Puertollano's house. An old Manila man was the caretaker, he was away most of the time working his fish traps and was glad they were there to occupy it during the day. They only had Dickie then. It was a couple of months after the move that Gregory entered their lives.

Gregory

Doug rode a Malvern Star bike to work and each day he passed a solemn looking little boy sitting on Unawei's verandah next door to Tang Wei's. Unawei had several hard wooden benches outside his shop where locals contentedly sat watching the world go by, idly gossiping between moments of contemplation and smoking. Each day Doug saw him sitting there when he called in to see his sister Lexie on his way home after work. The boy had obviously been sitting there all by himself for hours, no family, no friends to play with, possibly no food, just sitting there, so lonely, so sad. His legs dangled over the seat, not quite reaching the ground, just hanging without sandals. Every now and then he'd raise his hand to swat away a fly or sandflies. Broome water made your hair really stiff and wiry and there were grooves in his hair where he'd tried to comb it. His mother obviously didn't care about him, her interests were clearly elsewhere, so he spent most of the day sitting by himself waiting for some company. He was about four years old. He never smiled.

Doug told Laurelle about him and when he came home each afternoon she'd ask, 'Did you see that little boy?' One day Doug said, 'Do you think he could come and live with us, just for a little while?' and Laurelle replied, 'Yeah! Bring him home he'll be good company for Dickie. We'll look after him.' Laurelle could never refuse a child that needed a home. That afternoon Doug brought him home on his bike with a couple of shirts and pants and said, 'This is the little boy I told you about.'

His name was Gregory Hughes. When Laurelle saw him, she remembered him as a new baby three years earlier in Derby. His father, Billy Hughes, had proudly brought Gregory around to their place to show his friends Nellie and Tommy, saying, 'Isn't he beautiful?' Little did Laurelle know Gregory would become an important part of their lives. His mother was Martha Hughes, and she was pleased when Laurelle and Douglas offered to look after him. She was off to Darwin and glad to give Gregory up. 'He's better off with you and I'll write to him,' she said.

Gregory looked forward to a letter from his mother, a letter that never ever came and you could almost feel the pain it caused him. Just one little letter, that was all he wanted and when a note hastily scribbled on the back of a beer coaster arrived years later when he was a teenager, it was too late, he had given up.

At first Gregory was very forlorn looking. He had sad emotionless eyes, the type that kids get when they're not loved and cuddled. Laurelle and Doug sensed the hurt in him and they wondered if they could ever make his eyes light up.

Douglas junior arrived in 1949 while they were living at Puertollano's. He was nicknamed Doodie and in 1951 Mary was born. Gregory was settling in, starting to warm towards them and proving to be of great help to Laurelle. With him around she could go and enjoy a refreshing shower knowing that the little ones were safe.

The bathroom was well away from the house and instead of a shower there was a drum filled with water. You poured a tinful of water over yourself, soaped up, then poured another tinful to rinse off. That was the way they showered and during the winter months you went through the motions very quickly. Before Greg arrived Laurelle had to hurry because the babies were by themselves. She remembered one day when she had just ducked off to have a shower she heard Doodie crying, then he stopped; thinking nothing of it she continued. When she got out and checked on him, there was Dickie standing by the cot with his finger in Doodie's mouth. Doodie was happily sucking on Dickie's finger like a dummy. She removed it and could see where it was white from being sucked clean of dirt.

Laurelle could trust Greg he was very responsible and knew what to do. He would rock the babies, talk to them or push them around in the pram. They had a big yard so he pushed the pram around and around until they fell off to sleep while Laurelle washed and cleaned. Most children his age would have lost interest, but not Greg. He always seemed to know what to do.

Laurelle: *One day Greg wanted to make me a cup of tea and he went to light the fire and it had hot ashes in it so he threw some kerosene in to make it burn and it blew up in his face. I took him to hospital and by the time we got there his skin was blistering. Fortunately just the skin came off, there were no marks or scars. I said to him, 'What were you going to do?' and he sobbed, 'I was going to make you a cup of tea, I thought you'd like one.' He was very thoughtful like that.*

Doug and I never got any money for Greg. We never signed any paper when we took Gregory in. That was just the way it was with Aboriginal people. One day I went to the Roads Board to pay our electricity bill and the clerk, Mr McKenzie, said, 'Are you receiving any money for Greg,' and I said, 'No.' Then he replied, 'Are you getting any child endowment for him at all?' Again I said, 'No.' He told me I was entitled to it and should apply, which we did and got it. Naturally it was useful when it came through because we were battling for money with so many kids.

LIVING IN CHINATOWN

When Laurelle and Doug left Chinatown they had one baby. When they returned less than two years later they had four. Quite a record! They moved back into the small house owned by Doug's mother Goodji, and when she moved to Derby to go to the leprosarium she gave the house to Doug.

No one knows how long Goodji's condition escaped the health authorities. She walked around Chinatown with an overcoat on to hide the physical signs. A few of her friends suspected she had leprosy as she had been nursing Captain Scott who was suffering from the disease. He had transported patients on his lugger for the Health Department and was later admitted to the Derby Leprosarium where he died aged eighty-four. Goodji refused to go to the hospital. She was reported to the police who removed her from Chinatown and escorted her to the leprosarium. Doug did not want her to go and was very distressed knowing her destination. He was unsure when he would see her next but the matter was out of his hands. That was the way Aboriginal people were treated and he felt totally helpless.

Doug's younger brother Aubrey stayed on with them. He was working at Streeter and Male's shell house, sorting and packing pearl shells and there was no need for him to move.

Washing day was a nightmare for Laurelle. It was done manually, as the luxury of a washing machine was non-existent until her final years in Broome. It was not so much the hand washing but the dreadful quality of the water that made washing a daunting task, especially when it was for four toddlers and two grown men. The arduous process started with lighting the fire under the copper to boil the water before adding a tablet of Peak soap. When the scum frothed on the top it was scraped off and the clothes added to the boiling water. Washing took up the entire day and although Laurelle had the assistance of an Aboriginal woman, it was still a tiring job. The water was hard and left clothes, hair and skin hard. Drinking water had to be boiled to avoid getting stomach aches and bugs.

> Laurelle: *There was the time when Mary was watching me while I was putting blocks of wood into the fire. Broome was noted for its feral cats, particularly in Chinatown, they seemed to be everywhere. One day this cat walked into the house so I picked up this block of wood, took aim and threw it at this cat, knocking it out. Mary stood there and gave me this horrified look saying slowly, 'That's cruel you*

know.' I felt that guilty being lectured by a child. She made me feel like I had been sprung taking candy from a baby. I grabbed the cat, revived it in front of Mary, trying to save face in front of this child of mine. Mind you I never hit a cat again, certainly not in front of Mary.

In 1953 Iris was born and Laurelle and Doug were busy building dinghies. During the day Doug built luggers, and at night he worked on dinghies he sold to Sam Male. Laurelle was his assistant and together they built about eight dinghies in their backyard at the little house behind the pictures. Instead of receiving cash, they exchanged the finished dinghies for essential items such as a refrigerator and washing machine. With another baby on the way they needed these items more than ever.

After tea Douglas would start work on the dinghies. He did not have rivets so he drove a copper nail in then cut it off. Laurelle's job was to hold the dolly on the severed nail allowing him to hit the imbedded nail so it rounded off similar to a rivet. Douglas used this simple process for riveting dinghies and together they made a good team. Doug spent many hours searching for suitable bush timber to use as the stem and seating. Local timber was cheap, convenient and abundant. When Laurelle's pregnancy became too advanced for her to assist, Doug's boss, Jock Costello said, 'Finish the dinghy down at the boatshed. Let Laurelle rest for the baby. She's got enough kids to look after.' They got their fridge and washing machine and in 1954 another baby, Edith, joined the family. They had enough children to make a basketball team.

Laurelle: *The children used to play in the dinghies rocking from side to side pretending they were sailors at sea. One morning I heard the kids screaming and yelling so I raced out only to see Doodie yielding one of Doug's huge saws in the air like a wild warrior. Gregory, Dickie, [and his cousins] Gordon and Noel had been teasing and picking on him, so he hopped in the dinghy and picked up the closest thing he could lay his hands on. The boys were ducking and weaving. I was horrified, I had visions of him taking one of their heads off so I quickly got the saw off him, I don't know how I did it. I think I gave him some lollies. Anyhow the boys never teased him again.*

In 1956 Heather arrived and in November 1958 Neville made the fourth boy. Laurelle had double decker beds in the alcove, passageway and on the verandah.

The kids loved the little house, especially the way the tide surrounded them when it came in. During high tide it came right up to the backyard, lapping the stairs. The children loved to go swimming. Frolicking in the water, they entertained themselves for hours on end. On spring tide Chinatown flooded and the kids in the neighbourhood simply loved fishing and jumping from their back steps into the water. Some children literally jumped from the verandah into the water as the tide went under the concrete stumps the house stood on and rose to just below the floorboards. There was no Paspaley Shopping Centre, town oval or basketball

Alfred Brown and his daughter Kathy on her wedding day, 1956.
(Courtesy Laurelle D'Antoine.)

courts as there are now, just tidal marshlands. The tide was like a magnet drawing the white, Indian, Asian and Aboriginal kids who lived in the area. Mothers like Pearly Tack, Mercedes Gregory, and Lexie Tang Wei supervised their children and kept a watchful eye on any others that turned up. There was always a hive of activity when the tide was in and no shortage of people to watch the children. Living behind Sun Pictures had its advantages.

> Laurelle: *There was Ada D'Antoine, Margie Roe and myself. We used to hire this bus that Lofty Cavanagh had and go down to the beach — if not, Ada and I would walk down to the beach and take the kids. If we were going out to Gantheaume Point or Morgan's Camp or Ridell Beach we'd hire this bus and then he'd come back and pick us up in the afternoons. We had some good times, that was before Broome started to go ahead. Pearly Tack was another one I got to know. She gave me a lot of clothes for the boys that her son Victor grew out of. Doodie's second name is Victor, after him. Then there was my sister-in-law Lexie, who was always there for us. Much later I got to know Uni and Mow Gower. I wasn't a person that socialised much, I guess I was a shy person, you could say. With Doug having a big family I didn't really need anyone else. The women I got to know in Broome were very strong loyal women, good to me and the kids.*

GROWING UP IN BROOME

> *Life in Broome was very free for the kids. They could go to the pictures and you wouldn't worry about them. If they started mucking around an adult would say, 'Get*

home, it's getting late.' You had no fear of anything, there was nothing going on. Sure there were drunks, but they stayed in the pubs.

Laurelle

With their extended family, Laurelle and Doug were never short of company. On the weekends they joined Doug's cousin Henry and his wife Ada on camping trips out of Broome. They packed Henry's old truck full of kids and food then headed for either Willy or Bard Creek. The truck had no sides on the back so the older children and women sat around the edges with the little ones tucked safely in the middle. When they arrived, the call of the sea got the better of everyone. The little ones played near the water within safety of the women while the older kids speared fish and collected crabs, octopus and bait to fish with. They caught any number of reef fish including bluebone, snapper, bream, salmon and other species.

Henry had a drum rigged up on the back of the truck with a tap attached to it. He kept the drum filled with water so the children could have a wash and clean up for the return trip home. Having a belly full of food and exhausted from the sun, fishing and sea, they fell asleep to the rocking of the truck as it clattered and rumbled over the dirt track.

The D'Antoine kids loved fishing at the old Broome jetty. Fenton, one of the oldest of the

Laurelle and Yogi, 1956.
(Courtesy Laurelle D'Antoine.)

cousins, looked after the little ones. They loved catching and cooking whiting at the beach, trying not to burn their fingers as they juggled it from one hand to the other in an effort to cool it down. There was a chap by the name of Horrie Miller who was always down there, he kept an eye on them. Like all kids they got up to the usual mischievous things kids did but he was there if the kids got into any serious problems with the tide. He loved his fishing and the kids liked him.

Most afternoons Horrie flew his plane over the town and the kids waited and listened for it, racing outside and yelling and waving to him. One time, when Gordon, Gregory, Dickie and Fenton were coming home from school when mangoes were in season, Horrie put a pile of mangoes by the road for them then hid behind the bushes, peeping through the branches to make sure they found them. If any other kids looked like discovering the mangoes before them, he raced out and chased them away. The highlight was watching their faces when they found the fruit and devoured it. He was very good to the D'Antoine kids, I don't know if they ever discovered it was old Horrie who left the mangoes for them.

When the children were sick Laurelle walked them to the hospital or caught a taxi. It was a return trip of around five kilometres and she got to know every crevice in the road between their house and Broome Hospital. Nevertheless she never complained and took everything in her stride. Having a large family had its benefits — she quickly trained the boys to collect and chop firewood for the combustion stove that graced many Broome homes.

She was a trained seamstress so she saved money by sewing clothes for the children. Alfred frequently sent clothes from Cockatoo Island. Workers often left the island leaving behind clothes that had only been worn once or twice and the material was perfectly good. Laurelle would unpicked the garment and cut a pattern for a pair of shorts or a dress for one of the children. She was given an old hand-operated sewing machine that she sewed endlessly on; it passed the time of day and the children got their own designer clothes.

The family lived on fish and cheaper cuts of meat purchased from the local butcher's shop. Feeding the family on a shoestring budget was something she got on with and did not complain about. Cool drinks and lollies were luxuries, brought into the house only by visitors as there simply was not any money available for such extras, besides it kept the dentist bill down. They had no telephone, car, radio, gas, hot water or TV. They had electricity, a roof over their heads and were a healthy, happy and contented family. Laurelle and Douglas were doing a fine job raising a family the best they could under reasonably hard conditions.

The three older boys, Gregory, Dickie and Doodie, were at school by the mid fifties, leaving Mary, Iris, Edith and Heather at home. The boys went to the state school and started their formative years of education in Broome. Mrs Costello was their teacher and knew the family well, having taught Douglas in the late 1920s. School brought out a range of abilities in the boys.

Gregory was a bright boy, getting very pleasing results and becoming very popular. Dickie had to work twice as hard as Gregory and Doodie spent most of year one under the school playing trucks. Doodie was only five years old and had a very understanding teacher, Mr Paganini, who told Laurelle not to worry too much and that he was only a toddler and not quite ready for the rigid structure of a formal class.

While Laurelle was kept busy at home in the little house

behind the Sun Pictures with all the kids, Douglas continued to build luggers for Streeter and Male.

> Laurelle: *One day Doug left home and forgot to give Iris a kiss, she was only about two then. She sobbed and complained about her father going off to work without giving her a kiss, so I put a handkerchief on her head and she walked the short distance to the boatshed, got her kiss from her father and came home in a happy mood. Doodie would often go to work with Doug, playing within eyesight with his toys. He was the sort of kid that was happy with his own company.*
>
> *When he grew older he had this dog called Stinky and it went everywhere with him, it was a collie. He walked around Chinatown with his dog and nobody was game enough to touch him because the dog would snarl at them. One day Doodie went into one of the shops owned by Unawei, a Chinaman. Doodie wanted to buy some chocolates and lollies and when Unawei asked for his money he threw what looked like a sixpence on the counter and ran off. When Unawei discovered it was a tinny medallion he yelled out, 'Ah! What wrong with this kid! No good this kid.' He'd never chased him knowing if he did the dog would snarl and turn on him. Doodie was forever putting one over Unawei who wasn't game to chase him because of Stinky.*

Saturday night was pictures night. The children sat down the front while the adults sat towards the back, reclining on deck chairs and taking the time to socialise while waiting for the movie to start. Sun Pictures had distinct sections. There was a reserved area for people fortunate to have phones to ring and reserve seats. These people were noticeable by their code of dress and where they sat: they had the good seats. As the family grew, the older children would climb onto the roof of the house next to the picture theatre and watch the movie from there. It was in Laurelle and Doug's interest to ignore this behaviour. The financial burden of sending all the children through the front door of the picture theatre was considerable, not to mention the cost of treats that went with a night at the pictures. Cowboy movies featuring John Wayne and Audey Murphy seemed to attract the crowds. Everyone loved a good western.

On a quiet night you could hear the sound of the movies wafting throughout Chinatown. After the shopkeepers and restaurant owners closed their shops for the evening they'd relax on their verandahs, smoking and listening to the sound of the pictures.

Laurelle: *The kids in Broome were good. Our boys had the usual fights. I remember one time when Dickie and his cousins were fighting with the Djiaween boys. This particular day Dickie and Gordon were at the courthouse and Gordon climbed the boab tree. He threw the nuts down to Dickie. Gordon fell and knocked himself out and Dickie sat there and waited for him to get up. When he got up Dickie said, 'Are you all right to go home?' and Gordon said, 'Yeah!' so Dickie came home. When Gordon got home his mother Ada noticed he was walking funny so she asked what had happened and he told her about falling out of the tree. She said, 'Was anybody there with you?' and he said, 'Yeah! Dickie was and he sat there with me.' Later in the afternoon when we went to visit them Ada asked Dickie about it and he said, 'Yeah that's right Aunty,' so she said,'Why didn't you come and tell me?' and Dickie's reply was, 'Oh I couldn't leave him Aunty Ada, I had to stand guard in case the Djiaween boys got him.' To Ada that was a good enough explanation and she was good at explaining to Dickie the importance of telling an adult. She was good like that, she was very patient with all the children. Ada told me later that she kept laughing over Dickie's comment, 'I had to stand guard so the Djiaween boys wouldn't get him.'*

Mrs Tack owned a clothing and haberdashery shop in Chinatown and she had some material that Doodie took a fancy to. He went to Laurelle and said in a very low voice, 'Mrs Tack's got this material there,' not explaining in great detail, just saying enough to make his point. It was curtain material, but it had Davy Crockett and Indians on it and Doodie wanted it come hell or high water. They went down and bought some material so his mum could make him a shirt. She ended up making shirts not only for Doodie but for Dickie, Gregory and Mikey Manolis. When Mikey went up to the hospital he proudly wore his shirt and the resident doctor, Dr Peasley, asked his mother where she got his shirt from. He was more interested in the shirt than his patient. She said, 'His godmother made it for him,' meaning Laurelle. 'It's curtain material and they sell it at Tacks.' Dr Peasley sent his wife down to get some and instructed her to make shirts for his boys.

Another time Doodie wanted a shirt made of material that had a pink background with elephants on it. Laurelle made it up for him but Gregory and Dickie wouldn't have a bar of it because of the pink elephants. Pink was for girls. This didn't worry Doodie, who proudly wore his shirt with pink elephants on it.

My own earliest memory of Broome was a visit to the hospital. Gregory had taken me to one of the shops in Chinatown to get a cool drink. I was walking up the front path clinging to my bottle of cool drink. I was around four years old and I wanted to prove I could do things by myself and Gregory, being the tolerant brother he was, allowed me to express my new-found independence. The bottle slipped from my hand and one piece of glass managed to cut me in the face and another on the foot Mum said I was pretty shocked by the whole ordeal and by the sight of blood dripping down my face so she and Gregory took me to the hospital. We did not have a car so Gregory had to carry me all the way. The rest of the kids stayed with close friends of the family called Uncle Pango and Aunty Molly Barber. Gregory talked to me all the way to the hospital to keep me from bellowing. When we arrived the doctor examined the cuts, told Mum they didn't need stitching, then sent us home. Mum seemed to handle our childhood dramas with ease and just got on and did what had to be done without complaining.

12
Return to Derby

I didn't mind leaving Broome because it had such hard water and I was glad to see the end of it. You had to filter it as it was saltish and brackish. By comparison the water was beautiful in Derby. By then the pearling industry had changed and they were going into cultured pearls and there were no jobs, no boat building going on. I knew I'd miss the company of Ada and other womenfolk I'd made friends with but Dickie was sick so we had to shift to Derby.

Laurelle

When my parents moved back to Derby we stayed with Uncle Alwyn and Aunty Tilly who lived in Loch Street, next door to where the police station is today. Uncle Alwyn worked for Lou Kent driving trucks. Having an established family of their own meant we were never short of playmates and paired up with cousins of corresponding ages to entertain ourselves.

Living with extended family has always been a way of life for my parents and rarely were there times when there was just our nuclear family. It was the tremendous support of Uncle Alwyn and especially Aunty Tilly that helped Mum and Dad through the traumatic time in their life when they had to face the harsh reality that Dickie had contracted leprosy at a very young age.

Laurelle: *We used to take Dickie to Doctor Peasley in Broome for any little thing. So when I first suspected he had leprosy I felt so sick, a kind of sick feeling that is hard to describe overcame me. In the back of my mind I think I knew he had leprosy but did not want to believe it. Doug's mother used to hold him a lot in Broome, then she was taken to the leprosarium. But I was trying not to think of that. Anyhow I rang Tilly and told her about Dickie and she told me to bring him to Derby. We took him to Derby to the Native Hospital to Doctor Day, who said, 'Why don't you take him to the front hospital? You don't have to bring him here.' I said, 'Well I want him checked for leprosy. I believe you're the doctor in charge.' He took some tests and sent them out to Sister Francis at the leprosarium for analysing. Tilly warned me that he might have to go out to the leprosarium but I didn't want to think about it. I tried to forget about it, thinking he wouldn't need to go out there. I kept shutting the thought out of my mind, silently hoping he wasn't sick.*

Anyway the day they took Dickie, he was sitting down mending a bicycle with his cousin Joey when the Sisters pulled up and said, 'We have to take him out there, he's sick.' Well, I only had a few minutes to throw some clothes together for him, I hadn't even done his washing, how was I to know they would take him away. He didn't even have time to put a shirt on, or say goodbye to his brothers and sisters. They were taking away our little boy. It upset me a lot to see them put him in the car and take him away. I knew nothing about leprosy and didn't know what to expect. I felt confused and cheated. During this whole time Tilly was very good to us, she'd comfort us and kept saying, 'He can only get better now, he's getting the right medication.' He was so young and didn't know anyone out there. He was only eleven, he was only a child, my child.

My parents were very aware of the fatal effect of leprosy at the time and felt they were grossly cheated when Dickie became ill.

They waited for Grandad's weekly visit to Derby on the *Yampi Lass* to tell him the news about Dickie. They didn't know how he would take it. He had taken many leprosy patients on the *Watt Leggatt* to Broome, but this was different, suddenly his own grandchild was sick with the disease. Grandad was shocked at the news and advised Laurelle, 'You've got to feed them up, give your kids a lot of vegies.' Although the advice was well meaning it made Mum feel responsible for Dickie's condition. She felt she had not been a good mother. It wasn't until they visited Dickie that her mind was put to rest. She overheard Grandad asking the nun in charge, Sister Francis, 'Where did he pick it up from?' and she replied, 'He's picked it up from his grandmother, Goodji.'

When they were living in Broome Granny Goodji often held Dickie and cared for him, not realising she would pass leprosy onto him. Grandad tried to see Dickie as much as possible but this was difficult to juggle with work demands. He made arrangements with Bill Ayling, the local newsagent, to send comics out to Dickie, who looked forward to receiving them. Reading at least took his mind off his illness and in the imaginary world of comics he could forget where he was.

Laurelle: *Dickie didn't know why he was taken out there and didn't understand he was sick. He wasn't running a temperature, or vomiting, or having headaches or pains. He just wanted to be with his brothers and sisters, who also didn't understand what was going on. When we went out to see him he kept asking, 'When am I going home, when am I going to see the kids?' and we'd have to explain that he was sick and Sister would let him out when he was better. It was times like that, that I felt helpless. I found it very hard to comfort him. On one side I had Dickie begging to come home and on the other side I had his brothers and sisters asking to see him. Nagging me to see him.*

Dickie's first term at Bungarun, the leprosarium just out of Derby, was for three years. While he was there Mum and Dad visited him every weekend, leaving us kids with relations. Visitors were only allowed on the weekend. I can't even remember how they got there as we did not have a car.

When Mum and Dad returned home after their visits we would run up to them, demanding to know how Dickie was. At the time very little was known about leprosy and it had a strong social stigma attached to it but Aboriginal people never closed the door on their family. They never allowed the stigma to stand in the way of their strong concept of extended family kinship. The large number of Aboriginal visitors to the leprosarium each weekend was testimony to this. Dickie, like all other patients, was lucky. Family support was forthcoming and although he was separated from them, his parents kept his place in the family alive for his return.

Laurelle: *The Aboriginal people out there were very very*

good to him. I can't say enough good things about the way they cared for him. He started to get used to the people, and I've got a lot of time for them. People like Gabby Dolby used to take him fishing and camping so he wouldn't have time to think about his illness and family. He had an aunty there, who would give him wheat to go down and feed the wild ducks after school. They were the sorts of things they'd do to take Dickie's mind off his illness.

Looking back, Mum and Dad managed to face Dickie's leprosy with exceptional tolerance, understanding, and faith that he would return to the family. They took comfort in the fact his illness was not terminal and that the drugs were constantly improving, knowing one day he would be healthy. They appreciated the good education he was receiving from the St John of God sisters, and the opportunity that was provided to learn and play a musical instrument. Mum and Dad always kept a brave face and positive attitude. They spoke highly of the superintendents and I think they felt satisfied knowing Dickie was cared for by dedicated staff.

Laurelle: *While he was out there Mother Alphonsus taught him to play the cornet, which he became very good at. They had a band out there and he joined that. The band would often put on Christmas concerts for the visitors. They had a small school out there that he attended and once again Mother Alphonsus taught him and the other children that were out there. I remember one day his teacher wasn't well and he had to take the class. So he got them singing and the kids started to laugh while they were singing, so he gave them a piece of paper each and made them write 'I must not laugh while singing.' Then he'd take them out and make them play his version of cricket. As he grew older he spent a lot of time out fishing, then we'd meet him out at the fishing grounds. The nuns, Sister Antoinette and Sister Francis, were very good to him, I'm just glad they were out there for him. At the time the townspeople were very understanding about leprosy.*

Bungarun had the makings of a small town, complete with a band that performed concerts for patients, relations, staff and the occasional visiting dignitary. Bungarun became quite famous for its band. Then there were cowboy movies that entertained the patients, helping them forget the loneliness and isolation of their surroundings. The Aboriginal people held corroborees, with competing dancers from different language groups. In later years during Derby's annual Boab Festival, the leprosarium entered into the spirit of the occasion. Most years they entered a float in the parade and won their share of prizes. All these things kept the patients occupied and helped with the grieving process of being separated from their families.

By the time Dickie finished his first stint at Bungarun he was a competent player of the cornet. Learning a musical instrument helped the residents keep their mind off their illness and increased stimulation to their fingers and joints. He went to school in Derby and each Anzac Day he was given the honour of playing the last post. We were so proud to see our older brother up there playing the cornet.

Hundreds of Aboriginal people were institutionalised at Bungarun. It was established in late 1936 to hold ninety patients and closed in 1986. During the early years patients were sent to Bungarun for isolation reasons rather than treatment. They went there to die as there was no cure. The care and nursing given by the St John of God nuns smoothed their passage. Medication used to treat the disease was ineffective and it was not until the 1940s that chemotherapeutic agents and antibiotics such as sulphones, penicillin and streptomycin helped control the manifestation of the disease. Patients ended up with clawed fingers, club feet and faced amputation in severe cases.

The epidemic years were the forties and fifties with three hundred and fifty at its peak. Leprosy attacked the nerves and eventually resulted in infection to the bone if wounds didn't heal. Patients lost all sense of feeling and were unaware they had hurt or cut themselves. Some went blind from the side effects of medication. The new drugs made the patient non-infectious so physical isolation was no longer necessary. Nevertheless some patients freely chose to remain at Bungarun well after they were cured because they were so entrenched in institutionalised life and they found it difficult to compete outside.

By 1973 the medical facilities had greatly improved, with a network of skilled field staff to provide outpatient treatment and reduce admissions to the leprosarium. By 1986 there was no further use for Bungarun so it was officially closed leaving a relatively well-resourced leprosarium with no patients. Bungarun was handed over to the Aboriginal Lands Trust and in July 2001, officially became a work camp for minor offenders who had previously been placed in prison.

Kunmunya to Mowanjum

By 1958 most of Laurelle's sisters and brothers had young families of their own. Alwyn and Tilly had a well-established family of five children. Edie had married Dave Conway and happily settled in Riverton in Perth with several girls of her own. Kathy had married Alwyn Scott and together they ran a small welding business in Guildford. Ivy was working in Perth. That left Yogie who remained a bachelor and worked for a plastics business in Perth. They were a close family and Laurelle kept in touch with her sisters through letters and the occasional telephone call.

Alfred was still working on Koolan Island as a bosun on the *Yampi Lass* and loving every minute at sea.

When Laurelle and Doug moved back to Derby in 1958 the Aboriginal people from Kunmunya had settled on a pastoral lease about ten kilometres out of town, just past the airport. This was their third move since Laurelle last saw them in 1942. Initially it was decided they should move to Munja, then Wotjulum and finally Derby.

After the war Kunmunya seemed to go downhill. The number of Worrorra people appeared to be dwindling. Some went bush, the birthrate was very low, diseases had affected the population and the drive and direction of former years seemed almost non-existent. The mission itself had changed. The buildings were in a state of disrepair, the stock had not been cared for, the vegetables and crops were failing, especially the peanuts, and there was a general shortage of staff. Added to this was an outbreak of hookworm. The mission would need a massive injection of staff, finance and resources to restore it to the successful venture it was in the thirties and forties. The church simply did not have these resources and neither did the government.

About seventy miles from Kunmunya was the government settlement of Munja. It was having the same problems as Kunmunya and, like the church, the government didn't have any realistic solutions to the problems. The government offered Munja to the Presbyterian Church as a 'walk in walk out' deal. The church agreed to the deal and decided to move the people from Kunmunya to Munja.

The Aboriginal people around Munja were mainly Ngarinyin and Wunambal, sister tribes to the Worrorra. Neither the Kunmunya nor the Munja communities wanted to move, for cultural reasons, but agreed that if a move was to be made, it needed to be to a neutral locality free of domination by an individual tribe.

The church decided to move the people and buildings from Munja and Kunmunya to a place called Wotjulum, meaning *a place of living water*. Wotjulum was near the Coppermine Estuary nearly opposite Cockatoo Island where BHP was mining iron ore. The new location brought them closer to civilisation. There were the mining islands and the town of Derby. This meant improved medical services, education, employment and better living conditions. When the notion of a merger was adopted people started to move freely between the two places, with the relocation of everyone to Wotjulum completed by September 1951.

In 1956 the people of Wotjulum were on the move again, this time their sights were set on Derby. The merging of the three tribes had worked, and if this was all that Wotjulum achieved then all was not lost. But the dream to develop a successful settlement for the Aboriginal people didn't come to fruition. It was sheer hard work growing vegetables, mustering cattle, building houses and keeping the morale of people high. The elements were against them as water was not plentiful, the soil infertile and the country hot and unforgiving. On top of these were limited financial and human resources: together they did not add up to success. The Department of Native Welfare and the Board of Missions settled on a pastoral property about ten kilometres out of Derby on the road to Broome. It was large enough to run cattle and was called Mowanjum, an Aboriginal word roughly meaning *settled at last*.

Living at Mowanjum meant coping with town life. The children went to school, hospitals and shops were within walking distance, employment prospects were available and isolation and communication were not problems. The women were employed as housekeepers while the men worked as labourers. Although the move appeared to be for the better, the Mowanjum people were displaced and this started to take its toll on their culture. No longer were they close to their traditional land. Opportunities to practise cultural ceremonies were very limited and the freedom they previously had was suddenly restricted. Many were working in town with their children at school and, like other Aboriginal people across the Kimberley, they faced problems handing down their culture to their children. They were a long way from the bones of their ancestors and were exposed to alcohol.

Many of the elders alive during Reverend Love's days had passed on. The leadership had changed to men like Albert Barunga, Watty Ngerdu, Paddy Morlumbun, David Mowaljarlie and Allan Mungulu. On the women's side there were Elkin Umbagai, Buruwolla, Pudja, Daisy, Gudu and Patsy. The enormous responsibility of carving a new life for the next generation in a town starting to embrace technology rested heavily on their shoulders.

Many still had living memory of walking in from the bush to experience their first encounter with missionaries. These same people were expected to embrace a society on the verge of a technology boom.

When Mum returned to Derby she saw the Kunmunya people again, and as always they were overjoyed to see her. The women made a fuss of us and wanted to know about Alfred and the rest of her family. Mum wanted to visit them regularly but this was impossible as we did not have a car. Some of the women cleaned houses for various families and a few of the men worked in town. Later Albert and Watty worked as gardeners at the school and David began working with anthropologists. They joined in the town basketball competition and it wasn't long before they excelled at the game, representing the town in matches against Broome.

> Alfred: *Before they moved the people from Wotjulum I was working at Cockatoo Island. A Mr Coombe, I think he was Reverend Coombe and I think a protector of Aborigines, visited me on the island to ask my opinion if they moved the people to Derby. I said, 'Well, I think there's two points here. See, I think it's good for the little ones to have schooling and all that. But the old people will die off.' There's a lot of them that died here* [Derby] *through contact and drinking habits.*

> Laurelle: *When I came back to Derby in 1958 the Worrorra people were at Mowanjum. Pearl, who I knew from the mission, would often come and do the washing for me and I gave her a little bit of money, whatever I could afford, but mainly meat or fish. Pompey helped clean the yard and I'd give him the same too. They had no understanding of money and it was food that they wanted.*

I remember one day Gregory came home from work and there was Pearl perched on a pile of washing with Neville in her arms. She was trying to put him to sleep because I was busy cooking and she was rocking him and singing hymns. They love babies, the Aboriginal women. In walked Gregory. He didn't know the Mowanjum people. All he knew were half-castes. He was horrified that this old Aboriginal lady was holding his baby brother so he grabbed Neville, gave him his bath, powdered him up and put him to bed. Pearl got on with the washing and I explained to him that Pearl was one of the old ladies who grew me up at the mission. He could trust her. He seemed happier after I'd explained things to him.

The next day I saw Tilly and she was talking about a chap she kept calling Paddy who was a star basketball player. She said, 'He's always asking about you.' I said, 'I don't know a Paddy.' Alwyn, overhearing our conversation said, 'Laurelle, that's Morlumbun from the mission.' I'd only ever known him as Morlumbun, his Aboriginal name. How could I forget him when he had saved my life when I was stung by a bluebottle. I think a lot of them were given European names when they got to Derby.

Silvercity and Delawarr Street

When it was teatime Granny Goodji would say, 'You seen Iris? Tell her it's teatime. Tell that girl to come home now.' Then the message would be relayed to the next house until I got it. You felt safe and you didn't have to lock things up, everyone cared and supported each other. I guess I was privileged to have lived with Granny on the marsh because

> *although Aboriginal people were not allowed to openly practise their culture I was fortunate to experience much of it through living with her.*
>
> Iris Prouse (Laurelle's daughter)

When my parents moved back to Derby, Dad landed some casual work with the Public Works Department. The foreman there heard he was in town and had boat building skills. They got him to repair a dinghy and he did a very good job so they offered him some permanent work. Needing the money to feed all of us he took up the offer and worked for the department for the best part of three decades.

In early 1959 Mum and Dad moved to 5 Delawarr Street, a state house in the westerly section of the street, where we stayed for just over ten years before moving five houses down to a larger government house. Mum and Dad tried to make a good home for all of us — there were eight children at the time. The house had three bedrooms and probably seemed small for a large family; however, it was our own turf, it had a big yard, a friendly neighbourhood and the family dog called Buster.

He was an odd sort of a dog, happily letting visitors up the front steps, then growling at them with flared nostrils and flashing his teeth if they made any attempt to leave the yard without speaking to a member of the family. I think Doodie owned him. Doodie always had dogs with flared nostrils that showed their rather large sharp teeth at the sight of visitors. We all got on with Buster. I guess it was because we treated him like another member of the family rather than a dog. I don't know what happened to Buster in the end.

Laurelle: *Delawarr Street was a short street. We lived next door to Benny Birss and she had four children and her sister lived next door to her, she had two children, then across the road were the MacMillans, Horsboroughs, Jimmy Ah Chee and the Cousins. There were a lot of children in that street and they used to play on the street, it was very wide and safe as there weren't many cars around, not like today, every family has a car. The kids found friends in Derby. Television was unheard of and the children entertained themselves in a variety of ways from regular visits to the town pool to playing marbles and fishing.*

Apart from the odd fight and scrap or two, the kids in Delawarr were pretty good mates and looked out for each other. As we were by far the largest family in the street you were either brave or stupid to take one of us on. There were plenty of kids to play hopscotch, skipping, marbles and lots of other simple games that didn't cost money.

Across the road was a family called Cousins and they had a big box of comics so we quickly made friends so we could read all their comics. Heather would grab a handful and park herself on the front steps of our house and read her life away. We had to step over her to get into the house and that resulted in the occasional fight. Mum was often yelling at her to put the comic away and help clean the kitchen but she seemed to have a way of tuning out her voice.

Comics were the only source of literature that graced our home. Later Mum purchased a set of large booklets on early explorers that was sold to her by a shonky sales person that bravely entered our yard. It was rare to see a book, magazine, or novels lying around the house.

If a child in the neighbourhood had a birthday, every kid in the street was invited; if not they went anyway.

Kids moved freely from yard to yard playing and skylarking when they knew they could escape retribution from the adults. It was an accepted rule that everyone was home by sunset and if this was ignored the culprit was reminded by the stinging sensation of a leather belt around their bare bum — we certainly were. Our street was a family street where kids and dogs were safe. There was no need for security and I don't ever remember Mum and Dad having to lock the house up. Mind you, with all of us there was always someone at home.

The antics of my brother Doodie kept Mum amused, it helped keep her sanity with all of us. He loved animals and at one stage was fond of beetles which he found in the garden, under logs, in the bushes and places where only boys ventured. You would see him out the back scavenging through rubbish Dad left lying around, collecting beetles of all shapes and sizes. He even managed to find a psychedelic coloured beetle that changed colours when he held it up to the light. That was one of his favourites, I think, he even gave it a name. They had to have a bath with him, that was until one went down the plughole. He was so distraught, he never let them loose in the bath tub again. Mum caught him shaking a glass jar and said, 'Doodie what are you doing?' He said, 'Can't you see, I'm cleaning my beetles.' He was furiously shaking his beetles to a froth. He insisted on clean beetles, it didn't seem to bother him that some drowned during the process, so long as they were clean.

It was around this time that Granny Goodji, Dad's mother, returned to Derby and took up residence on the marsh, at the back of the Derby Caravan Park, towards the pensioner units on Rowan Street. It was a gathering place for squatters.

We religiously visited her after school every day

knowing she always had a cool drink, or peanuts, or lollies for us. Granny had a little shack on the marsh, where she lived with her friends and family. She had been in Bungarun for several years before moving to Sunday Island Mission then finally returning to Derby.

> Iris: *I was living with Granny Goodji at Sunday Island before we moved to the marsh and when they closed it down the Bardi people were moved by barge to live in Derby. I was about four or five when I first went to live with granny and it was because I had a bad temper and she seemed to be the only one who could control me. While we were at Sunday Island Granny spoke Bardi and several other Aboriginal dialects and I guess I understood the language because she'd speak to me in Bardi and I'd answer in English. I had friends like Christine and Ethel Lennard while we were at Sunday Island. When we moved to Derby she never spoke much Bardi, only when she was mixing with her own people from One Arm Point and this included Granny Annie, who stayed with us too. Garloo lived with us also and together him and Granny built the house on the marsh.*
>
> *The house was well designed and made from timber and corrugated iron and had steel poles, materials Granny had acquired from wheeling and dealing. It had a lot of louvres to control the amount of breeze, dust and rain that came into the house. In places the floor was made from wooden shipping pallets pushed together to make a raised floor and in other parts Granny had lino. She had a forty-four gallon drum in the kitchen that she'd fill every day with fresh water because we didn't have kitchen taps and that was where we got water from. My job was to watch the waterline inside the drum as it was filling up and make sure it didn't overflow. At the back there was an ablution*

block that had concrete washing tubs, a makeshift shower and toilets that had a portable dunny pan. Men from the Roads Board would come on a regular basis in a truck and replace the pans. Granny's place was the first house coming off the main road.

At the time a lot of Aboriginal people lived in marginalised areas such as the marsh. The Panton Street reserve was on the marsh, commonly called the Native Reserve with the Native Welfare Department opposite it, largely to control the movements of the Aboriginal people.

Iris: *Other families living on the marsh included Granny Topsie O'Meara, the Bin Kalis and I think even Jerome Manado lived there as well. There was a man called Abdullah, who may have been an Afghan, he was living there as well. The place was called Silvercity and I grew up with kids like Irene and Elizabeth Bin Kali and Francis and Michael O'Meara.*

Silvercity was a small community, a bit like a big extended family on the fringe of Derby and there was also a Chinaman by the name of Ali who sold Chinese takeaway, but the shire closed him down because he didn't have hygienic cooking facilities. There was no alcohol consumed and there was the usual menagerie of animals such as the family cats and dogs and even a pig that was everyone's pet. After school the children would play together and we'd play games like hopscotch, skipping, dodge-the-ball, knuckle jacks, french cricket and then there was marbles, the cause of endless fights. Granny had many visitors, people like Helen Rider, Lexie Shaw, Bob and Mary Hutchinson, Jack and Biddy Dale would come to see her and the place was never short of visitors and relations like Granny Gypsy and Aunty Lexie.

Later Granny bought a half acre block on the corner of Rowan and Hardman Streets, Derby. Being the smart person she was, she managed to save money acquired from her only vice, cards, and put her winnings towards a block of land. Granny Goodji's luck didn't stop there; later she bought another half acre in the same street about four blocks down going towards Neville Street. Garloo lived with Granny Goodji, he was a Ngarinyin man she met at the leprosarium and the relationship started there. He was always at Granny's place and as kids we grew up with him around. At the time I had no understanding of the highly significant role he had as an Aboriginal law man and the standing he had among the Ngarinyin people. He was part of the family and grew us up.

> Iris: *One morning at about 4.30am Goodji woke myself and Edie up, shaking us on the shoulder saying, 'There's a big snake under the blanket on my bed. Pull the blanket back and Garloo will hit it with the stick.' When we pulled the blanket back there was no snake but an enormous pile of money stashed under the blanket from her winnings at cards that night. There seemed like hundreds of notes in a range of amounts, there was silver everywhere. We thought we were rich. Granny loved playing cards and often when she'd go over to Granny Topsie's place to play cards, I'd wrap her dress around me and go to sleep with it, it had a comforting smell about it.*
>
> *When Granny had a bill to pay off she'd go and play cards and when she had the amount required to cover the bill she'd stop and come home. The people she played cards with would say, 'Goodji what bill you paying off now?' and she'd say, 'Oh! Just my water bill.' The water bill was*

about the only expense we had because there wasn't any electricity.

Sometimes I'd follow Garloo onto the marsh and watch him throw his boomerangs which he was extremely skilled at doing as he would tell me what he was going to do with them and sure enough that's what would happen. While we were out there he taught me how to ride a bike and I think this was because Granny ordered him to rather than asked him.

Occasionally I'd listen to him singing in language and I'd say, 'What are you saying Garloo?' and he'd reply, 'I'm chasing away that rain now because they having law business.' It was his job to keep the rain away while his people were having their cultural ceremonies. I learnt a lot about Aboriginal culture from him.

Granny never drank alcohol or smoked and kept an extremely clean house with ample food in the house. She hated the effect alcohol had on people and whenever Uncle Adrian or Garloo came home drunk she'd give them a tongue-lashing that made them hang their heads in shame. Although I lived permanently with granny for many years my brothers and sisters would come there after school and stay over on the weekends.

By 1960 Mum and Dad had been married for fourteen years. We did not have a car and Dad rode to work on a bike, the same bike he had in Broome. A return trip to work each day was about four kilometres, so Dad kept reasonably fit riding his Malvern Star. In the afternoon, when it was time for him to come home we would meet him at the corner and clamber over him so we could ride the last few yards on his bike. Dad became very skilled at riding a bike with at least three kids hanging off him.

Mum would call a taxi to do the shopping, banking,

paying bills and to take us to hospital. If we behaved we got to go shopping and ride in the car. The taxi drivers were reliable and responsible people like Bill and May Smith, Kenny Ah Chee and Dave Bickley. The taxis were all the same, smelling of disinfectant with plastic covers on the back seat that stuck to the back of your legs, making you slide out when it was time to hop out.

> Iris: *Every Saturday morning we'd walk down to do our shopping. First Granny would get her meat from the butcher shop, where Elders now is. Then we'd go to Aylings, where Le Lievres now is and Kimberley Traders, which used to be next door to the Chinese restaurant. After we finished Dave Bickley would pick us up in his taxi and take us home. Saturday shopping was like a ritual and Dave knew that at about twelve o'clock Goodji and her granddaughter had to be picked up from outside Kimberley Traders.*

Between 1960 and 1963 Mum had three more children, Andre, David and Cherie, taking the family to eleven children. The attractiveness of my mother went unnoticed and I was at an age where I took her for granted, not seeing what a strong selfless person she was. Years later I saw a photo of her when she was in her late twenties and I was immediately struck by her flawless skin, perfect bone structure and slim build.

By now my parents had enough kids to make a formidable cricket team. We learnt to play hopscotch with a baby on our hip and, believe me, it takes a certain skill to master the art of skipping with a baby clinging to you. It didn't faze us when Mum had another baby, we didn't think we could get any poorer but we were happy. Each night we queued up to use the showers and some fell asleep waiting to use the toilets after pictures on Saturday night, that's if we were too frightened to go out the back. Mum served tea in two sittings, lunch came and went that quickly it managed to just happen and breakfast was mainly toast, cereal or something light like spaghetti and baked beans.

Mum and Dad lived from one pay day to the next and looked forward to a bonus in June when they received a few extra dollars from the tax man for having so many kids. When the tax cheque came in Mum spoilt herself and bought an ornament or knick-knack for herself. She loved to collect them but never at the expense of food on the table for us.

David, Cherie and Andre at Granny Goodji's, c. 1964.
(Courtesy Laurelle D'Antoine.)

The bedrooms housed more double decker bunks than the local hostel, with the younger ones sleeping top to tail. A room to yourself complete with privacy was something you dreamt about and a bed to yourself was a privilege reserved for the older children. In spite of this, there always seemed to be space for a relative or two to bed down when they popped in for a visit.

As we grew older we helped out preparing meals, washing, cleaning and ironing. Mum could sew anything so we grew up wearing homemade clothes and rapidly got used to hand-me-downs. As I was third in line for the girls' clothes I had to grin and bear it. Being sixth wasn't so bad because by then they had fallen apart and had to be replaced with new ones. When it was our birthday or Christmas Mum always went to a lot of trouble to make us something special, often staying up late at night to finish it.

We looked forward to Grandad's visits. He always stayed with us and spoilt us with lollies and cool drinks. Looking back the extra helping of food coincided with Grandad's visits.

In many ways our house in Delawarr Street was very similar to the little house behind the Sun Pictures in Broome. Nothing flash, very small, sparsely furnished but brimming with people, children, babies and dogs. We were happy.

> Laurelle: *When we could afford it, the children were allowed to go to the pictures once a week, on Saturday as they didn't have school the next morning. Doug would take the older ones down first to get tickets and save seats. The children enjoyed the westerns, comedies and cartoons. During the week they weren't allowed out because we thought their homework was more important. Having such a big family we took up two rows of seats at the pictures. The younger ones had seats at the front, while the older ones tended to sit with us adults. At intermission everyone went across to Ayling's shop to get their drink and ice cream.*
>
> *The theatre seemed to be divided into three sections. As you walked in the Mowanjum people sat towards the left hand side, the little ones would wander over and talk to them. The adults sat at the back and the children sat at the front. Often we'd leave the pictures thinking we had all the kids, only to find that when we got home, a child was missing.*
>
> *One night we arrived home to find Andre missing. By*

the time Doug went back looking for her the gates of the pictures were locked, and he had to climb the fence to get in. He ripped his good pants and wasn't very happy at all. He eventually found Andre curled up on one of the deckchairs sound asleep, snoring. Another time Neville was missing, and there was a knock on the door and I heard someone say to Doug, 'You missing a son?' In walked Neville who was about seven then, he was full of fight, threatening to do this and that to us for leaving him behind. We managed to quieten him down and get him to bed before midnight. Then there was the time we left Heather behind, so she started to walk home. Doug met up with her in front of the Royal Flying Doctor's base. Like the others she blamed us for leaving her behind. If we left a child behind we'd never panic because Derby was such a small town then and we knew they were safe.

Later on when the kids grew into their teens they used to walk down to the pictures and you could hear them all coming home after the pictures, they'd all be talking and as each child went into their house the talk got softer.

SCHOOL IN DERBY

Spit flew across the space between the headmaster and the students, landing in very small droplets on the brown arm of the unfortunate child sitting in the closest desk. Everyone copped his spit at some stage, especially when he was angry and the veins on the side of his temple protruded. The headmaster had arrived unannounced at the classroom only to tell the students what they'd become accustomed to hearing in high school. Their teacher was away. 'Right, Wally, I want you to take

Science today. The rest of you get on with your work. There's a teacher next door to keep an eye on you. I don't want any fooling around from this class. Do you all understand?' 'Yes Sir,' chorused the class. Wally scraped his chair on the lino floor as he took his usual spot on the platform in front of the science lab. Surprisingly the students got on and did their work, though that was far less painful than facing the wrath of the nagging English teacher next door. Her high-pitched shrill gave you a headache that lasted all morning. The absent teacher was probably sick from a hangover or in jail after a scrap at the Spinifex the night before.

Teachers at Derby Junior High School came from Perth and didn't stay very long. They contributed very little to the community, living totally separate lives and staying only long enough to score a transfer back to the city while their sanity was still intact.

Like most schools across the country it was highly institutionalised in appearance and administered in the same vein. The classrooms were very basic with windows opening out onto the verandahs, so that when the children raced down them they had to skilfully dodge the open windows, as well as the kids, teachers and family dogs that found their way to school. The windows were covered with rusty flywire that served more to catch the dust than keep mosquitoes and flies out. Every student walking past flicked the flywire sending dust onto the desk of the poor student sitting on the other side. Another common pastime was scurrying around after pieces of paper scattered by fans turned to full blast by an inconsiderate student. There seemed to be lots of inconsiderate students at the school.

Airconditioning was unheard of and fans were the only source of relief during the build-up to the wet from

October to Christmas when the temperature hovered around ninety-nine degrees fahrenheit on most days. When it hit a hundred we rejoiced as we got to go home. The school closed when it got too hot to work. Constant high temperatures, sweaty, smelly bodies and dirty hands resulted in low levels of productivity in the afternoon and on days when the mercury rose, schoolwork looked more like *Blue Poles* revisited than a frustrated attempt at handwriting. There was always handwriting after lunch.

The students in the classes along the verandah thought they were pretty special; they had built-in radios in their rooms. During the closing months of the school year, when tempers flared along with temperatures, the teachers allowed the kids to put their perspiring heads on the desk and listen to what few educational programs the ABC broadcast. Every child knew the soothing sensation of falling to sleep to the lullaby of ABC serials. The radios are still in the classes as a legacy of the changing face of education.

The school was in Clarendon Street. It wasn't anything fancy, it just had basic facilities. Tucked away at the end of the verandah was the School of the Air and in front of the verandah was an asphalt basketball court. The toilets were located close to the courts so you got a strong whiff of them during class. The headmaster lived in a government house directly across the road, which was still used to accommodate teachers until the end of 1990.

As in most country towns my parents had the choice between Catholic or state schools. There was the usual rivalry between the two schools with kids indulging in the usual banter and teasing. Chants like 'state school dogs' and 'catholic frogs' were often chorused on the way home with the occasional insult graduating to a harmless fight at the closest park or boab tree.

We lived across the road from the school, which had its drawbacks as Mum would lean on the front gate, craning her neck to make sure we made it through the side gates in the morning and after lunch for the afternoon session. Truanting was unheard of and we did not dare miss a day of school for fear of a visit from the police the next day requesting an explanation.

We kept Mum and Dad broke with the endless cost of books and school fees. They escaped the expense of school shoes though, as we never wore them. The first decent pair of shoes I recall having was when I went to boarding school many years later.

By the time I went to school my older siblings had carved the way for me, and my entry into school was nondescript and uninteresting. The only time Mum went to school was to enrol one of us or for a parent interview dealing with our misbehaviour. It was always Mum who faced the music as Dad was always busy at work.

My class was on the verandah and I often wandered out of class to watch the rain. Mum said that as a kid I was fascinated by rain. I don't think the teacher was too fascinated when I leisurely took myself off in the middle of a lesson to watch the rain.

> Laurelle: *I was having problems with the kids at school with their lessons, they needed tutoring and I didn't know what to do about it because we didn't have a good education and besides we didn't have the money to pay a tutor. Ron Yates offered his services to come home and tutor the kids for a couple of hours at night. For that I'm really grateful to Ron for what he did for our children. He made them see that education was a very important part of life.*

Ron was a strange man. He was single, walked on his toes, and was an academic, having come from Melbourne as an electronic engineer. Fixing radios was his hallmark, though if you took one to Ron to fix you ran the risk of not seeing it for several years. Extrovert by nature and slightly eccentric, the town seemed to take pride in having a person like Ron around.

The seats in his car were wooden crates and there was more daylight coming through his floorboards than the window. You could study the patterns in the bitumen as you drove along. When the car turned a corner you had to grab the dashboard to stop the crate sliding around. When the buttons fell off his shirts he'd use pieces of wire to secure them together. I'm sure the wire was from remains of the radios he failed to return.

He had long hair and a matching unkempt flowing beard, and wore sandals that were bound to his feet with insulation tape. You didn't dare risk passing Ron as you entered Ronny Ah Chee's bakery. He'd immediately stop you and proceed to explain Pythagoras' theory in great detail, drawing vivid formulas in the pindan, making you feel totally embarrassed as people passed you on their way in to buy their bread. Teaching had no boundaries with Ron, he loved it and if he had the chance to revise a maths concept in front of the bakery, then he did just that. Along with all his other students we constantly dodged him for fear of being still cornered hours later.

His timing was impeccable, however, arriving at home just as Mum was dishing up tea. He loved rib bones. In spite of Ron's idiosyncrasies his heart was in the right place. He tutored other children in town and refused payment for his services, just a free meal occasionally, the warmth of a family and the satisfaction of knowing the children benefited from his help. Mum and Dad appreciated his assistance and deep down we knew he genuinely cared about our education.

By now Dickie was back with the family. The doctors had released him from Bungarun, allowing him to attend school while he was still on medication. When his tablets ran out he rode down to the Native Hospital to see the nuns to get more. He didn't like going to the main hospital, he felt more comfortable with the nuns and felt no sense of shame when he went to see them.

Dickie found it difficult socialising in school but our cousins, Joseph and Annette Brown helped him through those difficult times. It was in dealing with the wider public that he had problems. One night he went down to the town basketball courts with Doodie and our cousin Gordon and quietly slipped away without telling them. Later, when they caught up with him at home they asked, 'Why didn't you tell us you wanted to go home? We'd have come with you.' Dickie found it difficult to explain that the noise, the people, the seeming confusion, and the social expectations were things he didn't know how to deal with.

By the end of the 1960s the school had grown, and now attracted children from well outside the town boundary. Students from Mowanjum came in each day on a bus, making their presence known in athletics and basketball. Apart from the students around town they came from as far south as Roebourne and Onslow and as far north as Wyndham to attend the high school. They boarded at Saint Joseph's, a hostel operated by the Catholic Church, and went home during term holidays. They brought a richness to the school through their enthusiasm to perform well in the classroom and on the sports field; everyone integrated well into the school.

The enthusiasm even seeped into relationships that

started at school and continued in the front rows of the Derby Pictures. The budding romances were all very innocent and discreetly played out so parents had no idea who was pairing up with who after the lights went down.

After high school Gregory began working at the post office in Derby. He had to sit for a qualifying exam to get into the post office, which he had no problems with. His first job was delivering letters and telegrams, then working at the counter dealing with the public. He worked at the old Post Office, where Elders is now, then joined the navy.

> Laurelle: *One day Greg came home after work and told me he had made his first telephone call and naturally, as a young eighteen year old, he wanted to make a good impression. He said, 'Mum, I had to make this call to Mowanjum so I cleared my throat, ready to be nice and clear. I felt a little nervous but I made the call and when they answered it was this person with this strong Aboriginal English saying, "'Ullo, who there?" I nearly dropped the phone because I wasn't expecting to hear that. I was expecting to hear, "Good morning, this is the superintendent of Mowanjum Mission. How can I help you?" I didn't expect to hear an Aboriginal person on the end of the phone.' I didn't know what to do. Anyhow Greg must have got over the shock and finished the call. That was Greg's introduction to ringing telegrams through. He used to tell me these little things when he came home after work.*

13

The Death of Gregory

The early 1960s was a harrowing time for my parents. Raising a family of eleven was not easy and Mum relied heavily on Gregory for help with the children. It was a responsibility he took in his stride. Being a patient brother, he managed us with a great deal of ease and had a knack of giving us all a bit of loving each. He always found time after work to play a game of cricket or dodge with us. When it was bath time Greg was there to supervise before our innocent splashing graduated to strangling one another. While Mum was busy preparing the evening meal, Gregory read to us. He never complained; he was always there reading, supervising, soothing and controlling.

Gregory was turning into a fine adult and Mum and Dad were proud of him. He regarded them as his parents, refusing to acknowledge his biological ones, especially his mother, who finally started to take an interest in him when he became a young adult. He was popular, dependable and a great role model for us. We doted on him and you couldn't ask for anything more in a loving brother.

In 1962 when Greg was eighteen he joined the navy

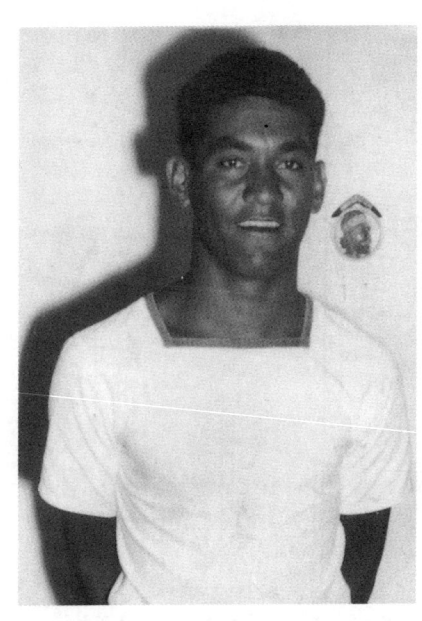

Gregory Hughes, c.1962.
(Courtesy Laurelle D'Antoine.)

and we were all so proud that a member of the family was in the navy.

He was a sentry for Queen Elizabeth when she visited Australia in 1963 and he sent Mum a newspaper clipping of the Queen walking down the gangplank with Greg in the background. Mum made the mistake of showing us and we all took turns to take the clipping to school to feature in class news. You can imagine, with all of us, teachers got sick of hearing about Gregory.

In December that year Gregory announced his plans to spend Christmas with us and we were so excited by the news the teachers had to put up with another session on Gregory. He came home several days before Christmas and never returned to the navy as he had a tragic accident and died.

Grandad was in Derby at the time. He had come across from Koolan Island to spend Christmas with us and was staying a few streets away with Aunty Ivy who was living in Derby for a short time. Christmas was shaping up to be everything we dreamed of. We knew we had Grandad and Gregory to spoil us and Mum made the best Christmas pudding filled with threepences and sixpences. She had a secret stash of loose change she kept hidden from us especially for her pudding. Occasionally we would get a glimpse of her counting the money in the secrecy of her room making sure she had enough for her famous pudding. Mum and Grandad had been shopping and were in the kitchen with Aunty Ivy when the accident happened.

> Laurelle: *Gregory came home in 1963 for Christmas and he had an accident at home. He died on Christmas morning. It was a very sad day for us all. He'd brought presents home for the kids and he was looking forward to seeing their reactions to the gifts when they opened them on the day.*
>
> *On the day of the accident my nephew Gordon was at the back of the house using Doug's buffer, polishing a pearl shell butterfly that he was making for his aunty and uncle for Christmas. We had these plastic chairs, I'd only just bought them, and they had thin iron legs with rubber caps on the bottom. Gregory was sitting on the back verandah rail flicking one of the chairs up while he was talking to Gordon. He overbalanced and fell off the verandah, pulling the chair over with him. The next thing I heard was Gordon screaming and yelling for us to come out. I rushed out and Gordon pushed me back in the kitchen saying, 'No, no, Aunty, don't come out here.' Doug rushed out and he grabbed the chair, he just thought it was lying on top of him him. Doug lifted the chair off his face, not knowing the leg of the chair had gone through his eye socket. He tried to pick Gregory up but he was totally unconscious so he rushed and phoned the ambulance and police and everything.*
>
> *Greg was immediately rushed to hospital and they said they had to fly him to Perth and that he couldn't breathe so he had to have a tracheotomy. It was Christmas Eve when they flew him to Perth.*

The following morning, Christmas Day, was one of the darkest days of our lives. Mum and Dad were yet to face the worst.

> Laurelle: *Sergeant Weaver knocked on our door to tell us that Greg had passed away that night. I think the whole of Derby mourned his death because he was such a popular boy. The bottom fell out of Christmas then. The kids wouldn't unwrap the presents Greg had brought them, they were grieving for him. They'd huddle together and talked and cried. They loved Greg very much. I didn't know what to do. His passing away really left the family grieving and it was something I couldn't accept for months and months. I think a part of me went with him. I relied so much on him and now he wasn't there any more. He attended to all my letters. He used to do all my business letters for me. If I had to send any letters away he'd do the writing, even when he was in the navy. I'd write and tell him about it. He'd write the letter and send it to me to sign and send away. All those little things he'd help me with, you see he was a very smart boy. I never got over his death.*
>
> *They gave Greg a navy burial at Karrakatta cemetery in Perth. Doug and myself and Cherie flew to Perth, Cherie was a baby. At the funeral there were a few navy officers and close relatives and friends. It was a very sorrowful occasion but we were thankful for having the short time with Gregory. Every now and then a person comes along and touches your life, for us it was Gregory.*

After Gregory's funeral Dad flew back straightaway as he had work but Mum stayed in Perth for a while with Aunty Edie. Mum had Cherie to care for and the death of a son to deal with and the last thing she needed was a houseful of children to cope with.

After that Mum seemed to become over protective towards us. She constantly wanted to know where we were, what we were up to and her sense of protection towards us seemed to sharpen.

14

Work and Recuperation

Dickie applied to join the navy but was unsuccessful because his hands were clawed and he failed the medical examination. He got a mechanical apprenticeship with a government department called Mechanical and Plant Engineering. Although he did not have manual dexterity he coped very well and was able to use spanners and other tools that required the use of fine motor skills.

Dickie went to Perth to have several operations on the nerves in his hands to regain his sense of feeling. His hands were becoming very claw-shaped and he was starting to lose a great deal of feeling in them. On one occasion he went fishing and a catfish barb got caught in his hand. The barb can cause excruciating pain but Dickie didn't feel a thing and watched unflinchingly while it was cut free with a knife. After his trips to Perth, Dr Holman stopped his medication for fear of side effects. Dr Holman blamed himself for the relapse Dickie had that led to his return to the leprosarium for a second time in about 1969.

Greg's death and Dickie's return to Bungarun was starting to take its toll on Mum. Dad had his work to occupy himself with and this was starting to take him out of town for several days at a time. Mum was at home all day with us kids and no outside interests. Suddenly our highly capable mother was showing signs of fragility and we became worried she would have a nervous breakdown.

Mum must have gone to see Dr Holman because he said, 'Would you like to come and work at the hospital? I think it's the pressure and stress that is making you feel this way.' We knew she wasn't coping very well with Gregory's death but as we were kids we didn't quite know what to do about it.

WORKING AT THE HOSPITAL

Work was a welcome relief for Mum. It was a change for her to mix with other people and not sit in four walls sewing, cooking and caring for us. Mum worked as a second cook in the hospital beside Aunty Tilly and the breakdown she was on the verge of having did not eventuate.

Work was like a new lease of life and together Mum and Aunty Tilly planned the hospital menus. When Aunty Tilly had days off Mum took over the full running of the kitchen. Mum worked with a good team, everybody worked well together and helped regardless of whether it was their job or not. The Marshall girls, Rhoda and Elaine and later Madelaine, helped serve the meals and there was a chap by the name of Ralph Kelly Mum talked about. He insisted, 'When you dish up you've got to make sure the presentation is done properly. Now you put the potatoes here, put the carrots there and the greens between them to give it colour.'

Ralph had learnt his culinary skills from the nuns at Bungarun. He was exceptionally clean and neat and took immense pride in keeping the kitchen floor spotless along with shining stoves, ovens and other cooking implements.

Mum and Aunty Tilly were excellent cooks and their reputation extended beyond the hospital. Derby must have been the only town in the Kimberley where the townspeople happily went to hospital knowing the meals were great. Starting work early in the morning wasn't a problem for her as we were old enough to get the little ones and ourselves to school. After school we went down to Granny Goodji's until it was time to go home around five o'clock.

Laurelle: *Christmas at the hospital was a good time, the administrator, Denis Evans, used to play the organ. At about ten o'clock we'd shut down everything. Matron Farmer would say, 'Come on down and sing some Christmas carols.' There'd be Dr Holman, all the doctors and all the nurses there and we'd be saying to Tilly, 'I wonder if our Christmas dinner is burning?' and she'd say, 'No, I don't think so, it's turned down low,' and things like that. We used to join in and sing Christmas carols then rush straight back to the kitchen and check on dinner. Dr Troupe would say, 'No china plates, no washing up this time.' We'd use paper plates and it was good. We'd prepare the tea and put it in the coolroom. For tea they'd have cold meat and salad and the nurses on duty would serve it up and distribute it. Later when the hospital became bigger there would be one lot of staff in the morning then another shift in the afternoon when it became too much for the nursing staff to give out meals on Christmas Day.*

Working at the hospital agreed with Mum and the extra money allowed her to lash out and buy a few nice things for herself. Whenever she went somewhere special she was always smartly dressed. Mum made a lot of her clothes and this helped the dollars go a bit further.

Of all the doctors Mum worked with it was Dr Holman she respected the most. When Dad was constantly sick with stomach pains she said, 'Why don't you go to Dr Holman and discuss what's troubling you in the stomach,' but he wouldn't listen to her. Eventually the stomach pains resulted in the need for surgery.

One night he became very ill and who should be the doctor on call but Dr Holman. Mum rang the hospital in a panic and he answered the phone saying, 'Calm down Laurelle, I can't hear what you're saying.' She explained Dad's condition, so he sent the ambulance around. The ambulance driver knew the front lights would be on in their house, but because of the commotion the whole street had their lights on. Iris stood out the front of the house waving the ambulance down. The ambulance picked him up and took him to hospital, rushing him immediately into X-ray. All the time Dr Holman kept saying to Dad, 'You have to stand up, I know it hurts, but you have to stand up, I have to find out where the pain is coming from.'

There was a nosy patient in hospital at the time with blood pressure problems. As they were wheeling Dad towards the operating theatre, obviously in a lot of pain, this nosy patient, wanting to help, got in the way, forcing Dr Holman to angrily say, 'Get the bloody hell out of here, you're either bloody dying, or getting in my way. Now just get out of the bloody way. Can't you see I've got a sick patient.' Looking back now it was pretty funny, but not to Dr Holman, who had an emergency on his hands.

He had to operate on Dad and just before they took him into the operating room Dr Holman calmly said to Mum, 'You go home to bed now, I want my breakfast in the morning. I'll let you know if anything goes wrong.'

Dad had intestinal problems. He survived the surgery and that was due to Dr Holman who was a very caring doctor, abrupt at times, but extremely dedicated.

He did not like sick patients waiting around to see him. As they arrived at outpatients he always stopped and found the time to see them straightaway, even late at night.

Dad had previously gone to doctors in Broome and they told him they couldn't find anything wrong with him. Dr Holman restored his faith in them again. Now you can't hold Dad back from visiting a doctor.

Taking a Break

Mum often came home exhausted after a busy day at the hospital to a verandah full of grubs.

David was the grub collector in the family. He played with his grubs for hours, lining them up regimentally for the neighbourhood kids to look at provided they kept their distance. Under no circumstance were they to lay a finger on them. After he outgrew grubs it was kangaroos. He had a pet called Joey, who was allowed into the house each morning to join him for breakfast. It was a common sight to see David sitting at the table sharing his cereal with Joey. One day Joey bit him on the cheek and after that was banned from the house and eating cornflakes.

Then there was the rooster, Neville's pet. It started to attack people out of the blue. When entering our yard visitors had to be on the lookout for the rooster as it would fly out of nowhere and peck you. It simply terrorised the kids in the neighbourhood. One day it pecked one of the children and met its fate with the stroke of an axe. Neville was devastated but Mum explained, 'The rooster was going for the kids' eyes and we can't have it doing that.' Neville's emotions subsided only to explode at the dinner table that night when he unknowingly consumed his pet for tea. 'Why did you let me eat it!' he demanded. 'You could have warned me I was eating my pet.'

After Gregory's death it was years before we started to enjoy Christmas again. The usual excitement leading up to the occasion was not there. The wharfies' Christmas parties helped ease the pain, especially for my parents.

It was the highlight of the year for nearly every child in the town and this excited the members of the family who were too young to remember Greg's last Christmas. Mum's brother Uncle Alf (Yogi) was a wharfie and lived with us, so the D'Antoine children were automatically invited.

> Laurelle: *The wharfies put on a show for the children. Whatever wharfies had any relatives in town they would dob in for presents and things like that and I remember one of the blokes by the name of Helmut, he was a wharfie and he said to my brother, who also was one, 'Well I'll buy a present for young Chuckie,' my younger son. If they didn't have a relative to buy a toy for they would buy one for their mates' relatives. Having a big family, we really appreciated things like that.*
>
> *Father Christmas would arrive on a forklift, then the kids would get their presents and then it was open house*

for all kids in Derby to come to the party. To see all these people, who were referred to as alcoholics — well it was a sight to see. They would serve the kids ice-cream. They never had a glass of beer while they looked after the kids, they served them ice-cream and lollies and gave them a real good time. They waited on the kids and made sure they had a good time. Then after the kids had all gone home they'd settle down to the adults' Christmas party, but not one of them would touch a drink before that. That's what I liked about Derby, for the handful of wharfies there was, they always put on a good Christmas party for the children. It's a lost tradition because the town doesn't have any wharfies anymore.

Dad worked for Public Works Department, which entitled him to air fares every second year for the family to go to Perth. If it wasn't for the airfares we would never have had the opportunity to visit our family in the city, it was simply too expensive for my parents. We flew to Perth on MacRobertson Miller Airlines in a DC3, filling up three-quarters of the plane.

We stayed with Aunty Kathy and Aunty Edie, who must have dreaded the sheer enormity of feeding, bedding and entertaining all of us. I often wondered how they felt when they knew we were visiting them. They needed at least four cars to collect us from the airport.

> Laurelle: *The first time we got on the plane I overheard one of the hostesses whispering to the other one, 'Here comes that family now.' We had reserved seats all down one side of the plane, it had single seats on one side and double on the other. The air hostesses got us to board first to settle the family before inviting the rest of the passengers on board.*

One day we went out to the airport to catch the plane but it was delayed. I think it had to go to one of the stations. Tilly said, 'Don't go home, come and have lunch with us,' so we did. We eventually got on the plane and we had to travel at night. As we got closer to Perth, Iris said, 'Look Mum, there's Perth there,' and when I looked down it was just a little township just outside of Perth. When we did get to Perth the pilot flew around the city to show us the sights and it was just on daybreak and Perth was really beautiful to see and it was still lit up. Iris saw this and she was so taken by it she couldn't talk. She was so surprised to see how big Perth was. She was only a little girl then and she'd never seen a city before.

If we got on the milk run, we'd stop all along the coast and the trip took about twelve hours to get to Perth.

Then there was Mary who would take herself off and sit with the air hostess asking endless questions. It wasn't so bad travelling at night because the kids slept through it all.

It was expensive taking the family to Perth for the holidays. When various family members heard we were in Perth they chipped in to help pay for excursions. Grandad seemed to be in Perth the same time and made sure we all had a good time, including those living in Perth.

On one occasion Uncle Alfie decided to shout us a trip to the zoo. That was pretty game of him. Taxis were sent for and the driver was so stunned when we all piled in, saying, 'My God, where's the end of this? Where did all these kids come from?' When we got to the zoo he said, 'When do you want me to pick you up?' Dad said, 'I thought you'd be glad to get rid of us,' but he said, 'No I'll pick you up.' He must have counted all of us because when he picked us up again he did a head count to make sure we were all present.

At the zoo Uncle Alfie took us on a train ride. He had a mate running it and although tickets had been bought, he let the kids on free. I kept saying, 'He wouldn't take our tickets, he wouldn't take our tickets,' and Uncle Alfie whispered through grinding teeth, 'Shut up and use it for something else.' I wanted to enjoy the novelty of handing the tickets over to a collector as I had never seen one before.

When we walked over to line up for the elephant ride we took one look and scattered, we had never seen anything so enormous and threatening. The younger kids went to see the lions and tigers and turned around to their cousin and said, 'Gee! look at that striped nanny goat there,' but it was a tiger. The kids had never seen a tiger before, they didn't know what it was.

We were fascinated with the idea of getting refunds on empty cool drink bottles. Once we found out you could exchange them for cool drinks and ice-cream we spent most of the day collecting empty cool drink bottles. One of us even went to the extreme of asking people for their bottles before they had finished drinking. It became a competition to see who returned home with the most money.

> Laurelle: *Then we went out to Yanchep and Georgie and Fenton* [cousins] *were with us. Fenton was carrying Neville on his shoulders and we went to look at the caves. We went in and we got to this big pool you had to walk around and Neville started yelling, 'No! no! there's crocodiles in there, there's crocodiles in there.' Everyone turned around to see who this kid was who thought there were crocodiles in the caves. Georgie and Fenton thought it was funny watching the kids' reactions to different things in the city.*

The Golden Days of Fishing

I remember one day, several years ago, Iris rang me up, it was Easter, and she said, 'You know Mum, for the first time in my life I had to buy packet fish for Good Friday. Can you imagine D'Antoines buying fish?' And I said, 'Well! we never had to, did we?' and Iris replied, 'I didn't have fish, usually we always have fish. I kept thinking about those days when we used to go out fishing and now here I am buying packet stuff.' It makes me wonder, will those days come back? But days never come back, not ones like those.

Laurelle.

Our first car, in about 1964, was a Toyota Stout. It heralded a very distinct phase in our life. Mum had stopped working at the hospital and having the car gave her the opportunity to develop an interest away from the house. She had a professional fishing licence and sold her fish to Ronny Ah Chee. The older boys were working by now but the rest of us still had to be fed, clothed and educated, so the extra dollars were great.

Dickie was still at Bungarun but as an employee now, working as a mechanic. He spent most of his weekends at home and when we went fishing he did most of the driving. Dickie was an excellent driver on the single lane dirt track that he knew like the back of his hand. He also knew every fishing spot on the Meda River. Mum knew when Dickie took us fishing she did not have to worry about the car breaking down or us getting lost as he always got us home safely.

Laurelle: *One day we went to a place called Snags.*

Timmy Hogan was fishing further down, then there was my nephew Joey Brown who had a line in. I had thrown my big line out, not far from Joey. Doug and I went further down the river to get bait. I was carrying the bucket and Doug had the throw net to catch bait. Before we left to get bait I said to Andre, 'I want you to sit on this reel.' She was sitting on the reel doing exactly as I asked and I said, 'If you feel anything big, yell out to Joey or Timmy so they can come and pull it in.' They weren't far away. Anyway we came back and she said, 'Something took me for a big ride.' You could see where the reel had spun and her little footprints in the mud making a full circle around the reel and she proudly said, 'It done that two times Mum.' I said, 'Why didn't you yell out for Joey?' and she said, 'I couldn't, I was too busy spinning around on the reel.' When Doug pulled the line in, it was minus the hook and the bait.

We only fished for barramundi, starting at Langi and Telegraph Pool on the Fitzroy River before working our way down to Jaraninga. When these spots became popular Dad moved further north to Snags, Milli-milli, Pelican Pool and Opening Bay, which were virtually unknown then.

Dad covered our tracks to the fishing spots using markers. An adult walked ahead and marked different trees for the driver to follow to find the place, returning a different way. Good fishing spots were like gold so we learnt at an early age not to publicise where we went. I'm sure the phrase 'secret spot' had its origins in the D'Antoine household.

We were the only family fishing at Pelican Pool until one day a fisherman called Bill Hailey slyly followed Dad into the spot. Bill bragged to the local anglers that he had cut a track into Pelican Pool, not realising that it wouldn't take long for every man, woman and dog to go there making it almost impossible to catch a fish. My parents were forced to explore other fishing grounds, so they fished further down towards the mouth of the Fitzroy in search of new locations. The process of entering using markers was used yet again.

Mum and Dad didn't mind people following them but it made them very angry when tracks were cut into the spots and their fishing places were exploited. We needed the money that came with a good catch.

Ronny Ah Chee bought all the fish my parents could catch. He owned the Golden Shower Bakery. He bought their barramundi as whole fish or fillets, paying around fifty cents a pound for fillet and thirty-five cents a pound for whole barramundi. As the recovery rate of fillet from a barramundi is about fifty percent it made better economic sense to sell the fish whole. The average return for a trip would be ten fish at fifteen pounds clean which would give a nett return of around fifty dollars. This was roughly a week's wages in those days and Mum managed to make good money on her licence.

> Laurelle: *One Sunday Dad, Doug and I went out to Pelican Pool, we went out there and were catching sharks all morning. Dad said, 'I'll shift down to where the truck is, maybe I might have some luck down there.'*
>
> *We were catching shark after bloody shark. Doug gave it away and went and lay down under a tree. I got this bloody big thing on my line and it was huge and I thought I had a swordfish. Doug was still snoring his head off under the shade of a tree and I'm yelling for him and he is ignoring me saying, 'It's only another bloody shark,' and I'm saying, 'I can't turn it.' If it was a shark it would have*

cut the line because we didn't have any traces or anything. Then this huge barra surfaced. Well, I've never seen Doug move so fast, he got up running. While he was pulling it in he kept thinking, I better not lose this one or else I'll be in terrible strife with Laurelle. Anyhow he landed it and the fish was only just hooked up. We got about five that day, nothing under twenty-five pounds.

We came back home and Neville and David had gone out to Mudhole, another fishing spot. David came running up to me very excited, tugging at my arm saying, 'Mum, Mum, look what we got. We've got fish and this is the smallest, and we've got bigger ones than this.' He was proudly holding his smallest fish, then he rushed off to get the next biggest. They did have some big ones. By the time he had his catch laid out Doug pulled out my barra and the rest of our catch. Well poor old David he walked away devastated. We had pinched his thunder. Poor David. He picked the wrong day to brag about his fishing trip. Between both of us we cleaned up that day and made a bit of money. We used to get some barras on hand lines then.

My parents frequently took other members of their family fishing and Dad taught a lot of his nephews to fish. There were even times when the kids in the neighbourhood managed to find their way out fishing with us. If you wanted to catch the elusive barramundi you befriended a member of the D'Antoine family. If you were lucky to get a berth on a fishing trip you did as you were told. Your first task was to carry the bait bucket, without complaining, and under no circumstances were you allowed to tell anyone the name of the fishing place.

Everyone had a job to do, which included setting up camp, collecting the firewood, carrying the bait bucket, swimming the net across the river, throwing the net for bait, watching the tethered fish, carrying the star pickets and many more. If you were not prepared to pitch in and help you were never invited back.

One of the best barra weekends Mum and Dad had was a trip to Meda River. Our cousins the Browns were with us. We picked up Aunty Tilly and the kids and Dickie drove us out. The barras were biting that day and Aunty Tilly got onto this barra. She got bogged knee deep in the mud trying to hold it. Eventually she had to give the line to Dad who managed to pull it in and it was the biggest barra we ever saw. While Dad was landing it Mum was silently praying, 'I hope he doesn't lose it, don't lose it please.'

Garloo and (l–r) Andre, David, Neville and Cherie, Doctors Creek, 1969.
(Courtesy Laurelle D'Antoine.)

While Dad was trying to land the barra Neville, who was a very young kid, was sitting up on the bank crying because his Aunty Tilly was bogged. After Dad caught it Dickie carried the barra up to the car and found Neville still sobbing, 'Aunty Tilly's bogged, why can't someone pull Aunty Tilly out of the mud.' Here was this little figure hunched up with his little blond head in his hands, sobbing because his Aunty Tilly was stuck in the mud, while the adults were praying the fish wouldn't get away. Dickie went off to rescue her.

My parents and Aunty Tilly caught a lot of fish that day, even the kids were catching them. The trip back home tested the strength of the old Toyota Stout as it was loaded down with barras and kids.

When Dickie walked into Aunty Tilly's place with the barra, the head was as high as his shoulders (Dickie was just under six foot) and the tail was dragging on the ground. Alwyn said, 'How did you pull it in? It's a wonder it didn't pull you in,' and Tilly said, 'It couldn't because I was bogged knee deep in mud. I had to get Doug to pull it in.' Alwyn was surprised to see anything so big. We all were.

> Laurelle: *We relied on fishing, as we needed the money to help feed and educate the little ones. We used to net them. It was big money in those days. The boys used a throw net to catch bait for the kids to line fish, they were very good at it. There was Dickie and Doodie and Joey and even Timmy used to get bait. Dickie was the best net thrower. He could throw the net under overhanging mangroves and still made it spread the full circle.*
>
> *In 1973 I gave up my professional fishing licence to return to work at the hospital. It was like giving up a way of life for our family. We went fishing every weekend and the kids practically grew up on the banks of the Fitzroy.*

There were no eskies to keep the fish in. My parents used a method of tethering the fish live until they were ready to leave. This involved tying them to a common line that allowed the fish to swim around in the water. The fish remained alive and fresh for hours. The only problem was the occasional crocodile that took one or two. Another common practice was burying them in a small pool on the bank. When they were ready to leave the fish were still alive and they took them back home wrapped in canvas ready for cleaning, gutting and filleting.

We frequently stayed out overnight and everyone slept under the stars on a canvas. There were always fires going around the camp, which served to keep everyone warm and keep the occasional crocodile away. The net had to be checked regularly so there was always someone up to stoke the fires.

Timmy Hogan, a local Derby identity, spent many weekends over the years fishing with Mum and Dad. He was a schoolmate of Doodie and Dickie's and seemed like another member of the family. He could tell a few stories about Mum's skill at fishing. He can even tell a yarn about a crocodile attack he survived when they went fishing one day at Meda River.

It happened on the weekend when Dad, Mum and Timmy, only a young kid then, decided to go fishing the night of an eclipse of the moon. They didn't think anything of it. Mum had her professional fishing licence so they were planning on putting a net across the Meda. Doug had a homemade canoe which they tied on the back of the Stout. The canoe was just big enough to carry the net across the river. When they got to their fishing spot further up from Meda Rocks they met up with a couple of friends, Mary and Bob Hutchison. They unpacked the car and canoe then put the gill net in the canoe along with Dad's rifle, a .22.

By now it was dark but there was enough moonlight to see what you were doing. They knew they had to get the net into the water as soon as possible before the eclipse of the moon. Timmy happily hopped in the canoe and took it around to where they wanted to set the net. Mum and Dad walked along the bank opposite him, however before they got very far they heard a bone-chilling cry for help. It was Timmy screaming, 'Help! Help!' They could hear this banging noise, but didn't realise it was the canoe being hit. Bob ran towards the scream saying, 'He's hit a reef, he's hit something.'

By then the eclipse of the moon had started and the light was fading. All Doug had was a torch with a flat battery that gave a dull yellowish light. Timmy was screaming at the top of his voice, yelling over and over for help. It was then Doug realised it was a crocodile attack. Doug felt totally helpless and the reality of the situation hit him. 'Oh my God,' he kept repeating.

The screaming and banging seemed to go on for five minutes and all Laurelle and Doug could do was listen helplessly. The rifle was in the canoe but even if they had it, they couldn't see Timmy. The next thing they knew there was this canoe heading straight past them up the bank. It was Timmy. Shocked and shaken he eventually told them what had happened in between spasms of shivers.

A crocodile had attacked him and when he realised what it was he had the good sense to lean the canoe towards the croc, knowing it would counterbalance the attack. The banging that they heard was the crocodile hitting and banging the canoe trying to get at Timmy, and Timmy trying to hit the croc with the paddle. Although he had the rifle he couldn't get to it because he was too busy balancing the canoe and defending himself.

Just before the attack Timmy had seen ripples in the water. Assuming it was a barramundi he thought nothing of it, except to think, 'We're going to kill the pig tonight.' Then the croc attacked.

After settling Timmy, Mum and Dad packed up and took him back to town, leaving the canoe with Bob and Mary. Timmy was still in a state of shock when they arrived in town. It's difficult to say if he ever really recovered from the attack, but he did make an effort to come to terms with it a short time later when he went out fishing again with Dad. When Dad got the canoe ready to put in the water Timmy said, 'I'll get in, I have to get rid of this fear,' and Dad said, 'You'll be okay. I'll walk beside you on the bank.' Dad had a rifle just in case anything happened, but fortunately nothing did.

Timmy continued to fish with Mum and Dad but they never netted Meda again, that was one place they stayed clear of.

The old Toyota Stout earned Mum a lot of pocket money in those days. We loved that old car, it opened up a lot of the fishing spots along the river. But it wasn't so much the places it took us but the number of kids and barras it carried. It was never the same after it caught fire, so Mum and Dad traded it in for a Ford International, which was a bigger vehicle and could hold plenty of kids and fish.

> Laurelle: *One day the faithful old Toyota Stout caught on fire. The wiring caught alight and Dickie told the kids to get out and head for the bush while he put it out. It was petrol and I thought it would explode and he didn't want the kids getting hurt. Looking back now it was funny, with all the kids and myself with a baby slung across my shoulder racing for the bush. You could see these little faces poking up behind the bushes watching Dickie's every move. He got it under control and called us all back. How he got the car going, I don't know. Eventually he got it started and we headed back to town. Dickie was a damn good mechanic and always got us home when our car broke down.*

My parents were always happy to take young men fishing with them. It meant extra help for throwing the net, swimming across the creek with star pickets and generally getting bait and checking set lines. It was around this time Geoff Wright started fishing with them. Apart from boarding school, he had spent most of his life inland and had a lot of catching up to do. He loved fishing with the zeal of someone long denied the chance.

> Laurelle: *Another time we took Geoff Wright out fishing, this was in 1971. At high tide we decided to give it away and return to the vehicle. All the fishing gear was loaded into the dinghy, I got in also, and Doug and Geoff started walking the boat up the creek towards the car.*
>
> *Now the water in the creek was chest deep and halfway back Doug let out a shout and reckoned he had been spiked by a stingray. He got into the dinghy, sporting a nasty wound on his foot and was in a lot of pain. The tide was starting to go out and Geoff ended up pushing both of us back up the creek.*
>
> *We got back to the pool opposite the vehicle and the tide had dropped off the mudbank by a foot or so and on the bank was the belly track of a very large crocodile. It had either passed us on its way down the creek or was still in the hole between us and the vehicle. The pool was about twenty-five metres wide. Well we had to get across so Geoff tied a light rope around his ankle and swam across then pulled the boat over. I am not sure if they keep records on the twenty-five-metre swim but I would be extremely surprised if Geoff's time has ever been broken!!*
>
> *When we got back to town Doug was admitted to hospital and it took nearly a week for him to recover from the stingray spike.*

Fishing on the Fitzroy was a special time in our lives. Everyone in the family can tell you a fishing tale or two. It was a way of life for us, it was something we accepted, loved, and sometimes hated, especially when Elvis Presley was featuring at the pictures and we were forced to go fishing. Looking back it was a time in our lives when my parents had us together before we all moved on. It would have been great if Gregory had been there with us.

15

Times of Change

By the mid sixties conditions for Aboriginal people throughout the state started to change. The *Native Administration Act* (1963) in Western Australia signalled the dawning of a different future. In 1967 an Australian referendum allowed indigenous people to be included in the national census and gave the Commonwealth concurrent powers with the state to legislate on the welfare of Aboriginal people. The last restrictive policies of discrimination and segregation were dismantled and abolished and Aboriginal people were encouraged to access mainstream education and employment, and the medical and social welfare systems. It was not until the 1970s that institutions perpetuating past segregational practices dissolved and Aboriginal people started to experience the benefits of these changes. It was a rags to riches scenario in the space of an exceptionally short time for a culture with living memory of its introduction to non-Aboriginal society. Old attitudes, behaviours and values die hard and the acceptance and self-determination Aboriginal people wanted continued to elude them, and to some extent continues to elude them today.

Derby become a place for displaced Aboriginal people to gather. The people from Kunmunya had moved. In 1950 Kunmunya Mission was closed and the people moved first to Wotjulum then in 1956 to Derby, with the long-term plan of integration in the town. At Mowanjum displaced Ngarinyin, Wunambal and Worrorra people lived hundreds of kilometres from their traditional lands. In 1949 Derby Reserve was established in Villiers Street and by the 1950s the town was a place for Aboriginal people to spend their holidays.

In 1962 the United Aboriginal Mission on Sunday Island closed and the Bardi people were sent to Derby. By the late 1960s Aboriginal people had access to award wages. This affected those working in the pastoral industry as station owners could not afford to keep them, and they drifted into Derby and Fitzroy Crossing and other major towns seeking employment at the wharf, the shire, hospitals and wherever they could find it. By the early seventies, Derby was a melting pot for many different Aboriginal groups who were starting to come to terms with their new-found independence from the Native Welfare Department. It was an independence they had no control over. They did not have the skills to make a successful transition into a society on the verge of a technology boom.

> Laurelle: *Aboriginal people could quite easily get jobs in the town. Men were working on the new jetty and main roads or the shire. A lot were working at the hospital in the kitchen, or the laundry, or the workshop. There was work for them if they wanted it. Some of them wondered if it was worthwhile working. There was one young girl working with me in the hospital and as soon as she got her pay her family would chase her up for money. I said to her,*

> *'Why don't you open up a bank account and get the office to bank it for you before your family get it.'* She said, *'No use doing that, they'll find out and get it off me somehow.'*

By 1970 quite a few Derby parents were sending their children south for further education. The government school only went as far as year ten, forcing parents to look at the option of boarding school and hostels in Perth or Geraldton. Not all parents could afford this and had no choice but to sent their children to work as soon as they finished their Junior Certificate. A few students were gifted enough to get a Commonwealth Scholarship and went to Perth, subject to their parents' financial ability to meet the extra costs involved.

My four oldest brothers and sisters were too late for the educational benefits that were put in place in 1970 for Aboriginal children. Dickie was a mechanic and auto electrician and Doodie was into his third year in the navy visiting exotic places abroad. Mary had just returned to Derby after doing her nursing training at Swan District. In 1968, after obtaining extremely good results in her Junior Certificate, Iris went to work at the Water Authority. The remaining six of us were still at school, plodding along.

BOARDING SCHOOL

By 1970 the Commonwealth government had introduced a program called the Aboriginal Secondary Education Grant Scheme. It was designed to improve educational opportunities for Aboriginal children so they could access and pursue further education. It meant Aboriginal parents, for the first time, could apply for financial support to send their children to Perth for further education.

In order for Aboriginal people to qualify for the assistance they had to acknowledge their ethnicity. This was very confusing for many Aboriginal people who, for many years, had been penalised for doing so. The guidelines and financial benefits were in keeping with other schemes operating that assisted non-Aboriginal parents living on remote farms and stations to send their children south for schooling.

> Laurelle: *It was heartbreaking sending the kids away to boarding school, but Doug and I knew they could only benefit from it. In 1970, Edith was the first to go south, to Saint Brigid's, and while she was there the nuns heard her stringing the kids along telling them she came from a tribe up north. Anyhow the nuns twigged she was Aboriginal so they sent us some forms for Aboriginal Study, which we didn't know about. Doug took the forms to John Turich who filled them out and encouraged us to apply for it. Financially it was a big help and it helped with the other kids, it was good because it was paid to the school and you didn't have to worry so much about the big bill that came at the end of the term. We also got airfares for her.*
>
> *At that time the local school here only went to year ten and she organised herself to go away to boarding school. We'd always told the kids how important it was to get a good education. At one stage there we had three kids away at the one time. There was Neville, Andre and David away all at the one time. They found it hard going away; they were in a culturally different environment, something they weren't used to, but they knew they had to go.*
>
> *When it was time for Andre to go back to school she'd*

hide her air tickets because she didn't want to go back. The first day she had been at boarding school one of these bullies made the mistake of picking on her so the nun in charge, knowing Andre could hold her own, turned her back while Andre promptly put the bully in her place. Then she got into hockey and she liked that and she talked a lot about that. I remember the year she finished we drove down to pick her up from Stella Maris in Geraldton and she was that anxious to get out of the place she was packed and ready to go well before we arrived.

Then Cherie used to start getting homesick even before she went back and by the time holidays came around she was okay, then it would start again.

If it wasn't for Aboriginal Study, there was no way we could have given our children a good education, some would have missed out. But the best thing was they did something with their education and became something, even the older ones who didn't get the help. Doug and I always told them it was important to get a good education, and they all did just that. A lot of Aboriginal people didn't really know about Aboriginal Study then. I remember my brother-in-law asking how Doug and I could afford to send the kids away and we told him about Ab Study.

In 1970 I went to Saint Brigid's in Lesmurdie and it was a cold shock to the system. I had been to the city before but Perth in the summer is very different to the lonely winters it deals out mid-year. At first I was intrigued by the novelty of being away from home and generally enjoyed the new experiences that presented at a girls' boarding school. I was surviving at school although I did find the work challenging. There were about eight other girls I knew from Derby and Broome and this saved me, otherwise I would have been home like a flash.

The year rolled on and so did winter and that's what I hated the most. I did not have a lot of good winter clothes and associated Lesmurdie with blue hands, chattering teeth and utter wet, dark bleakness. I found the social dynamics of a middle-class boarding school totally confusing and offended a lot of people in my efforts to conform and please.

Kimberley Girls and Sister Claire, Saint Brigid's College, 1970: (l–r) Colleen Masuda, Loretta O'Meara, Colleen Puertollano, Denise Sariago, Faye Dean, Sr Claire, Anthea Bin Demin, Shirley Cox, Edie D'Antoine.

The girls from the Kimberley stuck together and we became good friends, finding the isolation easier to handle as a group. We found ourselves having to come to terms with a different environment and culture and the challenge drew us together. Many of us have remained great friends, still seeing each other today. It was a common sight to see us in full Saint Brigid's regalia perched on a stone wall sunning ourselves, looking for split ends and munching on raisin buns. How ridiculous and awkward we looked and felt. The smell, food, climate, language and culture were different.

In June that year I became an aunty for the second time. Mary had a daughter, Veronica, in January and Iris had Tammy in June. Mum stopped working at the hospital to take care of them while my sisters went back to work. They were adorable little things and I quite enjoyed coming home to them on the holidays, among other things.

Laurelle: *I rather enjoyed looking after my granddaughters when they were babies. One morning about ten o'clock I heard this Crash! Bang! Clatter! When I went to investigate Tammy had crawled right into the back of the cupboard and was throwing everything out of my kitchen cupboards. Behind her, sitting on the kitchen floor, was Veronica, neatly stacking things like a lady. It was the little things like that that you remember.*

A Larger House

Dickie had finished his apprenticeship as a mechanic and auto electrician at Bungarun. He was free to leave the leprosarium but had chosen to stay there as he had a job as a mechanic. This meant managing his time between Bungarun and home.

He was quiet happy clocking up the kilometres between the two bases, especially if it meant spending time with his younger siblings and two nieces who were becoming very fond of Uncle Dickie. The shouts and cheers from the little ones yelling, 'Uncle Dickie! Uncle Dickie!' when he drove into the yard brought a smile to Mum's face. She understood his need to be with them. Dickie spent a lot of time spoiling the little ones, showering them with lollies and goodies at every possible moment and taking them fishing when the opportunity arose. It was as if he wanted to make up for the time he didn't have with us.

My parents had moved five houses down to a larger furnished government house on the corner of Heytesbury and Delawarr Street. It was just behind the Boab Inn and this suited Dad because he had engineers from work who stayed at the Boab but came home for breakfast.

Dad couldn't boil water so Mum had to prepare breakfast for them, and that's when she brought out her good china. It seemed quite bizarre, this household with kids and grandkids running amok while Mum was fussing over engineers, serving them breakfast and toast on these dainty toast racks and good china. Dad often brought engineers home for Mum to cook for. She was an excellent cook and could whip up a delicious meal in no time. Chinese was her speciality and she earned a reputation as a great cook among Dad's work colleagues.

> Laurelle: *I remember when the grandkids were about two years old and we were getting ready to go shopping. I'd bathed them and was getting ready myself. When I came out of the shower the place was very very quiet. I sensed they were up to no good. They'd managed to get into the girls' bedroom and covered themselves from head to toe in Heather's creams and powders and they stunk of this sickly Avon perfume smell. They had powder all over their little faces, you could only see the whites of their eyes. They were enjoying themselves and I had to give them a second bath to wash the smell away, then clean up the room. They wanted to smell nice as they knew they were going shopping. When Heather came home she hit the roof, threatening them with a slow and painful death. She wrote a sign banning the kids from the room. The sign said, 'Veronica and Tammy banned from this room for life.' The grandkids couldn't read and the sign meant nothing to them. These were the little things the girls got up to, it's good to sit back and laugh about them now.*

Uncle Alfie (Yogie) was still living with my parents and working as a wharfie on the state ships, along with casual work with Ronny Ah Chee, helping in his bakery when the boats weren't in. Everyone squeezed into the house on the corner and there was hardly any room to swing a cat. Fortunately television hadn't hit Derby so the children spent most of their time outside playing when they weren't at school.

In 1971 I returned to Saint Brigid's, much to the dismay of the college board. One of the boarders from the Kimberley was diagnosed as having leprosy during the Christmas break and sent to Bungarun. The administration at the college stopped all the girls from the north returning except myself and another boarder from Broome called Maxine Chi. They saw us as a threat to the well-being of the other students and I was shocked that we were treated like this by a Catholic school. We were both doing year twelve and as it was a crucial time for us we were allowed back, but the other girls had to attend school elsewhere. Dad knew the politician Frank Wise and he pulled a few strings to get me back.

When I returned the other boarders were genuine in their concerns over the whole ordeal. Following this I had to have regular medical examinations every holiday break before returning to school to clear me of having leprosy. It was a requirement under the Health Act, Section 337 and my parents could not apply for the Aboriginal Study grant unless a medical certificate was forthcoming.

In a strange way all this made me more determined to see out my final year at Saint Brigid's. My parents believed a good education was the way of the future for Aboriginal people. 'If you want to get on in the white man's world you have got to have the same education,' they said. Thinking back, this was my first raw introduction to my awareness of being Aboriginal and I often wondered how the boarder diagnosed positive felt, knowing we were being treated like this. The regular leprosy examinations suddenly become a threat to any plans I may have had for further education. I felt totally uneasy, inferior and angry at being subject to this treatment and the concept of equity started to take a very different meaning for me.

ALFRED RETIRES

It was also in 1971 that Grandad had a heart attack while he was working on Koolan Island running his own launch. My sister Mary was working as an enrolled nurse at the hospital and on duty when he was admitted. When she went home that night she told Mum he had been brought in from the island after having a heart attack. He was placed in intensive care and fortunately made a full recovery with no permanent damage.

The years of hard work had taken their toll and it was nature's way of telling Grandad to start winding down. He decided to obey the signs and retire.

BHP were reluctant to see him leave. His knowledge of the coastline, the tide and boats were invaluable and the company wanted to retain his services. They offered him free accommodation on the island complete with meals at the mess in return for his assistance in emergencies. He would be required to help in emergencies, for example, when workers were stranded at sea. Grandad realised this was a good deal but he wanted to be on the mainland spending his retirement with his family. He eventually settled for an open invitation to visit the island whenever the need took him.

In 1972, in recognition of his twenty-six years of service

to BHP, the company gave him a trip around Australia. The manager of Koolan, Charlie Brownlow, wrote him a letter acknowledging his service, enclosing a fat cheque and making it clear the door was always open should he wish to visit the island.

Grandad took his trip around Australia visiting the capital cities and taking three months to enjoy every moment. He was extremely proud of the way his loyalty and services to BHP had been recognised and acknowledged by the company and the people of the island. It was an excellent note on which to finish his working life. He had been working since he was fifteen and you could count on one hand the number of different jobs he had. We were very proud of Grandad and knew he commanded a lot of respect from his mates and workers on the island.

After his retirement Grandad stayed with Mum and Dad in Delawarr Street. He purchased a caravan large enough to accommodate his needs and parked it in the back yard.

The best part of retirement was the endless fishing trips and time to read. He enjoyed books by Ion Idriess and other historical and factual literature. He was well-read and each week walked to the newsagent to pick up his standing order of *Pix* and *Post*. His ability to recall information meant he could confidently correct anyone who let a few facts stand in the way of a good story; they only ever did that once while Grandad was around. He was the person you wanted sitting at your table on a quiz night.

When he was working on Koolan he was well-known for his attention to detail when movies were shown and on picture nights people would say, 'I bet Alf will come up with something tonight.' He'd pick faults in the movies such as the use of zips on purses before their time and things like that.

Shortly after his retirement Grandad started to take a formal interest in the Catholic religion. He'd never stopped being a Christian, but attending church on a regular basis as he had at Kunmunya and Byford was difficult while he was working on Koolan and Cockatoo Island. We were all baptised Catholics and so were Uncle Alwyn's family. Grandad was very good mates with with the local parish priest, Father Lorenz, who he approached to receive further sacraments.

Marriage and other Family Changes

In November 1972, after a two year courtship, I married Geoff Wright. He worked as a clerk for Main Roads Department.

My older brother Doodie had received an honourable discharge from the navy and was in a relationship with a local girl, Margie Rose. My sisters Mary and Iris were also married. Mary had moved south to Bridgetown, taking my younger brother David with her to attend school there.

In 1973 Mum went back to work at the hospital. The kitchen staff hadn't changed much and everyone still chipped in and helped each other. It was easy for her to slip back into the hospital routine. Aunty Tilly was still the cook and her offsider was Betty Hunter and at some stage Ruby Rose, Margie's mother, assisted. Mum become the sweets cook and together they made a formidable team.

In March of that year Geoff and I had a son we named

Linton. This brought the total of grandchildren for my parents to seven. Grandad had around twenty great-grandchildren.

Heather was attending Perth Modern after completing a nurse's aide course the year before at Derby Regional Hospital. She was too young to do nursing so she went to Perth Modern, then continued on to the West Australian School of Nursing to do her registered nursing course. Years later she went on to Edinburgh to do her training in midwifery.

Neville and Andre were at boarding school in Geraldton, leaving Cherie at home. Dad was into buying cars and fishing gear through Tropical Traders in Fremantle, while Mum meticulously shopped for furniture, gifts for her grandchildren and knick-knacks. It was the first time my parents had some time, privacy and money for themselves.

Just when my parents thought they could get rid of the double decker beds in the boys' room Mum was told, 'Aunty, young Jimmy Greatorex needs a home.' In her usual caring manner she said, 'Bring him home, he can live with us,' and continued cooking rice for tea. Jimmy arrived wearing black boxer shorts and a sleeveless top. He became our brother.

16

Dickie's Death

In early 1974 Mum and Dad were dealt another blow. My brother Dickie was killed in a car accident in the Northern Territory. He was twenty-seven years old, in the prime of his life, and starting to enjoy the freedom denied him after spending many years in the leprosarium.

He'd gone to Darwin with a cousin of Dad's, Uncle Burro Hunter. He told Dickie, 'You're coming up to Darwin with me and you're going to mix with the young people.' Dickie was quite excited about the move to Darwin and Uncle Burro encouraged him to make friends and enjoy life. While he was there he had surgery on his crippled hands at East Arm, a hospital that specialised in surgery on leprosy patients. It was while he was there that he was involved in the car accident that ended his life.

Dickie had gone to Katherine for the weekend with some friends. They decided to go swimming at the river and were on their way back to town when they failed to take a bend. Dad's sister Aunty Peggy, who was living in Darwin at the time, rang to give them the tragic news.

Grandad, Iris and my parents were sitting outside

having a cup of tea when the phone rang and Dad got up to answer it. The look on Dad's face after receiving the call was enough to tell Mum something tragic had happened. Dickie was the only one of the four passengers to be killed.

Mum was totally devastated when Dickie died and Dad feared she might have the nervous breakdown that had threatened her health after Greg's death. We were all shattered by the loss of our brother and concerned with how Mum would hold up. Only Iris, Cherie and I were at home so my parents had to contact the rest of the family who were spread across the state to give them the bad news. The following day a steady stream of family and friends visited my parents to sympathise with them the loss of their son.

The blow of losing Dickie was eased the following year when Shaun came into their life. Shaun was Dickie's son, though we did not know about him until after Dickie's death. He was about eighteen months old when they got him. He had been living with his mother at Mowanjum and Doodie and Geoff went out and got him.

Shortly after that, Heather came home one afternoon to find Mum bathing Shaun in the back trough and said, 'Who is this?' and Mum said, 'It's your nephew Shaun.' Needless to say Heather was a bit taken by surprise. Although he never replaced Dickie, his presence seemed to ease the immense pain that was tearing away at Mum and Dad's hearts.

> Laurelle: *Dickie was really popular with the people at Bungarun and East Arm so when he died they were devastated. They used to rely on him to fix their cars and anything mechanical they had. After Dickie's death, when I got his stuff, I found this letter that he'd written to us*

but didn't post. He was just writing to us before he died, he didn't know he was going to die. He told us about this son that he had and how he was planning to send for Shaun so he could give him a better life. Anyhow I went to see Dr Spargo who confirmed what Dickie said. Spargo made all the arrangements between Shaun's mother and us so we could adopt him. His mother knew he'd be better off with us and everything worked out okay. He started school at Derby, then he went to school at Exmouth when we moved there.

I remember it was difficult getting him to wear his uniform to school. I'd send him off dressed in school uniform and shoes and he'd sneak back home and change into these old red shorts and basketball singlet. One day the principal sent for us and Doug made some excuse so I had to go up to the school only to find Shaun in the principal's office dressed in these old red shorts and I said, 'Why are you dressed like that?' and the principal said, 'That's how he comes to school all the time.' The principal made me feel as if I didn't take proper care of him so I said, 'I certainly don't send him dressed like that.' The principal had a chat to him about his dress and things improved.

Mum and Dad had Dickie's funeral in Darwin, as his plans had been to settle there after he had surgery on his hands. Dickie had been confident he could find work and raise Shaun in Darwin. They wanted to respect his wish and decided to bury him in the place he planned to call home.

17

Some Big Moves

In 1978 Mum and Dad decided to move to Exmouth. Dad had been offered a transfer to Exmouth as the District Officer with the Public Works Department.

He had been working with them since 1959 and the years of hard work had paid off as he had made his way to a senior position within the department. The accomplishment may seem unimportant to most people; however, for Dad it was not easy. Competing in the mainstream with an education that stopped at third grade was difficult enough, without the racism that reared its ugly head now and then. In spite of this Dad rose above these barriers and become a District Officer at a time when Aboriginal people were mainly employed as labourers. He was also a Justice of the Peace and a voluntary parole officer for the Ministry of Justice.

Often his job took him away from home as he supervised construction of the Wyndham and Broome jetties and the land-backed berthing facility in Port Hedland. He was a key person in the building of the Derby jetty and responsible for pile driving during its construction. We were proud of Dad and the level he had risen to in the department.

The younger children were now away at school in Geraldton and although Jimmy was living with them he was well into an apprenticeship in carpentry with a local businessman. When they moved he came to live with us in Archer Street. Shaun was at school and, like most children that age, exploring the intricacies of an educational institution that would rule his life for the next ten years. Shaun fitted neatly into the family, as he was the same age as his cousins. He often spent time with Iris, myself or down south with Mary. He was not short of homes and seemed like just another kid around the place.

Mum wasn't keen on the move; it meant a shift away from her family. I don't think she wanted to leave Grandad, Uncle Alfie and the grandchildren. I did not want to see them go but knew the move would be good for them.

Just before they moved to Exmouth Mum was working for Uncle Alwyn. He had bought Graysmark's shop, where the Assembly of God Church is now, and ran it as a Fish and Chip business. Mum cooked for him in the evenings and although she missed her friends at the hospital she preferred the social interaction to the busy demands of the hospital. As my parents were planning on moving, Uncle Alfie moved to the shop with a friend to caretake. He hadn't married and was starting to take to alcohol. Mum and Grandad were very concerned about his drinking habits but as he was an adult there was very little they could do except advise him to drink in the safety of his own home.

Grandad moved his caravan to Uncle Alwyn's and Aunty Tilly's place, a few blocks down in Delawarr Street. He was happy to stay home and look after the house during the day while they worked at the shop. His mornings were spent pottering around the garden and in the afternoon after his nap he socialised with the steady stream of visitors who came to see him. They included workmates and friends from Koolan and Cockatoo, family and even adults he knew as children at Byford Home. His friends from Mowanjum often visited, popping in to say hello and have a chat. It was a common sight to see Father Lorenz's Falcon utility parked at the front while he sat on the verandah having a yarn over a cuppa with Grandad. Added to this was the constant stream of great-grandchildren who visited him knowing he always had some fruit, biscuits or cake to satisfy the hunger pains that surfaced after school.

Grandad shopped at Reid's Drapery in Clarendon Street and one day he went there to do his usual shopping and found ten dollars up against the fence. Being the honest person he was he went inside and handed the money to the owner, Mr Reid, saying, 'I found this money outside your shop. Can you find out who owns it and give it to them.' Mr Reid explained that it was almost impossible saying, 'Keep the money, Alfred. You deserve it, you found it. Others wouldn't be as thoughtful as you.' Thinking nothing of it Grandad bought a couple of pillowslips and a lottery ticket. He did not put his name on the ticket and when an announcement was made over the air that an unnamed ticket sold by Reid had won a large sum in the lotteries he thought to himself, 'Gee! I've got an unnamed ticket.' Sure enough, he'd won a nice sum of thirty thousand dollars to help with his retirement. It took several days to get the beaming smile off Grandad's face.

It was while Mum was living in Exmouth that Grandad

received a phone call from a member of his family from Queensland. She was in Darwin for a conference and her name was Jeanie Jimmy. She met another Derby person at the meeting. One thing led to another and Jeanie was able to get Grandad's phone number and gave him a ring. They spoke for a short time before they were cut off during their conversation, leaving Grandad completely distraught. He sat by the phone for hours waiting for a return call that did not happen. He was on the verge of tears when he reported the incident to Mum. That was his only contact with his people since he left in 1926.

LIFE IN EXMOUTH

Initially Mum found it difficult to settle into Exmouth. Suddenly she found herself alone at home during the day for the first time in decades. Shaun was still with them, and Cherie and David, who were schooling in Geraldton, visited during the school holidays.

> Shaun: *At school you mixed with Americans, New Zealanders, Filipinos, Negroes and children from other races. Every day the children would assemble under the pavilion and the prefects would raise the American and Australian flags, then we would sing the American and Australian anthems. In the afternoon the prefects would take the flags down and were expected to fold them in a special way otherwise they would have to redo it. In this way Exmouth was different to other schools. I didn't enjoy it much and preferred being out of school where I wasn't picked on and had my friends to mix with.*

For the first time since her mother died in 1937, Mum had a lot of free time on her hands so she applied for a position as a domestic at the hospital. The management knew she had a flawless work record in Derby and she had no problems securing work. Once again she found herself cooking in a hospital, and worked there for five years, during which time she made many friends.

Dad was frequently away working at Onslow and Carnarvon. The towns came under his jurisdiction and he visited Onslow fortnightly to oversee the management of the department. Visits to Carnarvon occurred monthly to attend meetings and to discuss general administrative issues with the engineers and other colleagues.

But, in Exmouth, Mum and Dad still found time for their favourite leisure-time activity.

> Laurelle: *We went fishing this day, just Doug and I. We carried our fishing gear and water down to the edge. The beach ran down, then there was a reef that you could fish off. I threw my line in and away it went and I pulled in this big snapper, then Doug pulled in another. Doug said, 'I better start cleaning these fish, so we can go home.' We had to go home because we didn't have an esky to keep the fish in. That day we got nine big snappers within about an hour, then we came home. That was the best day's fishing I can remember at Exmouth.*

They lived at Carr Way, then moved to Nimitz Street. It was great having my parents in Exmouth as it gave us a place to visit during the school holidays. It was a good family place for the kids to spend their holidays. I don't know who missed whom the most, them missing the family or the family missing them.

Geoff and I often sent our son Vernon to visit them. His

birthday was on the 4 July and he looked forward to the celebrations hosted by the Americans from the military base at Exmouth commemorating Independence Day. Being his birthday, he thought they were putting the celebrations and fireworks on especially for him. It was a huge let down many years later when he discovered the real reason for the festivities.

By now Mum and Dad had over fifteen grandchildren and Grandad had around twenty-eight great-grandchildren. They were very proud of their record.

Zina Howieson (friend of Laurelle's): *I can't remember the year Doug and Laurelle came to Exmouth to work and live but it was wonderful for me as it was like having family there. Laurelle is the sister of a very dear and close friend of mine of years ago, Ivy. I had met Laurelle briefly in 1959 when Ivy introduced us.*

The main character in this relationship was Alf Brown, Laurelle and Ivy's Dad. I met Alf in my Cockatoo Island days. Alf introduced me to Ivy and over the years our friendship grew from there. Laurelle became a good friend and we shared many friends and lots of jokes. She has a wonderful sense of humour, would tell a story or a joke and crack up before the punch line. We laughed a lot, it didn't take much to make Laurelle laugh and it took a lot to make her mad. She is a wonderful person, very close to her family and adores her kids and was very proud of them.

Laurelle was the cook at Exmouth hospital and was and still is (I hope) one of the best cooks I've ever met. No one can roast a chook like Laurelle. Between her job and running a home, Laurelle put on some lovely feasts. We had many memorable meals at the D'Antoines' residence. Not meals — banquets! I just hope Laurelle thinks kindly of the miserable barbecues I used to put on. Laurelle's attributes didn't stop at cooking, she was a wonderful dressmaker and made lots of clothes for her family, especially the grandchildren. And as for fishing, Laurelle was magic, she never came home empty-handed. One day she caught eight cobia in about half an hour. We were always in her shadow and rarely caught anything. Being the good-natured person she was, we'd always get a feed from her catch.

I think Laurelle enjoyed Exmouth, she never had any culture problems, well she never told me if she did and I think I would have sensed it. It was a wonderful experience having Laurelle and her family in Exmouth with us and I was sad when the D'Antoines moved back to Derby. Much has happened since those days at Exmouth, but I will never forget Laurelle. She was a friend and confidante.

In 1979 Uncle Alfie died in Derby aged forty-five. He had been ill for several years suffering from cirrhosis of the liver. Mum was pretty cut up but powerless to help Uncle Alfie, seeing he was reluctant to acknowledge he had a problem with alcohol. Grandad took it badly; Yogi was the first of his children to go. He knew his son was very ill but the reality of seeing his son go before him hurt badly.

Laurelle: *I had to fly to Derby for the funeral. Dad was pretty cut up and I think he blamed himself for Alfie's death. Dad used to growl at him for drinking and I'd say to Dad, 'You're not achieving anything. He's a grown man. Let him have his beer, just get someone to bring it home for him so he doesn't have to drive.' When we were at the graveside Dad was sitting on a fold-up chair near the coffin. He wanted to get up and kiss the coffin. I guess that was his way of showing he still cared for Alfie. Dad felt he'd also let Mum down because he couldn't help Alfie deal with his drink. He kept saying to me, 'I'm glad you came.' I had to get back to Exmouth and I knew Tilly would take care of Dad.*

Shortly after Mum returned to Exmouth she received the devastating news that Grandad had cancer of the spine. Aunty Tilly rang and told her that when he got these back pains it would set his heart off so she went to the doctor to find out the cause and was told he had a slow growing cancer in the spine.

After Grandad was diagnosed Father Lorenz visited him in hospital and found him almost crying. Father Lorenz said, 'What's the matter?' Grandad replied, 'I've got cancer.' Father said, 'Well, let's go over and do something about it.' Following this, Father held a special mass and administered the Sacrament of the Sick to Grandad in front of his family. Father said the mass in such a way the sadness was taken away from the occasion. I thought it was a touching ceremony and a way for the family to come to terms with Grandad's illness in a positive way.

Retirement

In 1985 Dad retired from the Public Works Department, aged sixty-three. My parents flew to Perth for a formal ceremony organised by the department for eight employees retiring at the same time. Dad received a silver tray as a retirement gift from the department.

The local member of Parliament, Tom Stephens, an

acquaintance of my parents, contacted Dad and asked if he was interested in caretaking Cape Leveque. He knew Dad was retiring and would keep the place well maintained until a decision was made regarding the future of the lighthouse. It was an isolated lighthouse approximately one hundred and eighty kilometres north of Broome and, being fully automatic, needed very little maintenance. The airstrip was operational in case of emergencies. The army had expressed an interest in Cape Leveque but that did not amount to anything. One Arm Point was not very far so my parents could visit Dad's extended family in the community there.

Doug D'Antoine receiving a presentation on his retirement, 1985.
(Courtesy Laurelle D'Antoine.)

> Laurelle: *The funny thing about it was when we went up to One Arm Point for a holiday Doug's family were talking about the future of Cape Leveque. I said to Doug, 'Why don't we put in for the caretaker's job there.' Doug said, 'We can try.' When we got back to Exmouth Tom Stephens got in touch with Doug and asked him to caretake the lighthouse, so that was how we came to caretake Cape Leveque. Anyhow we packed up and towed our boat up to Leveque. On the way we had to leave our dinghy at Beagle Bay because of car problems. We finally got there and the feeling of seeing the old lighthouse was*

so strong for both of us, it was like we were back in our own country, coming home. Doug was on the verge of tears and I wasn't much different. This was where he was born and grew up. He knew every creek and bush fruit in the area.

The decision to give Cape Leveque back to the Aboriginal people took some time to make. It gave Laurelle and Doug time to think about their next move. The logical step was to go to One Arm Point. The community needed people of their own kind with administration skills and experience. Doug could help with the management of the community and Mum could go fishing when the tides were right. Dad's mother, Granny Goodji, had died but his brother Charlie was living there. Dad's people were pleased he decided to become involved in the politics of the community and promised him their support.

18

Grandad Passes On

In September 1986 Grandad died. Mum was out fishing with Uncle Tony and Aunty Gypsy when Dad met them at the boat ramp as they were coming in. He greeted her saying, 'I've got some bad news for you. Your father died.' Doug had been worried how to break the news to her. She was so close to her father and it seemed there was no other way than to be straight to the point.

Although Grandad had been diagnosed as having cancer of the spine, it was almost as if he had recovered from it. He never had the usual chemotherapy that most cancer patients undergo and didn't take any medication. Apart from using a walking cane there was little indication that he was sick. The pains and ailments he experienced seemed more to do with old age. Occasionally he complained of back pains, but nothing serious, and we thought he had a few years in him yet and would always be around.

Uncle Alwyn and Aunty Tilly took him to hospital the night before. They were working for the Main Roads Department as cooks, at a camp in Broome. Aunty Tilly said to Uncle Alwyn, 'Well, you better stay here. I'll go and set up camp and come straight back and let someone else do the cooking.' And Uncle Alwyn said, 'Well, what can I do because Dad's in hospital? It will be better if I went and helped you and we can be back quicker.'

That night Grandad's health was stable and the family thought it was another passing stage in hospital. Aunty Tilly and Uncle Alwyn never made it back to the MRD camp that day because Grandad died the next day.

Annette O'Connor (Alfred's granddaughter; Alwyn and Tilly's daughter): *He was still living in the house by himself and he'd say to me, 'When you go past in the morning, check to see if the door's open. If the door's not open come and check me.' I'd drive past every morning, check the door and make sure it was open, then I'd keep going to school and come back in the afternoon.*

The night before he went into hospital he was around home having tea. It was my daughter Catie's birthday and she wanted to have her party with the old people. Grandad was supposed to be going to Perth and Aunty Theresa was planning on going to Beagle Bay so Catie decided to spend her birthday with them. Grandad was in high spirits, laughing and joking, so when we heard the news the next morning that he was in hospital I thought he'd be out soon.

Grandad was independent right up until he died, living by himself, cooking, cleaning and gardening. The only time he used a wheelchair was many years before when we had the mass where he received the Sacrament of the Sick and that was only because Jock wheeled him across from the hospital.

Grandad's funeral was huge, an indication of the respect he had both in and out of Derby. It was the largest funeral that year as friends and family came from as far south as Perth and north from Darwin. Sympathy cards and phone calls came from around Australia. Mum was contacted by many of Grandad's work mates from Koolan Island who wanted to share with her the great times they had with him. They all thought he was very special and a credit to his family.

The last time I saw Grandad was at the viewing held at Aunty Tilly's place. He looked aloof and at peace. A requiem mass was said by his mate and long time friend, Father Lorenz, who fittingly recalled the characteristics that made Grandad so unique. It was a good day and his children laid him to rest in the Catholic section of the Derby cemetery.

> Laurelle: *I initially felt anger at Dad's death. I reckon he had no right to leave us behind. Doug warned me he was ailing but I was used to him being there for us, he was always there to give us advice, he supported us, it seemed like he would always be there. I guess I didn't want to believe he was getting old. Then I realised that he was old and sick and that it was time for him to go. I was close to my father in my own way, and so were my brothers and sisters. He didn't seem to show any emotion but we knew he cared for us. He always remembered our birthdays and Christmas and never remarried because our needs came before his own. I tell you what, I never back answered him, never in my life, because I knew whatever he told us, it was for our own good. I would never have wanted another father. He was both a mother and father for us.*

After Grandad died his Queensland family contacted Aunty Edie in Perth through an advertisement placed in the *West Australian*.

Laurelle: *Just after Dad died there was this article in the paper about him. Alwyn came up to my place. I was living in Barnett Way in Derby and he said, 'Have you seen this? Beryl Ah Chee showed me this.' He handed me this clipping and it was seeking the whereabouts of Alfred Brown, last known to be working in Broome. It gave a contact number. Anyhow I'm not sure whether he brought it to my sister Edie's attention or whether she saw the advertisement herself but she followed it up and rang the phone number given in the paper. A chap answered the phone and Edie said, 'I understand you are trying to contact Alfred Brown. He's my father.' The chap passed her onto his wife Ellen Breyze who was trying to make the contact. Ellen is Edie's niece. At first Ellen seemed scared, I guess she didn't know what to expect and felt frightened. Anyhow they got talking and were really pleased to make the contact. Edie invited Ellen over to her home to meet the family. I think my sister Kathy went up from Bunbury to meet her, along with Joey, Donella, Neville and Edie's own kids and their family. That's how we made the contact through an advertisement in the paper. They were all happy they met each other and spent hours talking about the family.*

Mum was emotional about making contact with her family in Queensland. It seemed to bring her a step closer to Grandad's past that had remained a mystery as he shut the door on it. He only told her what he wanted her to know and was very selective in the information he provided. The reunion meant a lot to her and she discussed it with Aunty Kathy and other members of the family including myself.

19

Djarworrada

David Mowaljarlie used to always come home to see me. We'd talk a lot about Kunmunya and the old people. He'd come and have a cup of tea or a meal or a yarn with Doug. Then he'd disappear for a couple of weeks then you'd hear this knock on the front door and there would be David. We'd say, 'Where have you been?' He'd tell us he'd been overseas to Germany or to Paris or to other places to promote Mowanjum and get money for his people. Much of David's time was spent with anthropologists, land councils and overseas, dealing with cultural issues. When he was broke I'd feed him and say, 'Have you got any tucker in the house?' and he'd say 'Little bit mangari, food,' so I'd send him home with meat, fish and whatever I had in the house. I'd never give him money. When I was in Exmouth and came back to Derby he told me to put in for some land. He used to talk about land and how concerned he was about his people. Sometimes he'd come home very depressed and he'd say, 'You know sister (he called me sister), I don't think we'll get our land, not in my time, not in your time.'

With a good education David could have been another

Nelson Mandela. He was always trying to do things for his people in the best possible way he knew.

Laurelle

At the end of 1986 my parents moved back to Derby. Living at One Arm Point did not turn out as Dad hoped. The support was not forthcoming and Dad became disenchanted with the management and operation of the community so they decided to return to Derby. They lived in a rented flat before buying a house in Knowsley Street.

It was the first house they could afford to purchase themselves. Built in the sixties, it was an average sized house by Derby standards with overgrown bougainvilleas gracing the front fence and a huge back yard. It badly needed internal and external maintenance; however, what it lacked in appearance it made up for in personality. It did not take long for the house to take on the usual family atmosphere, with dogs, people, babies, cups of tea and plenty of noise. The house hosted numerous parties and a fight or two.

Dad pottered around the house mending things that had seen better days, but avoided any major renovation jobs that looked like taking him and Mum away from their beloved Saturday afternoon football or interfere with the good tides that meant fishing.

Mum became involved with the Catholic parish when she returned to Derby. Each week, usually on Sunday morning, Dad drove her to church, picking her up after mass. Although we were Catholics none of us was practising the faith so Mum went to church alone. Later Mum joined the choir and on the odd occasion I went to church I witnessed the depth of her faith and the ease with which she embraced it.

Four generations of Laurelle D'Antoine's family: Veronica Bamford, granddaughter (standing), Mary Cowley, daughter, Carly Hedlam, great granddaughter, and Laurelle, c. 1990.

By now my parents had eighteen grandchildren. They still had Shaun but he was living with Mary and going to school in Geraldton. We were spread out over four places. Doodie was driving heavy machinery for Leightons throughout the north-west and happily married. Mary was in Geraldton with her four children and embarking on a career with the Aboriginal Affairs Department. Iris was living on the corner of Delawarr and Heytesbury Street with her husband Rocky Prouse. She was working for Community Health and had five children. Neville was living in Perth with his wife Dale, and two sons, having just completed tertiary qualifications in cartography. Andre had become an enrolled nurse and was living in Broome with her partner Peter Cairns and baby named Courtney. David had finished an apprenticeship as an auto electrician and Jimmy had finished one as a carpenter and was working in Derby. That left Cherie, who was finishing her teaching degree in Queensland.

I had two sons of my own, Linton and Vernon, and was living in Derby. My husband Geoff was working for the Main Roads Department in administration and doing very well for himself. Our oldest son Linton was going to Mazenod, a boarding school in Lesmurdie.

In 1982 I took up the challenge and enrolled in an external teaching course coordinated by Holy Rosary School in Derby through Signadou College in Canberra. In 1986 I had just finished my teaching diploma and was working at the Holy Rosary School teaching an upper primary class.

Looking back, my parents had done a pretty successful job of raising us; we had all fared pretty well.

BACK TO MUM'S COUNTRY

Thinking back, Djarworrada became part of our lives, and the lives of those connected with us, when we made an effort to make Mum's dream become a reality. In 1991 Mum started an Aboriginal community and called it Djarworrada. I think it was her way of taking us back to her country where she was born and sharing it with us.

It is fair to say that initially my brother and sisters and their spouses were prepared to give the Djarworrada concept a go. We were all involved at various levels, depending on our locality and current commitment to our nuclear family and jobs. Mum certainly had the skills in her family to make her dream a reality. That it never came to fruition was due to differing family opinions on the direction for the community and the organisational politics she had to deal with. Above all the biggest barrier was its remoteness; it was accessible only by sea.

By the 1980s a massive demographic shift of Aboriginal people back to their traditional land was well underway in the Kimberley. Missions, stations and government settlements were handed over to the Aboriginal people. Both state and commonwealth governments ventured into programs to assist Aboriginal people to return to their traditional land. This was all done in the name of self-determination, a buzz word on the lips of politicians. Both governments also embarked on programs designed to improve the social disadvantage faced by Aboriginal people.

In 1989 the Aboriginal and Torres Strait Islander Commission was established, a Commonwealth initiative to assist Aboriginal people in their efforts to establish an economic base that would ultimately lead to economic independence and self-determination. In theory the concept was very good and well-meaning. In essence the notion of self-determination was about giving Aboriginal people the freedom to identify their needs, plan programs to address those needs, manage them and take responsibility for their outcomes. This means deciding and acting on priorities, but conflict arises over whose priorities they are. Outstations formed by family groups started to appear and by the mid 1990s there were over thirty Aboriginal settlements on the Dampier peninsula ranging in status from established communities to outstations and excisions on Aboriginal reserves.

Talking to David Mowaljarlie about land and seeing other Aboriginal people developing their own communities inspired Mum. Several years prior to this Geoff and I had encouraged Dad to get some land on the Dampier peninsula but he was reluctant. Others were not so reticent.

With a place in mind to develop her own Aboriginal community Mum approached the Mowanjum people for support. Eddy Bear was the chairperson at Mowanjum then. Mum felt nervous about asking them for help but she had no cause for concern. In true Aboriginal style the old people at Mowanjum showed their pleasure at her request and said, 'Well it's all right, you're Worrorra.'

Laurie Uttemorrah, a supportive council member said, 'It's about time you came to see us for help.' She was born there, grew up with them and still maintained her links with them and was accepted by them. They gave their support to assist her.

Shortly after her visit to Mowanjum, Mum lodged an application with the Aboriginal and Torres Strait Islander Commission to start the community. The terms outlined by the ATSIC Act were fulfilled, and the community was incorporated with a membership mainly comprising the family. Mum was the founding member and she named the community Djarworrada, a Worrorra name meaning, *spill over*.

> Laurelle: *A chap from ATSIC filled in all the forms and David Mowaljarlie was there making sure it was done correctly. When we got our certificate back, my daughter Mary set up things so we could become a community. I didn't know what to do. I did not understand some of the things you had to do. She went into ATSIC and did everything.*

The location chosen for Djarworrada was Camden Harbour, which coincidentally is very close to the site of a failed white settler expedition from Victoria in 1864. Kunmunya was already in the hands of Harry Shadforth, Mum's cousin, so the next best place was Camden, which had a harbour for safe anchorage and protection from cyclones. It had potential for a fishing and tourist industry with an old airstrip which could be renovated and used. With support from the government and family, Mum felt the concept of developing an Aboriginal community would work, given the skills among the family.

THE CAMDEN TRIP

In October 1991 a team of seven members of Djarworrada Aboriginal Corporation set out overland for Camden Harbour through some of the most rugged and remote country in the Kimberley.

The seven members included Alwyn Scott, Don Cowley, Peter Cairns, Jimmy Greatorex, William Prouse, Doodie D'Antoine and his wife Margie. In addition there was Ernie Hunter and Sam Lovell and an old family friend Garloo. He had grown up in the area; it was his birth place and he knew it well.

Mum wanted the location surveyed and the area assessed in order to start the community. The team needed to examine the possibility of constructing a road into Camden and check the natural sea landing and the state of the airstrip. Potential water sources had to be found and the fertility of the soil determined. Lastly they had to locate a suitable place to build the community. I remember Mum being excited and pretty confident the overland trip would be successful.

> Laurelle: *The trip meant we were getting somewhere and I was quite excited. ATSIC was supposed to go out but they declined at the last minute. There were a lot of bets taken that they would not get there. Everybody that had radios were keeping track on them. Timmy Hogan radioed them every night and let us know how they were. David Mowaljarlie said to me, 'They can get there, give them time.' He was right, they did.*

The team of ten people set out on 21 October and travelled in four Toyotas. Their first camp was on the

Calder River after passing through Beverley Springs and across the Isdell and Charnley rivers. They had covered four hundred and seventy kilometres that day and as the road was starting to deteriorate along with daylight they decided to call it quits. That night, and each night of the trip, they made radio contact with Timmy Hogan in Derby. He was the contact person who relayed messages to Laurelle. The following morning they drove for just over an hour then arrived at an Aboriginal community called Pantijan.

Doodie used the Pantijan community's tractor to make a crossing between two massive paperbark trees where the track had virtually disappeared. They were forced to pick their way along the old camel track and covered forty-four kilometres that day. It took them seven more days to reach their destination. The old camel track started to disappear so they had to push their way through the vegetation. Sam Lovell often walked ahead for hours trying to find the best possible route. At times they were forced to burn their way through and frequently spent hours moving rocks and boulders by hand, only to drive a few metres. They used chainsaws and car winches to cut a road through. At times like this they averaged roughly nineteen kilometres a day through thick vegetation and creek crossings that tested their road building skills.

The journey was not without its fair share of staked tyres, leaking radiators, near roll-overs and frayed tempers. Eight days into the trip Doodie, Margie, Jimmy, Don and William were forced to turn back due to mounting vehicle trouble, leaving two vehicles and five people to continue on to Camden. Those continuing on made their way across the Glenelg River before going around Mount Trevor and finally reaching Camden

Harbour on 29 October, dishevelled and exhausted but overcome with an immense sense of achievement.

Along the way they had stumbled over rusty old chains belonging to a set of harnesses probably used on camels. Closer to their destination they came across an old boab tree with faded names virtually undecipherable and a drawing of a very old sailing ship, raising the possibility that these were made by members of the Camden Expedition that came from Melbourne in 1864. At Camden they saw the remnants of the Second World War airstrip and at Sheep Island they saw the lonely grave of Mary Pascoe, a pioneer on the 1864 expedition. This is the grave Laurelle and her cousin Amy used to visit and decorate as children.

After carrying out the necessary assessments they returned to Derby on 3 November. It was only the exemplary bush skills of Sam Lovell and Garloo's knowledge of the area that allowed them to reach Camden. Their knowledge and understanding of the bush was so sharp and comprehensive they were able to drive through harsh rocky country that was virtually trackless after Pantijan. Every time they came to a dead end or creek crossing that seemed insurmountable Sam picked a way through thick vegetation, pointing them in the right direction with his impeccable bush skills. Garloo recognised hills, ridges and other geographic landmarks

Camden Harbour, 1991.
(Courtesy Ernie Hunter.)

that jolted his memory. It had been about sixty years since he had roamed the country as a young lad. Between the two of them they kept the expedition going.

Camden proved to be a suitable location but accessibility was a problem. The idea of constructing a track into the community was out of the question due to the prohibitive cost involved. Water was good, the area boasted a safe harbour and the soil seemed good. It was decided access had to be by sea. The enthusiasm of those concerned with developing Camden was infectious and the keenness was almost intoxicating. A boat had to be purchased before any on-site construction could start.

However, the demands and frustrations of running Djarworrada started to take its toll on community members. Grant applications had to be completed and quarterly audit reports done; liaison with resource agents and other administrative duties had to be carried out on a voluntary basis. Liaising with ATSIC and other resource agencies was frustrating as local interpretations of guidelines underpinning grant applications made negotiations far from clear. Often priorities for the community were different to those ATSIC saw as important. Guidelines seemed to be constantly changing and the general operational structure of state and Commonwealth departments dealing with Aboriginal politics was totally unsatisfactory. Field officers were constantly changing, making continuity almost impossible.

Mum was often advised of programs that would benefit the community only weeks before closure of grant applications. This meant working parties had to be formed at short notice, placing additional stress on all concerned. All members had full-time employment and family commitments and the extra responsibility started to take its toll. Added to this was the highly sensitive issue of land tenure. Negotiating the various conflicting interests, including those of Aboriginal organisations, pastoralists, national parks and conservationists, tourism and state and federal governments, as well as local politics, was all very stressful.

The enthusiasm fuelling Mum's dream started to wither and factionalism began to rear its ugly head among members. Starting construction at Camden seemed years away. What originally seemed straightforward and achievable was developing into a nightmare.

> Laurelle: *By this time my children used to go into ATSIC and do all the paperwork for me. I found it hard to understand things and the way the department operated, so my children would explain them for me. But then other things started to happen that worried me and I started to feel sick inside.*

Down Memory Lane

In spite of the organisational politics Mum was still determined to go ahead with Djarworrada. In 1994 she was advised to move the proposed location of the community from Camden Harbour to Hall Point. The supply of water was not as suitable and abundant as anticipated at Camden. In October 1994 Doodie took her to Hall Point on the community boat *Solitude*. The trip would take two weeks and Mum wanted to look at the area herself so community development plans could be drawn up. They decided to kill two birds with one stone and survey the reefs for bêche-de-mer and trochus shell.

It would give her some idea of their availability and the prospects of starting a fishing enterprise.

By now her grandson Shaun was an adult and he went with them on the trip. They left Derby on Wednesday 12 October at 5.45am and sailed past Mary Island just before 7.00am. The seas were calm and everything was going according to plan, even the makeshift toilet in the boat was running like a charm. Their first sight of the mainland after Mary Island was beyond Stokes Bay. After passing Long Island and Lachlan Island on a calm neap tide they sailed through Whirlpool Pass, a passage of water that can be very treacherous if the timing of the tide is not right, even at neaps. Just after noon they crossed Bullock Bay to a pearling beds site, which stretched for miles. Anchored at Gibbings Island was the mother ship for the pearling beds.

It was when they neared Cockatoo that Mum started to cast her mind back to when she was a kid on the *Watt Leggatt* with Grandad. Allowing herself to enjoy the memories she recalled when there were only two houses and one shed on the island. There was a beautiful woman called Mrs Starkie who always met them at the beach armed with lollies and treats for her brothers and sisters. Then there was George Balsom, Maurie Donovan and a chap called Bluey who worked there and several others as well, but she couldn't remember them. At mid-afternoon they stopped at Koolan and tied up to the *Val-Elle*, a tug already anchored there. After having a shower on the *Val-Elle* Mum had stew, chops and rice for tea then turned in, leaving the boys to chat the night away.

During their trip they searched for bêche-de-mer and trochus at Augustus Island, Capstain, Perseverance, Champagny Island and several other spots, finding very little, as the tide was far too high. The presence of the sea slug gave Laurelle an idea of the feasibility of processing it. At one spot a large crocodile made its presence known, so obeying their instincts they left the bêche-de-mer and trochus untouched.

Going through these very dangerous seas Mum wondered how her father had coped with only a fourteen horse-power Hinke kerosene motor. She also thought of the Aboriginal people at the mission who sailed in a dugout canoe with little to protect them from the waves and crocodiles. As she looked at the unforgiving sea she also spared a thought for the missionaries of Kunmunya who did it hard.

On the return trip crossing Collier Bay the weather deteriorated and started to become very threatening. They had engine trouble and Mum was worried, but the *Solitude* managed to cross safely.

The trip was very special for Mum and she still talks about it and is determined to do it again. It gave her and the other members of the community the opportunity to consider fishing as an industry for Djarworrada. It unearthed memories and a suppressed passion to return home after over fifty years. Her desire to return was frightening and in some way has robbed her of the relaxing time she could have been enjoying with Dad in their retirement.

Towards the end of the year construction started at Hall Point. The temporary shed previously erected at Camden was moved to Hall Point. Building materials were transported to the community and a very large shed was constructed. There were setbacks, however. Dealing with Aboriginal resource agencies designed to assist Aboriginal communities proved frustrating and time-consuming. Delays in starting the fishing industry that the community badly needed in order to generate an income tested the patience of several members. Not to be put off by this, Laurelle kept her hopes and spirits up and her patience and persistence helped her soldier on.

> Laurelle: *I felt quite happy about starting Djarworrada, for me it was like going home and everyone was keen to do their little bit and I thought Djarworrada would really take off. At first I was happy with the enthusiasm. I had a dream to get a fishing enterprise off the ground and prove that with funding we could do it. We could get something going for the old people so they could go home. We could have an airstrip there and a processing plant for bêche-de-mer and the money could be put back into the community. I wanted to have a place for the old people from Mowanjum, somewhere they would be happy, and if the young ones wanted to come out there, then there would always be work for them. Djarworrada would also be a place for my grandchildren and great-grandchildren.*

The concept of Djarworrada is in limbo and it appears it will not be realised in its original form. Thinking back, the expectation of a family our size and with our skills, characters and professions, working together successfully on a shared vision is almost impossible to fulfil. At some stage we all brought a little baggage with us and, given the political climate, Djarworrada was like a festering boil just waiting to surface. Many family members have moved and for me it has been a lesson that life is too short for worries. My parents, especially Mum, continue to fight for its future and what they believe in and I fear it will be at the expense of their health and what little money they have. The future of Djarworrada is in the lap of the gods.

In April 1996 Mum and Dad celebrated their fiftieth wedding anniversary with over forty family and friends at Whiteman Park in Perth. From all accounts, it was a thoroughly enjoyable and memorable occasion. During their fifty years of marriage they raised twelve children and two grandchildren, giving them a stable and caring home environment and the best possible education they could afford. They have twenty-two healthy grandchildren and over fifteen great-grandchildren. Their family is very important and they enjoy nothing better than having them visit, especially the little ones who affectionately refer to them as Numpa and Greatgran. They see themselves as fortunate parents responsible for the upbringing of three healthy generations. Given their track record they are on course to see great-great-grandchildren.

Laurelle and Doug D'Antoine, Derby, 1993.
(Courtesy Geoff Wright.)

In February 1999 Mum turned seventy. A surprise party was held for her at Pandanus Park, which Cherie and her partner Ernie Hunter were managing at the time. On the morning of the event, Dad took her out to the park saying, 'Come on, Laurelle, let's go to the park for a drive.' He'd been given strict instructions by his daughters that it was his responsibility to drive her to the park without her suspecting anything. Naturally she thought they were going to a meeting about Djarworrada so she didn't question his request. She was taken by surprise when she arrived and discovered it was a party in her honour and not a meeting. Friends and family embraced her as she walked in and together we celebrated her birthday. We were all there to share the day with her and I think it was the last time we made the effort to be together for her.

20

Going the Full Circle

When I went to Weipa to represent Mum I met a lot of family. They knew her family existed but didn't know where we were. One of the things I found very interesting was there was no animosity, or didn't appear to be any, just acceptance. One of the old ladies made a comment that a lot of the people are coming home. I don't know what other Stolen Generation people had returned to Mapoon but it was an interesting comment. There were a number of people who went out of their way and came looking for me to tell me how they were related to me. It was quite incredible, quite overpowering that these people wanted to meet me.

Neville D'Antoine

After Aunty Edie had made contact with the family in Queensland I thought it would be good for Mum to go and meet them. Iris had met them on a recent conference held in Cairns and she experienced an overwhelming acceptance and eagerness to learn about us.

After talking to Iris about her trip I knew it was

important for Mum to meet her family while her health was good. I raised the subject with her and we decided to aim for April 2000 to go there. I was nearing the completion of writing Mum's biography and was intrigued to meet our Queensland family and share it with them. The trip was deferred to July, as I was now principal at Wangkatjungka School and finding it difficult to organise the trip.

> Laurelle: *When Iris went to Cairns they were overjoyed by her visit. They piled Iris up with photos and an open invitation to come back with all the relations. Then I decided it was time to go and see them.*

During the school holidays in July, Mum and I flew to Cairns to meet the family. I was curious about what the trip would hold for both of us. We were met by Florrie Uiduldam, my cousin. Through tears and hugs Florrie said to Mum, 'Aunty, I recognised you straight away when you were coming down the steps. You have that same look as Mum.'

It was an emotional time for Mum, catching up with so many members of the family at once for the first time. So many years had passed since her parents had left for Kunmunya in 1926. When she met her cousin Waiu Uiduldam the tears came, then they sat quietly holding each other's hand, savouring the special moment for them both and deeply appreciative of the opportunity to be together.

Mum quietly said, 'We didn't know we had cousins here. Dad didn't talk much about his family. Then when Mum died he was busy with work and raising us kids. We knew he had a sister called Jane. But he didn't tell us much more. It wasn't until my sister Edith made contact and met Ellen that we learnt he had a sister called Kitty, who had a big family.'

Waiu replied, 'Mum [Kitty] always spoke about her brother Alfred and she called her oldest son after him. We knew we had an Uncle Alfred but we didn't know what he looked like. They both grew up in Mapoon Mission. Mum was a dormitory girl before she married at nineteen. It was an arranged marriage to a Badu man. Then they moved to Badu Island where we were all born. Mum had a big family and we all grew up there. It was a hard life. Not much education and hospital, living in poor housing. Then in 1972 we moved to Cairns, by then all the kids were grown up and we moved here for jobs. In 1978 Mum died here in Cairns.'

Laurelle sat quietly thinking about what Waiu said before commenting, 'It's a pity Dad didn't know Aunty Kitty was in Cairns because when he retired from BHP they gave him a trip around Australia and he called in to Cairns. I'm sure this was before 1978 and if he knew Aunty Kitty and the family were here he would have made every effort to meet her.'

Together they spent hours catching up on each other's lives before the conversation moved to their dreams and hopes for their family. Laurelle said, 'I'm trying to get a community going so we can go back to my land. It's called Djarworrada and is near the mission where we grew up as kids and where Dad worked for nearly sixteen years. That's when him and Mum were sent to Kunmunya. Dad had to drive the mission lugger the *Watt Leggatt* and Mum taught in the kindergarten. That's before Mum died in 1937. I feel I want to go home and make a place where the young kids can work so they are not drifting all the time. It is very difficult because the government say one thing and do another. It's very hard.'

Waiu thought for a while then said, 'You know, Laurelle, we want to do the same thing, but the Land Council here are stopping us. We are trying to get land in Mapoon where Mum grew up but the lawyers are saying we do not have any solid evidence to prove Mum grew up in Mapoon. They are saying she was not taken there but we know she was there with Uncle Alfred and Aunty Jane. The lawyers say we have to get more evidence to prove she grew up there.'

Laurelle's replied, 'I know how you feel. I'm tired of government departments making it hard for people like you and me. They keep changing the rules. We have been trying for over six years to get occupancy at Djarworrada but they keep fobbing us off. No one really wants to help us.'

Over the following week we met countless members of the family. People who had links with Mapoon went out of their way to meet us, especially Mum. A young chap who grew up in Mapoon came to meet her saying, 'I know all about your parents, my grandmother Mabel Butta was great mates with your mother, they worked together in the kindergarten.' He left Mum with a photograph of them taken at the mission just before she left for Kunmunya. Mum was stoked, as it was the only clear photo she has of her mother. Another chap said, 'Next time you come back you let me know and I'll take you to Mapoon.'

Just before we left to return to Derby Florrie pulled Mum aside and said, 'You know, Aunty, why we put that advertisement in the paper — the one Edie saw and made contact with Ellen — Granny Kitty grew me up and I called her Mum. While we were growing up we always believed in our Torres Strait Islander culture. That's the way it was. Torres Strait culture is very strong in our family. Mum [Kitty] was Aboriginal. She was Aboriginal and she never complained that we didn't go to any trouble with her culture, but she told us about Uncle Alfred. When she died Mum came to me in a dream and said, "You fellows always turn to your Torres Strait for your culture. You never try and find your Aboriginal culture." I can clearly see her turning her face in the dream, almost scolding me, giving me a strong message. So when Ellen went to Perth I told her to put the advertisement in the paper so we could try and find out about Uncle Alfred. That's how we found each other.'

Laurelle grabbed Florrie's hand and squeezing it tightly said, 'I'm so very happy Kitty guided you. Without her we'd still be searching for each other.'

Florrie Uiduldam informed the Cape York Land Council that Mum was the oldest surviving child of Alfred and Ina Brown. Her birthright gave recognisable status to the traditional lands of her parents. Grandad was a descendant of the Taepadhighi people. Another piece of the jigsaw was starting to fall into place with the discovery of this valuable piece of information on Grandad. But while Mum's status as a traditional owner was explicitly acknowledged when we were visiting the family, at the time it meant nothing to her. Mum was caught up in meeting her Queensland family; she wasn't seeking traditional ownership, it came looking for her.

Months after the trip to Cairns Mum received a phone call from an anthropologist handling the land claim through the Cape York Peninsula. The land claim included Mapoon and the traditional lands of her parents. Grandad was Taepadhighi and Granny was Thanakwithi. As the oldest child Mum was invited back to Queensland to represent her parents and more importantly to get to know the family.

Although the offer surprised her, she felt immense gratitude at being accepted by her Queensland family. It was very short notice so she made arrangements for my brother Neville to represent her. Neville was living in Toodyay and working in Perth for the Aboriginal Affairs Department. His knowledge of land tenure was extremely extensive and he knew the policy governing land claims. I think Mum felt it was a little out of her depth and things were moving too fast.

> Neville D'Antoine: *When I went to Weipa I attended a workshop for the Thanakwithi mob which is where Granny Ina came from. She was adopted by the Thanakwithi people through Jimmy Jimmy and I understand she was regarded as one of them. Granny's mother Georgina married Jimmy Jimmy after arriving at Mapoon and as Granny was a very small child he adopted her and grew her up. It was quite amazing the reaction I had from the people there. Once they understood where I sat within the structure as the grandson of Ina and could relate it back to themselves, there was a fair amount of acceptance of who I was. They were accepting me and calling me uncle, brother and things like that because they could identify where I sat within their family structure. That was quite different to Aunty Susie Madua who is from quite a different tribal mob who regarded Granny as Ina Shadforth, claiming her from the Shadforth side. They were very distinctive in the surname they used for her. Even then there was acceptance of who I was because they could relate to where I came from.*

Neville's trip led to a return trip to Weipa for Mum. As the oldest surviving child of Alfred and Ina she had a cultural obligation to fulfil as a traditional owner and sign an agreement. On this trip my brother David accompanied her to explain the complex entitlements of all parties involved so she had a clear understanding of the agreement. A mining company wanted to establish a trust fund with the traditional owners. Royalties would go into the trust fund to be used for educational benefits, employment and training for the indigenous people involved. This suited Mum and the traditional owners.

> Laurelle: *If I didn't go over and sign the agreement any person that could prove they were related to Mum and Dad would be entitled to royalties. This way the money goes into education and jobs and that's better. Besides most of the family are in Western Australia so the Queensland families will benefit the most and they are entitled to it more than I am. I was more pleased they accepted me and respected me as Alfred and Ina's daughter. When I went to Weipa the people accepted me with open arms. They kept saying I was a traditional owner. It wasn't something I said. There was no animosity towards me or David, just acceptance and they made an impression on me because they knew me better than I knew them. Anyhow a week later we all came back for the signing. The traditional owners agreed to the royalties going into a trust fund and asked that before any mining was done they be consulted to make sure sacred sites are protected. When we had the signing a young chap said to me, 'You go over to the tent and they will paint your hand with bauxite paint and put your hand on the tiles then sign it.' The paint seemed more like an ochre Aboriginal people use to paint themselves for corroborees.*

No sooner had Mum returned from Weipa than she and Dad were off on a plane to Cairns in April for a family reunion for the Brown family. Florrie Uiduldam was the driving force behind it. I knew of twenty-two family members from Grandad's side spread over four generations who made an enormous effort to attend. Mum and Aunty Kathy were the two children of Grandad's to go. I would like to have gone but I had work commitments and had met the family the previous year.

The Brown family reunion, Cairns, 2001.
(Courtesy Iris Prouse.)

There was a photo of Grandad and his two sisters hanging in the hall as you went in with a traditional Torres Strait lei hanging around it. The photo touched the hearts of everyone who was there that evening, especially those lucky to know him. There was traditional Torres Strait Islander dancing along with an Aboriginal corroboree to celebrate the evening. People gathered and talked and cried together. Mum spent time with Grandad's sisters on the Hudson side. They held her hand all the time and did not want the evening to end.

Florrie welcomed everyone and Iris introduced the four generations of Grandad's family and there were more tears. Mary gave a speech on behalf of Mum and the older members of Grandad's family were given the royal treatment. The food and celebration were first class and from all accounts it was an exceptional reunion. Mum felt every conversation that night brought her a little closer to learning about her father. It was difficult for Mum to say farewell but she was appreciative of the opportunity to meet them and piece together the jigsaw of Grandad's life that eluded her for so long.

The last eighteen months has been an astonishing time for Mum, re-establishing links with her family. Mum is starting to slow down and I notice she is shaking a little, walking a little slower and forgetting where she left her bag. To me she is an incredible lady who in the face of adversity was able to overcome all the hurdles of life.

Mum's remaining wishes are for her family to be happy again and to visit her mother's grave in Kunmunya.

> Laurelle: *The reunion was very touching. I wasn't the only one that thought that. All of Alfred Brown's family, Dad's family, that went over there, they found it very touching. I still have to have a bit more to do with Mum's side of the family, the Chargers and people from Aurukun. I felt happy, a feeling hard to describe. I felt as though I had come a full circle in my life, from where it had started with Mum and Dad and then going back when I had my children. My children had all grown up and I went back to see where Mum and Dad had come from. It was very heartbreaking but I was really happy that I did go there. To begin with I didn't know whether I was very happy or very sad. It was a fulfilment. I feel I can say I've gone the full circle.*

Laurelle and Doug with their children and spouses, Derby, 1993.
(Courtesy Geoff Wright.)

Bibliography

BOOKS

Biskup, P (1973), *Not Slaves, Not Citizens, The Aboriginal Problem in Western Australia 1898–1954*, St Lucia: University of Queensland Press.

Bolton, G (1981), 'Black and White man after 1887' in C T Stannage (ed), *A New History of Western Australia*, Nedlands: University of Western Australia Press, pp 124–178.

Davidson, W S (1978), *Havens of Refuge, A History of Leprosy in Western Australia*, Nedlands: University of Western Australia Press for the Public Health Department.

Dickey, B (1994), *The Dictionary of Evangelical Biography*, Sydney: Evangelical History Association.

Haebich, A (1990), *For Their Own Good*, Nedlands: University of Western Australia Press.

Haebich, A (1990), *Aborigines and the Law: An Introductory Guide to Legislation Relating to Aborigines in the Western Australian Statutes*, Perth: Western Australian Museum.

Hey, N (1923), *A Visit to Mapoon*, Sydney: Presbyterian World Mission Association.

Jacobs, P (1990), *Mister Neville*, Fremantle: Fremantle Arts Centre Press.

Kidd, R (1997), *The Way We Civilise*, St Lucia: University of Queensland Press.

Long, T (1980), 'The development of government Aboriginal

policy: the effect of administrative changes, 1829–1977', in R M and C H Berndt (eds.), (1980), *Aborigines of the West. The Past and Their Present*, Nedlands: University of Western Australia Press, revised edition, pp. 357-366.

Loos, N (1988), 'Concern and Contempt' in T Swain and Rose D Bird (eds.), (1988) *Aboriginal Australians and Christian missions: ethnographic and historical studies*. The Australian Association for the Study of Religions.

Love, J R B (1936), *Stone-Age Bushmen of Today*, London and Glasgow: Blackie and Son Ltd.

Matthews, H C (ed.) (nd), *The Aborigines Calling!: by the Missionaries on the Different Stations*, Melbourne: Presbyterian Board of Religious Education.

McKenzie, M (1969), *The Road to Mowanjum*, Melbourne: Angus and Robertson Ltd.

Mounsey, C F (1979), 'Aboriginal education: a new dawning', in R M and C H Berndt (eds.), (1980), *Aborigines of the West. Their Past and Present*, Nedlands: University of Western Australia Press, pp. 395-405.

Paton, F H L (1911), *Glimpses of Mapoon*, Melbourne: Arbuckle, Waddell and Faulkner.

The Mapoon People (1972), *The Mapoon Story*, Mapoon Book 1, Fitzroy, Victoria: International Development Action.

Schapper, H P (1970), 'Legislation and administration', in H Schapper (1970), *Aboriginal Advancement to Integration*, Canberra: Australian National University Press, pp. 11-19.

OTHER PUBLICATIONS AND REPORTS

Annual Reports of the Chief Protector for Western Australia, 1904, 1906, 1910.

'Anorexia nervosa', *Kunmunya*, Issued by the Authority of the Board of Missions of the Presbyterian Church of Australia, (nd).

Balfour, H R, 'Report and Impressions of a visit to Kunmunya', Presbyterian Church of Australia, 1936.

Presbyterian Outlook, the Organ of the Presbyterian Church of

Queensland, Vol. 4, No. 57, May 1923.

Queenslander, 16 December 1916.

Report by the Queensland Aborigines Department, 1926.

Report on Mapoon Mission Station, 1913, for the Home Secretary in Queensland.

Report on Mapoon Presbyterian Mission Station, 1910, written by Reverend Nicholas Hey, Presbyterian Church of Australia Board of Ecumenical Missions and Relations, State Library of New South Wales.

West Australian, Friday 29 March 1935.

West Australian, Saturday 30 March 1935.

West Australian, Thursday 4 April 1935.

UNPUBLISHED MATERIAL

MANUSCRIPTS

Green, N (1990), 'Government Stations / La Grange, Wallal, Moola Bulla, Violet Valley, Munja and Udialla', Kimberley History Project.

Jebb, M A (1996), 'Jayida Buru Social History Timeline'.

O'Connor, Jocelyn (nd), 'A History of Mr Alfred Brown'.

Wharton, G (1997), 'Notes on the McDonnell Electric Telegraph Station, Cape York Peninsula, Queensland'.

OFFICIAL DOCUMENTS

Annual Report 1926, Committee on Missions to the Heathen, Presbyterian Church of Queensland, Presbyterian Church of Australia Board of Ecumenical Missions and Relations, State Library of New South Wales.

Correspondence Files, Committee on Missions to the Heathen, Presbyterian Church of Queensland, February 1926, May 1926, June 1926, Presbyterian Church of Australia Board of Ecumenical Missions and Relations, State Library of New South Wales.

Kunmunya Mission Register: Births, Deaths, Baptism, with

Communion Roll, January 1920–January 1960, Presbyterian Church of Australia Board of Ecumenical Missions and Relations, State Library of New South Wales.

Kunmunya Mission Diary: November 1934 January 1939 and April 1939–December 1943, Presbyterian Church of Australia Board of Ecumenical Missions and Relations, State Library of New South Wales.

Mapoon Register: Births, Deaths, Marriages, Presbyterian Church of Australia Board of Ecumenical Missions and Relations, State Library of New South Wales.

Minutes of the Heathen Missions Committee, Presbyterian Church of Queensland, 1924–1931, Presbyterian Church of Australia Board of Ecumenical Missions and Relations, State Library of New South Wales.

Minutes of the Proceedings of the General Assembly of the Presbyterian Church of Australia, 1924–1945, Presbyterian Church of Australia Board of Ecumenical Missions and Relations, State Library of New South Wales.

Report of the Royal Commissioner on Aborigines [Moseley Report], January 1935, State Library of New South Wales.

Western Australian Native Affairs File No. 265/44 on Laurelle Andrewina Brown, Aboriginal Affairs Department.

Western Australian Native Welfare Files No. 463/27 and 268/43 on Alfred Brown, Aboriginal Affairs Department.

Western Australian Parliament Act No. 14 of 1905. An Act to make provision for the better protection and care of the Aboriginal inhabitants of Western Australia.

Western Australian Parliament Act No. 43 of 1936. An Act to amend the Aborigines Act, 1905.

DIARIES, LETTERS AND ORAL RECORDINGS

Diary of Len Young, held by Len Young.

Letters written by George Holmes to the Board of Missions, 1940, 1941, 1942, Presbyterian Church of Australia Board of Ecumenical Missions and Relations, State Library of New South Wales.

Letter written by Zina Howieson to author, 1996, held by author.

Letters written by J R B Love to the The Board of Missions, 1938, 1939, 1940, Presbyterian Church of Australia Board of Ecumenical Missions and Relations, State Library of New South Wales.

Letter from Oakes, Wes and Hazel, 1996, held by the author.

Letter written by Father Albert Scherzinger to the Commissioner of Native Affairs, Western Australia, 8 April 1946, in Western Australian Native Affairs File for Laurelle Andrewina Brown.

Library Board of Western Australia (1981), *An Interview with Alf Brown, 30 July 1981*, Perth: Battye Library.

AUTHOR'S RESEARCH MATERIALS

Field notebooks and tapes of interviews from 1995 to 2001 are held by the author.

Tapes:

Barunga, Pudja, at Mowanjum Mission, 1995.
D'Antoine, Douglas Patrick, at Derby, 1995.
D'Antoine, Laurelle, at Derby, 1995.
D'Antoine, Neville, at Toodyay, 2001.
D'Antoine, Shaun, at Derby, 1997.
Oakes, Wes and Hazel, at Derby, 1997.
O'Connor, Annette (Marie), at Derby, 1998.
O'Donnell, Florence, at Perth, 1995.
Peters, Amy, at Mowanjum Mission, 1995.
Prouse, Iris, at Derby, 1997.
Uiduldam, Waiu, at Cairns, 2000.